Fly Fishing Yellowstone National Park

An Insider's Guide to the 50 Best Places

Nate Schweber

HeadWater
Books
STACKPOLE
BOOKS

Published by
STACKPOLE BOOKS
5067 Ritter Road
Mechanicsburg, PA 17055
www.stackpolebooks.com

Printed in the United States

First edition

Cover photograph by Guy R. Muto
Cover design by Caroline M. Stover

Library of Congress Cataloging-in-Publication Data

Schweber, Nate.
  Fly fishing Yellowstone National Park : an insider's guide to the 50 best places / Nate Schweber. — 1st ed.
    p. cm.
  Includes bibliographical references and index.
  ISBN 978-0-8117-1051-0 (pbk.) — ISBN 0-8117-1051-3 (pbk.) 1. Fly fishing—Yellowstone National Park. 2. Fishers—Yellowstone National Park. I. Title.
  SH464.Y45S39 2012
  799.12'4—dc23
                                    2012006960

For Kristen; *for letting me*
For my stepdad Bill Innes; *for going with me*
&
In loving memory of Carolyn Elizabeth Schweber

Contents

Introduction

Mountain man John Colter, the king-hell daredevil of the Lewis and Clark Expedition, is credited as having "discovered," in the frigid winter of 1807/08, the land that would later be hailed as a trout Shangri-la—the world's first national park, Yellowstone.[1]

Of course, this attribution slights the scores of Native Americans who already knew about Yellowstone. Bands of Blackfeet, Bannocks, Flatheads, and Crows all passed through.[2] A scrappy tribe of Sheepeaters, part of the Shoshone nation, even managed to eke out a year-round living in Yellowstone through the short summers and brutally cold winters in part by feasting on the rich flesh of the region's marquee fish, the Yellowstone cutthroat trout.[3]

Native Americans and early Europeans in Yellowstone west of the Continental Divide caught chunky whitefish; majestic grayling; and silvery, speckled westslope cutthroat trout in the Madison and Gallatin Rivers. Sheepeaters, and other native people who passed through what would be the park's torso, with awesome Yellowstone Lake at its heart, caught big, golden, and brilliant Yellowstone cutthroats.

When Colter's days of hopscotching ice floes, dodging grizzlies, and sprinting nekkid away from Blackfeet warriors were through, he retired to a farm in Franklin County, Missouri, to live out his final few years with his wife, a Native American woman named Sally.[4] A famous legend goes that his associates had nicknamed Yellowstone "Colter's Hell" after incredulously listening to the man's zany tales about jets of fire-hot water and boiling mud.[5] It's assumed that people at the time thought Colter's stories could mean only one of two very bad things. One, Colter was crazy. Two, God was angry.

Around 1810, an Oregon-bound explorer named Wilson Price Hunt, in the employ of John Jacob Astor, called on Colter at his farm. Hunt wanted to know the best route to take through the wild Pacific Northwest.[6]

Colter told him something else. Hunt listened in amazement as Colter described what he had seen in Yellowstone Lake, a cerulean alpine sea higher than any other freshwater body of its size in the country. Colter said he had seen an enormous petrified fish. The fish was fifty feet long. Fifty! For real.[7]

A famous, but unverified, Yellowstone legend has it that the notion to turn this land into a national park was first voiced in September 1870 by a group of explorers sitting around a campfire here at the junction of the Gibbon and Firehole Rivers—the headwaters of the Madison. PHOTO BY NATE SCHWEBER

Suffice to say, from its earliest written accounts, Yellowstone has been a place of fantastic fish stories.

This is a book of fish stories. Since time eternal, anglers have loved stories. Part of the reason for this, I suspect, is that stories contain the best fishing advice. Another reason is that nothing sends an angler's mind reeling like a great story about a cool spot. Hence, I took my publisher's assignment to write a guide to fishing in Yellowstone and set out to collect the stories about the best places to fish in the park.

I interviewed dozens of rangers, biologists, writers, tourists, locals, men, women, a famous person or two, and yes, fly shop owners and fishing guides. The end result is the widest array of voices ever collected in a guide to fishing Yellowstone. It is my hope that the diversity of insights here makes this book unique among the several Yellowstone fishing guides already on the market. I asked all the people I interviewed to tell me a vivid story about a single spot to fish in Yellowstone—their favorite spot.

Lest my motives seem too high-minded, Delores Marsh, whom I interviewed for my chapter about Ojo Caliente on the Firehole River, sussed me out over the telephone.

"When you're listening to my stories, you're fishing right along with me," she said. "You're going to live through someone else's fishing stories until you can go and see these places yourself."

She was right. Although I was born and raised in Missoula, Montana, I've lived in New York City for the past decade. Marooned in this sparkling metropolis, I do most of my trout fishing vicariously over the Internet, courtesy of blogs like Fly Fishing in Yellowstone National Park. I wanted to find a writing project that would bring me back home to Montana, or to Yellowstone. Right after high school I spent the best summer of my life flipping burgers for tourists at Mammoth Hot Springs and hitchhiking on my days off to catch giant cutthroats in the upper Yellowstone River (never knowing that those great fish were at the start of an awful decline). When I learned that this publisher was looking for someone to write a guide to fishing in Yellowstone, I snapped at it like a starved cutthroat to a flailing Salmonfly.

I spent eight more weeks in Yellowstone in the summer of 2011 and visited 47 of these 50 places, all but the remote Thorofare, which was inaccessible due to high water. I hiked about 300 miles, mostly by myself, and warbled like Freddie Mercury to avoid surprising any bears. I hit the pause button on my regular gig as a freelance reporter for the *New York Times*. I also put on hold recording sessions for my third rock-and-roll album. I took a break from my normal daily life with my lovely fiancée (*Hi baby!*) in the new Brooklyn condo on which we'd just taken out a mortgage (*I love you!*). I even sheared off my long Jim Morrison hairdo because I didn't want my locks turning to dreads during a summer when I saw more moose than showerheads. I packed my fly rod and tent; hopped a plane to Bozeman, Montana; bought an old pickup off Craigslist for a thousand bucks; and lit out for the land of grizzly bears, wolves, buffalo, and wild trout.

All in the name of research, friends. Weeks and weeks of glorious research.

Early on I had the idea to try and write about the 50 best places to fish in the park—based loosely on the Chris Santella books—but I realized the story wouldn't quite fit that template. There is a deeper drama going on underwater in Yellowstone. The quality of the park's fishery has ebbed and flowed throughout history and, sadly, we're in an ebb right now. Lake trout, illegally planted in Yellowstone Lake probably sometime in the 1980s, massacred that watershed's native population of cutthroat trout, the park's linchpin fish.

It's a sad story that I wove through these chapters, including transition chapters in which I go into more detail. But it's not the whole story. Yellowstone is vast, and miles of her streams and acres of her lakes still teem with wild trout, same as ever. In some places the fishing is getting better, more authentic, more *Yellowstone*. I tell these stories too, like how park biologists recently created a reservoir of genetically pure, native westslope cutthroat trout in High Lake.

I give extra attention to the park's most fabled waters, like the Firehole and Madison Rivers, streams so unique and at times prolific that they course through the dreams of anglers worldwide. Because those two rivers are so famous, as are the Yellowstone River, Yellowstone Lake, and Slough Creek, I wrote more than one chapter about each.

These chapters are organized chronologically, roughly based on the times during Yellowstone's late May through early November fishing season when each spot comes into its peak form. Also, I compiled facts, culled from my interviews, that give a quick synopsis for each spot including fish species, insects, suggested patterns and techniques, plus directions.

Mostly, I worked to weave into this text the voices of the people I interviewed.

I strove to make this book as accurate and truthful as possible, so I was pained to leave out a few classic, but unverified, Yellowstone yarns. Like this one: on the evening of September 19, 1870, as westslope cutthroat trout and grayling splashed at the junction of the Firehole and Gibbon Rivers, Cornelius Hedges, a member of the seminal U.S.-government-sponsored expedition to explore the Yellowstone region, first voiced the noble notion that this land be preserved for all time as a national park.

It's a great tale, and surely the cutthroats and grayling rose that day, but Yellowstone historian Lee H. Whittlesey says the Hedges part is just a myth. Out. With other stories here, I had to take my sources at their words, conscious of the fact that fishermen are known to spread their hands a little wider every time they talk about a trout. (Were the cuttbows Dean Reiner caught on lower Slough Creek *really* 30 inches?) Still, I checked and rechecked wherever possible, even going as far as to ask for photographic proof, and I'm confident that all the trout anecdotes in here are true, give or take an inch or two.

Considering the awful damage that lake trout have done to the cutthroat fishery in Yellowstone Lake and the upper Yellowstone River, it's hard to argue that those once-mandatory fishing spots could still be called some of the park's "best." But they remain some of the park's most iconic. And the fishing can still be unforgettable. A by-product of the sickened ecosystem is that the only cutthroat trout left, those that managed to avoid the gullets of lake trout, tend to be gargantuan.

On one trek, I hiked 36 miles over four days down to the tip of the remote Southeast Arm of Yellowstone Lake, Vice President Dick Cheney's favorite spot. I followed that lonely old trail past mutilated bison and elk

Releasing a rare, giant, Yellowstone cutthroat trout in a Yellowstone Lake spawning stream, the first cutthroat I was able to catch after hiking more than 30 miles.
PHOTO BY NATE SCHWEBER

carcasses, and I was on high alert because I literally walked on top of wolf and grizzly tracks. Then I experienced my weirdest animal encounter ever: a snowshoe hare sat next to me for hours on the lakeshore one night and warmed itself by my campfire.

For more than 30 miles, I didn't catch a single damn cutthroat. Then I explored up a small feeder stream that I dare not name, not far from a spot where fish biologists drove pegs into a tree so they could ladder up if mean ol' Mr. Griz came at them. I dragged an olive Woolly Bugger through a turquoise hole and watched a massive silver/gold/blue/green shape materialize. I saw a triangle of white—a huge maw opening—and I heaved back on my rod. The great trout rolled away from me, flashing pure gold as the sunlight hit it broadside. I battled that giant, pure-blooded buck to shore and gaped. Twenty-six inches! Cheeks, gill plates, and trademark cuts the richest red I've ever seen.

That, friends, is the kind of experience Yellowstone offers.

Bud Lilly, the granddaddy of Yellowstone guides who first fished the park in 1935, balked at my asking his favorite spot. "I think what you do when you tell people about spots is they lose their initiative to go out and find their own," he said. Indeed, that fantastic blog, Fly Fishing in Yellowstone National Park, never reveals *too* much about a spot. It makes readers imagine, scour topographical maps, and then get out and hike. I tried, as much as possible, to encourage that here. I even left out some spots.

I owe an enormous debt of gratitude to the mysterious author of Fly Fishing in Yellowstone National Park—for early inspiration, on-the-ground information, and hospitality, which I detail in my chapter on "Notellum Creek."

A question I kept circling back to in my interviews was, why Yellowstone? After all, four of the sport fish found in Yellowstone—rainbow trout, brown trout, brook trout, and lake trout—can be caught in abundance in plenty of places other than the park. *What is so special about catching them in this place?* I asked. Every answer revolved around similar themes: an incredible wildlife sighting, a geothermal phenomenon, a sense of history, an appreciation of wilderness, and a bond forged with a loved one—a realization that *this experience can't happen anywhere else.* Ranger Shelton Johnson, speaking about the Gibbon River, described it best when he said, "Fishing is just a way to connect with Yellowstone in a deeper way." I wanted this book to reflect that.

I also wanted to illustrate the tangential roles trout have played in park conflicts, both historic and modern. In my chapter on Nez Perce Creek, I uncovered fascinating new details about one of the most amazing human dramas in Yellowstone history: a remarkable 1877 encounter between a band of Nez Perce, including heralded peacemaker Chief Joseph, and an early group of park tourists—a husband who survived three gunshot wounds, and his wife who was taken prisoner. After months of digging through genealogical records in seven states, I tracked down relatives of those tourists, George and Emma Cowan, and they shared with me an unpublished transcript about the ordeal that George dictated to his daughter shortly before he died. Trout featured in that saga, as they do today in a dispute over access to the lower Yellowstone River in the park, which I discuss in the chapter on the Black Canyon of the Yellowstone. It is chapters like these that I hope make this book a contribution to the body of original reporting on Yellowstone Park. I also hope that the early Yellowstone stories folded into some of these chapters give this book appeal not just to anglers, but to lovers of Western history too.

On my long ramble to see these spots for myself, I saw eight grizzlies. I watched a double rainbow arc over a gray wolf posed on the edge of the Lamar River. I laid nekkid in the first morning's light in a hot pool at the base of a 100-foot waterfall in the park's remote Cascade Corner. I saw a bull buffalo roll another one over in a duel. I saw the whole, awesome Black Canyon of the Yellowstone; the bottom of the Grand Canyon of the Yellowstone; and 150-foot Osprey Falls in the middle of Sheepeater Canyon. I sniffed sage and tasted sweet wild raspberries. All summer long, I slept under creamy, navy skies in the bed of that old Craigslist pickup that I nicknamed "Scamper," and also in a little one-man backcountry tent that I nicknamed "The Bear Burrito."

Did I mention I even caught some trout?

The sun sets on the Firehole River as steam from geysers and hot pools wafts skyward. This is some of the most beautiful, and unique, scenery on earth in which to catch a trout. PHOTO BY NATE SCHWEBER

Alone in the wilderness, my mind often turned to my favorite nature writers—Walt Whitman, John Muir, and Edward Abbey. But most of all, I thought about a fascinating Englishman named Howard Back who was a World War I veteran, businessman, adventurer, and art collector. After his wife died suddenly, Back wandered Yellowstone and fished in the summers of 1936 and 1937, and the next year he published the first guide to fishing the park. Old-timers in the backs of shops selling feathers and hooks will tell you that it's still the best. Like me, Back had no professional business writing a guide to fishing in Yellowstone. It was just something he loved, something he wanted his grandchildren to experience in the exact same way he did, something he wanted to share with others so that they might lend their voices to a chorus that would sing this region's glories in perpetuity.

With that motivation as inspiration, I tried to write this book with the pluck of a city street reporter and the enthusiasm of a Prodigal Montanan. Herewith, *Fly Fishing Yellowstone National Park: An Insider's Guide to the 50 Best Places.*

Before You Go

BASIC FLY SELECTION

A general Yellowstone fly box should have a mix of attractors, terrestrials, basic nymphs, and streamers. A collection of patterns could look like this: Parachute Adamses size 10 to 20; Royal Wulffs, Royal Coachman Trudes, Yellow Humpies, and tan Elk Hair Caddis size 10 to 16; yellow and orange Stimulators size 2 to 14; hoppers size 6 to 14; ants and beetles size 14 to 18; Hare's Ear, Prince, Copper John, and Pheasant Tail nymphs size 14 to 18; and black and olive Woolly Buggers size 4 to 8. Make sure to check with local fly shops for the most up-to-date hot patterns.

OVERVIEW OF HATCHES

Opening day in Yellowstone Park means *Baetis* (Blue-Winged Olive) hatches on the Firehole, Madison, and Gibbon Rivers, usually followed by Pale Morning Duns along with the year-round midge. *Baetis* hatches, which span the season, are usually strongest on overcast, snowy, or drizzling days between eleven o'clock in the morning and four o'clock in the afternoon; PMDs usually hatch in mid to late morning on sunny days and in early afternoon on cold days stretching into mid-September. After rivers like the Madison, Gardner, and Yellowstone subside from runoff in late June and early July comes a couple of Yellowstone's most exciting hatches: Salmonflies and Golden Stoneflies. These big bugs are most active from midmorning through late afternoon. More mayflies come into the mix in June, including Gray Drakes, which hatch all day long on places like Slough Creek and the Yellowstone River and have spinnerfalls around breakfast and dinner times respectively. Green Drakes appear in mid-June and last through the summer, and Brown Drakes usually hatch from mid-June through mid-July. On lakes, *Callibaetis* usually hatch from midmorning through midafternoon, with a spinnerfall that directly follows. Also damselflies are an important stillwater hatch from midmorning through midafternoon. Many warm, calm evenings in Yellowstone bring great caddisfly hatches. Terrestrials like ants, beetles, and spruce moths become a part of trout's diets starting in June. By mid-July, trout begin feeding on small and medium-sized grasshoppers and crickets, and then trout feed on the adult versions of these terrestrials through August and September. The season winds down in Yellowstone much like it started, with *Baetis* hatches—smaller than their springtime cousins—usually on the Madison, Gibbon, and Firehole Rivers.

Again, be sure to check with local fly shops for hatch news.

WEATHER

Temperatures can bottom out fast in Yellowstone, so always be prepared to deal with hypothermia. Be sure to carry at least a waterproof rain jacket or a poncho on all outings, even in midsummer, as afternoon rainstorms are common. For longer hikes and overnights, consider rain pants as well and make sure to pack dry, warm clothes. Bear in mind that it can snow any day atop the Yellowstone plateau.

BEARS

Follow these rules for staying safe around Yellowstone's grizzlies:

1. Never approach a bear. Try to stay at least 100 yards away from any grizzly and at least 30 yards away from other animals, including bison (also referred to here as "buffalo"), moose, and elk.
2. Avoid hiking alone.
3. Make noise, particularly when traveling sections of trail where the visibility ahead is limited.
4. Stay away from animal carcasses; a territorial griz is often lurking nearby.
5. Remember berry patches can be "bear-y."
6. Stay on the lookout for griz sign, such as tracks, scat, and root diggings.
7. Be aware of the wind direction. Grizzlies downwind can smell you, but take care not to surprise any upwind bears.
8. Dispose of all fish entrails in fast or deep water after puncturing the air bladder.
9. When camping in the backcountry, remember to cook your food at least 100 yards away from your tent, and hang all food, trash, and other odorous items either on a backcountry bear pole or suspended from trees at least 10 feet off the ground at least 4 feet from any tree trunk. Don't bring anything with any odor into your tent, such as food, toothpaste, or toiletries. I try to sleep in different clothes than the ones I wear when cooking.
10. Carry pepper spray. Although guns are now legal to carry in Yellowstone, spray remains a wiser option. Spray can ensure that everybody leaves the encounter alive, such as in the case of a hiker who triggers a defensive charge from a mother bear protecting her cubs. Also, it's easier to hit a moving target with a cloud of spray than with a tiny bullet. Many people have shot at charging bears and missed or worse, enraged the animal with a nonlethal wound.

Remember how much more vivid your fishing trip can be in griz country. Because your senses are on high alert, you experience every sight, sound, and smell in a deeper, more urgent way. And like trout, grizzlies don't live in ugly places.

That being said, before I lit out for Yellowstone, I was very nervous about spending most of my summer alone in deep griz country. I interviewed Yellowstone bear biologist Kerry Gunther on the phone from New York City for a chapter in this book. After I asked him all the questions I had written down, I had to pick his brain about what I'd need to do to stay safe.

He mentioned the same tips I shared above, and perhaps because he still heard unease in my voice, he tried to end our conversation on a positive note.

"We haven't had a fatal griz mauling in Yellowstone Park in a quarter century," he said. "So the odds are with you."

The day after I arrived in Yellowstone, a grizzly bear killed a park visitor for the first time since 1986. Six weeks later, another hiker was killed by a griz.

Neither of the mauled hikers carried pepper spray, which could've saved their lives. I followed all the rules and never had a problem. So my advice is this: remember the odds, but pack spray just in case.

MOSQUITOES

If I was forced to carry only one kind of spray—bear spray or bug spray—I'd have to choose bug spray. Fortunately, it's not either-or. The bugs in Yellowstone can be maddening. Be sure to have plenty of mosquito repellant.

RECOMMENDED READING AND ONLINE RESOURCES

Fishing Yellowstone National Park: An Angler's Complete Guide to More Than 100 Streams, Rivers, and Lakes by Richard Parks. This stream-by-stream guide, written by a longtime Yellowstone fly shop owner, sets the standard for Yellowstone fishing books. Now in its third edition.

Hiking Yellowstone National Park by Bill Schneider. An invaluable guide for anyone looking to visit Yellowstone's more far-flung fishing spots, this book includes maps, essential backpacking tips, and rules for zero-impact camping.

Flyfisher's Guide to Yellowstone National Park by Ken Retallic. A recent Yellowstone fishing guide that includes details about area fly shops, accommodations, airports, and more.

Fishing Yellowstone Hatches by John Juracek and Craig Mathews. The most in-depth study of Yellowstone's trout food.

Yellowstone Fishes: Ecology, History and Angling in the Park by John D. Varley and Paul Schullery. An essential and hard-to-find read that details the natural migrations and stocking history of park fish.

The Waters of Yellowstone with Rod and Fly by Howard Back. The original 1938 classic.

Some of the best resources for fishing in Yellowstone are online. As of this writing, these web sites feature some of the most up-to-the-minute fishing reports, as well as other news, photos, stories, and curiosities.

Fly Fishing in Yellowstone National Park. The classic, the best; it features reports on hot streams, hot flies, and important news as well as excellent links. http://flyfishyellowstone.blogspot.com

Yellowstone's Volunteer Fly-Fishing Program. Founded in the early 2000s, the park's volunteer fly-fishing program helps biologists monitor trout populations in waters throughout Yellowstone, as well as harvest nonnative trout from certain at-risk fisheries. For more information, see the eplilogue. http://www.nps.gov/yell/naturescience/vol_fishing.htm

Park's Fly Shop. Features the most frequently updated fishing reports. http://www.parksflyshop.com

Blue Ribbon Flies. Beautiful photos and thoughtful essays. http://blue-ribbon-flies.com/blog

Chi Wulff. A collection of trout related news and stories, much of it dealing with Yellowstone and the Yellowstone region, plus great recipes and craft beer suggestions. http://chiwulff.com

TroutBugs. An eclectic mix of trout news and stories that features a helpful list of recently updated blogs from around the Yellowstone region. http://joshuabergan.blogspot.com

RULES AND REGULATIONS

All Yellowstone anglers over the age of 15 need to buy a license, which are available at most ranger stations, park stores, and area fishing shops. Each license comes with a printed copy of the most current Yellowstone fishing regulations, which are also available online and by request from most park rangers and shops. Make sure to check the rules for any body of park water before you start to fish. Key points include: Yellowstone is open for fishing from sunup to sundown starting the Saturday of Memorial Day weekend and ending the first Sunday in November; catch-and-release for all native species, including cutthroat trout, grayling, and whitefish; mandatory kill for all lake trout caught in Yellowstone Lake and no limit for lake trout caught in Heart Lake; and barbless hooks only and no lead weights. Creel limits for nonnative fish vary, as do special closures on short sections of streams; check the latest rules.

Make sure all gear used in one body of water is cleaned thoroughly before it is used in another; this protects against the spread of invasive species, such as whirling disease and New Zealand mudsnail. It is illegal to transport any fish from one body of water to another.

Remember to be courteous to both the environment and to other anglers. Try to stay on established trails, and give other anglers plenty of room. Yellowstone is huge, so there is no need to crowd.

THE FISH
Yellowstone Cutthroat Trout

The hero of this book. Yellowstone cutthroat are native to the Yellowstone River drainage and have been stocked in parts of the Snake, Gallatin, and Madison drainages as well. Yellowstone cutthroat grow large and are gold, silver, or toasty brown with black spots concentrated most toward their tails. They also have rosy gill plates and crimson slashes under their jaws. Key waters to find them include Yellowstone Lake, Yellowstone River, Snake River, Fall River, Lamar River, Gardner River, Soda Butte Creek, Slough Creek, Hellroaring Creek, Cache Creek, Pelican Creek, and Trout Lake. A native species that shares the park's namesake to boot, all Yellowstone cutthroat trout are to be released unharmed.

Westslope Cutthroat Trout

The comeback kid of this book. Pure westslope cutthroats were native to the Madison and Gallatin drainages before they were wiped out in the park save for just a few hundred specimens in a tiny unnamed tributary of Grayling Creek. While they tend to grow smaller than Yellowstone cutthroats, westslopes are silvery and often sport red bellies along with the trademark red cuts under their jaws. Key places to search for aboriginal westslopes in Yellowstone include upper Cougar Creek and the North Fork of Fan Creek. Thanks to park officials' restoration efforts, High Lake and the East Fork of Specimen Creek are now reservoirs for westslopes. Soon Goose Lake will be filled with westslopes, too. All westslopes must be released unharmed.

Snake River Finespotted Cutthroat Trout

The mirage of this book. Snake River finespotted cutthroats may swim only in the portion of the upper Snake River that flows through Yellowstone. These trout are scientifically classified in the same subspecies as regular Yellowstone cutthroats, but they look different. Finespotted cutthroats, as their name implies, are speckled with tinier, denser black spots than regular Yellowstone cutthroats. See the Snake River chapter for more information. All finespotted cutthroats must be released unharmed.

Arctic Grayling

The ghost of this book. Silvery arctic grayling are easily distinguished by their large, iridescent, sail-like dorsal fin. They once filled the Madison and

Gallatin Rivers, as well as the lower Firehole and Gibbon Rivers. Today they thrive in Grebe, Cascade, and Wolf Lakes and occasionally wash down into the Gibbon and Madison Rivers. All grayling must be released unharmed.

Rainbow Trout

The leaper of this book. Rainbow trout are distinguished by the pink or crimson stripe that runs from their gills to their tails. Native to the West Coast, rainbow trout were stocked extensively in Yellowstone, particularly in large waters, including the Madison, Gibbon, Firehole, Lamar, Gardner, and lower Yellowstone Rivers as well as creeks including Nez Perce, upper Tower, Grayling, Fan, and Specimen. Because they spawn in spring, often at the same time as native cutthroats, rainbow trout can interbreed with the natives and dilute their genetic purity. In recent years, rainbow trout have infested the upper reaches of Slough Creek in the park, jeopardizing that stream's population of pure cutthroats. Park officials have set a creel limit of five rainbow trout in Native Trout Conservation Areas, and they encourage the harvest of rainbows in Lamar Valley streams and other tributaries to the Yellowstone River. Rainbows must be released in the park's Wild Trout Enhancement Areas, including the Madison, Firehole, and Gibbon Rivers.

Cuttbow

The quandary of this book. Cuttbows are born after a rainbow trout breeds with a cutthroat trout. A cuttbow is not genetically pure, and this hybridization is responsible for the widespread decimation of native cutthroat populations in Yellowstone. Still, because cuttbows and cutthroats are commonly mistaken for each other, park officials have instituted a policy in which any fish with a slash under its jaw—cutthroat or cuttbow—must be released unharmed.

Brown Trout

The trophy of this book. Brown Trout are gold with black spots, like river leopards. Originally from Europe, they have a reputation for being the cagiest, savviest trout, giving extra gravitas to any angler who manages to catch a big one. They swim in Lewis and Shoshone Lakes; the Madison, Firehole, Gibbon, lower Yellowstone, Gardner, Lewis, and Snake Rivers; and creeks, including Nez Perce and Solfatara. Browns must be released in the park's Wild Trout Enhancement Areas, except in the Lewis River where two brown trout may be creeled, only one more than 20 inches. Park officials set a creel limit of five brown trout in Native Trout Conservation Areas, including the lower Yellowstone River, Gardner River, and Snake River.

Brook Trout
The dangerous jewel of this book. Brook trout have green bodies; orange bellies; white-edged fins; and spots of yellow, orange, and red with blue halos. Originally from the Northeastern United States, brook trout were stocked widely in Yellowstone, and because they are such aggressive feeders, they can outcompete native cutthroats. Key places to find brook trout are Lava, Obsidian, Tower, and DeLacy Creeks, as well as Grizzly, Joffe, and Fawn Lakes. Park officials set a creel limit of five brook trout anywhere in the park, and they encourage the harvest of any brook trout caught in Soda Butte Creek, where brookies have leaked down in recent years from outside the park and now threaten native cutthroats.

Mountain Whitefish
The survivor of this book. Silvery and often looked down on by trout fanatics for their sucker-like mouths, mountain whitefish are Yellowstone natives and have shown the tenacity to hold on where other native species, like grayling and westslope cutthroats, have gone extinct. Find mountain whitefish in the Madison, lower Yellowstone, and Snake Rivers. All mountain whitefish must be released unharmed.

Lake Trout (Mackinaw)
The villain of this book. A tremendous gamefish and a tremendous scourge, lake trout are native to the Great Lakes and were stocked in Lewis Lake in the late 1800s. From there, they colonized Shoshone and Heart Lakes, and a century later they were illegally stocked in Yellowstone Lake, sending that watershed's population of native cutthroats into a disastrous tailspin. Lake trout are dark blue with white splotches. Boat anglers using deepwater fishing rigs often target lake trout. They can also occasionally be taken from shore. All lake trout caught in Yellowstone Lake or the Yellowstone River must be killed, and there is no limit on lake trout caught in Heart Lake. Anyone who doesn't want to eat a lake trout from these watersheds can puncture the fish's air bladder and hurl its body out into the deepest water possible. There is a limit of five lake trout in Lewis Lake, Shoshone Lake, and Lewis River: only one more than 20 inches.

1 Firehole River at Biscuit Basin

Leslie Dal Lago, John Juracek

In the middle of the great park snakes a river like no other, a stream that at first glance seems uninhabitable to fish and inhospitable to humans.

Its banks seep plumes of steam, and gallons of scalding water pour in from gullies that smell of egg rot and bloom bloodred with strange algae. Hairy, horned, clawed, and toothy beasts from the last ice age stalk the banks in search of food or places to give birth, or both.

Trout: Rainbows and browns averaging 10 to 14 inches, with a few bigger ones too; brookies in the upper reaches; whitefish below Firehole Falls.

Bugs: Mayfly hatches, including Pale Morning Duns and *Baetis*; caddisflies, including *Nectopsyche* and White Millers; also Salmonflies, midges, and terrestrials.

Suggested fly box: Parachute Adamses size 14 to 20; Pale Morning Duns, Blue-Winged Olives, and Sparkle Duns size 16 to 18; Iris Caddis emergers and Elk Hair Caddis size 14 to 20; Hare's Ear, Copper John, Pheasant Tail, and Prince nymphs size 14 to 20; soft-hackle wet flies size 14 to 20. Also, black and olive Woolly Buggers size 6 to 10.

Key techniques: Match the hatch; fish nymphs when no fish are rising. Swinging soft-hackle wet flies can also be very effective here.

Best times: May through June; also September through November.

Directions: Grand Loop Road parallels the Firehole River from its junction with the Madison River up through Old Faithful.

Special rules: Fly-fishing-only; catch-and-release for browns, rainbows, and whitefish.

"As you pass the geysers on the way to the Firehole, you think, I'm going to fish *that?*" said Leslie Dal Lago, who first fished the Firehole on an opening day weekend in the mid-1990s just after she moved back to her hometown of Idaho Falls.

This is opening day in Yellowstone National Park, where scores of anglers flock to spots like Biscuit Basin on the Firehole River to ring in a new season, and new lives.

Dal Lago walked Firehole's banks, gaping at the same steam clouds that in 1936 reminded Yellowstone's first fishing memoirist, World War I veteran Howard Back, of the Second Battle of the Somme.[1] After spongy steps to the riverside, she saw dozens of yellowish Blue-Winged Olives hatching under the overcast sky. Dal Lago tied on a size 16 imitation dry fly and cast.

Moments later, she was hooked to the most beautiful rainbow trout she could remember, all silver and strength, with perfect angles and an unforgettable band.

"Its bow was so red it was almost scarlet," she said. "I'd just never seen a red like that."

Like Dal Lago, longtime West Yellowstone resident John Juracek also became infatuated with the Firehole River. The river, probably named around 1850 by mountain man Jim Bridger,[2] seized Juracek's dreams a half century ago, when he was a teenager in the flatlands of Cedar Rapids, Iowa, pouring over books by early Yellowstone fishing writers Ernie Schweibert and Ray Bergman. Juracek moved to Yellowstone country in 1976 and never left. He cofounded the Blue Ribbon Flies shop in West Yellowstone with Craig Mathews and has written several books about fishing the park, particularly his favorite stream, the Firehole.

"There's an infinite amount to learn in the Firehole," Juracek said. "And that's what keeps people like me coming back."

The first lesson Juracek took from the Firehole River is to approach with stealth. Firehole fish are wary, he said, and stomping up to the bank and sloppy casts send them darting away. His second major lesson was that paying attention to the Firehole's hatches could make the difference between a big fish and a little fish, or no fish.

One of the river's best hatches is the early season appearance of Pale Morning Duns, which Juracek calls "the main springtime emergence, good-sized flies." He likes to match this hatch with a size 14 Sparkle Dun.

Baetis, a smaller mayfly, often hatch in tandem with the Pale Morning Duns. The *Baetis* also come on strong in September and October, Juracek said. Nymphs of both these mayflies take fish all season long.

"A caddisfly called *Nectopsyche* has in the past decade become a major source of trout food on the Firehole," Juracek said. Twenty years ago, he would only see a handful of *Nectopsyche* caddis along the banks. "You'd never

The Firehole River just downstream from the bridge at Biscuit Basin. Here, thermal features send up mysterious clouds of steam and the river is filled with lively trout.
PHOTO BY DR. GUY R. MUTO

think about imitating it," he said. Today *Nectopsyche*, a warmwater insect, is "the most important caddis," on the Firehole, Juracek said. He imitated it with a size 16 Iris Caddis emerger.

The skies can be the best indicator of which type of fly to use.

"If it's skuzzy and nasty, you're probably going to fish mayflies," Juracek said. "If it's warm and sunny, you're probably going to fish caddis."

Conscientious anglers skip the Firehole in July and August, when hot air temperatures combine with geyser runoff to make the river too warm to be healthy for trout. Firehole trout died by the thousands in the record-breaking temperatures of drought years in the last decade.

In recent years, the Firehole has taken heat for being a foot-long-fish stream. The Firehole's waters have warmed gradually due to geothermal shifts underground that today pour more geyser runoff into the river than in the twentieth century. Juracek said the Firehole's trout grow fast but then burn out before they reach their 16-inch-plus sizes of yore. Still, the river holds some big surprises, and, Juracek said, based on observation, "there are more trout in the Firehole now than there ever were."

"When a hatch is happening and you see the surface of the river boiling with rising trout, it's just an incredible experience," he said. "And if you can't appreciate a 12-inch wild trout in a place like this, you need to adjust your perspective on this sport."

The Firehole River at Biscuit Basin is one of the most popular spots to fish along this fabled trout stream. It is home to beautiful and hard-fighting rainbow and brown trout. PHOTO BY NATE SCHWEBER

Wild is the optimal word on this river. Not long ago, Dal Lago guided two clients in Biscuit Basin in the fall. On the opposite bank stood an enormous bugling bull elk and his harem of cows. For more than an hour, the clients cast a Parachute Adams trailed by a Blue-Winged Olive emerger to crimson rainbows in front of this elk's majestic silhouette.

The clients were so focused on their flies that they missed the drama brewing behind them.

A smaller bull elk on their side of the river approached and challenged the giant bull. Dal Lago watched it unfold.

"That big boy got up and ran right through the river where those fish were rising," she said. "He was like, 'Bring it on, you want to fight? Let's do this now.'"

Dal Lago hurried her clients out of there. But she returns often, as does Juracek.

"The Firehole gets under your skin, and you can't get it out," Juracek said. "On opening day, the water is still cool from snowmelt, the fish are very active, and the animals are calving. It's the regeneration, the start of a new year for fishing."

Open Season

Trout season began in Yellowstone National Park around 12,000 years ago when the great glaciers pulled back and a little stream in the high country south of today's park border split in two in a mountain meadow. One branch, Pacific Creek, flowed west. The other branch, Atlantic Creek, flowed east, toward Yellowstone Lake and beyond. Their junction marked a spot where a fish could actually cross the Continental Divide.

After the last ice age, ancient cutthroat trout, whose ancestors ran up from the Pacific Ocean via the Snake River and evolved into today's Yellowstone cutthroats some 3.5 million years ago,[1] swam from Pacific Creek into Atlantic Creek.[2] Other pioneer cutthroats followed, as some still do today, and they flushed down the Yellowstone River. They tumbled over the Great Falls of the Yellowstone and climbed up the Lamar River and the Gardner River. They branched out to creeks like Pelican, Tower, Hellroaring, Soda Butte, Pebble, Cache, and Slough. Vitally, these cutthroats colonized giant Yellowstone Lake, and it began to beat each spring like a heart pumping millions of red spawning trout up into her rushing blue veins.

Some of the Yellowstone cutthroats in the upper Snake River system were covered with smaller speckles than others, like ground pepper instead of peppercorns.[3] These special trout would later be called "Snake River finespotted cutthroats," and although scientists consider them to be identical to Yellowstone cutthroats, anglers celebrate their difference.

A third native species of Rocky Mountain trout, the westslope cutthroat, filled streams bound for the upper Missouri River, like the Gallatin and the Madison, plus the Gibbon and Firehole Rivers below their respective falls. These westslope cutthroats lived alongside two other gamefish—the arctic grayling and the mountain whitefish.[4]

These aboriginal trout were the ones the Sheepeaters harvested and the ones that splashed in the Yellowstone River when Jim Bridger threw a huge party for mountain men in the Hayden Valley in 1838.[5] When pioneer hook-and-line anglers arrived in Yellowstone, many of them dismayed by the industrial pollution that had already diminished so many once-great trout streams of the East, they were ecstatic.

A spawning Yellowstone cutthroat trout leaps a chute of water in the LeHardy Rapids section of the upper Yellowstone River. These fish originally crossed the continental divide at Two Ocean Pass and washed down the Yellowstone River. They colonized Yellowstone Lake and ran up the rivers and creeks in the park's eastern and northern parts.

In 1870 Army Lieutenant Gustavus Doane wrote that the fishing in Yellowstone Lake was so "perfectly fabulous" that "even the most awkward angler" could catch "mule loads" of cutthroats.[6] In 1874 tourist Windham Thomas Wyndham-Quin, 4th Earl of Dunraven and Mount-Earl, visited Yellowstone and wrote, "Every lake and river teems with trout," and added that he ate them "till I was ashamed to look a fish in the face."[7] An 1877 memoir by Jack Bean, a trapper, scout, and Native American fighter, tells of fishing for cutthroats in Yellowstone Lake with Sir William Blackmore, a wealthy British venture capitalist.

"He thought it would be wonderful if he caught one for each year he was old—fifty-four. He soon caught the fifty-four and tried for a hundred. He was not long making this and tried for fifty-four more—and kept fishing for another hundred—and another fifty-four," Bean wrote.[8]

The iconic Yellowstone fishing story, that of hooking a cutthroat and cooking it in a geyser, came in 1883 courtesy of Henry J. Winsler's book *The Yellowstone National Park: A Manual for Tourists*. Winsler claimed to have "tempted a trout to its doom" in the Gardner River and poached it in the scalding runoff from Mammoth Hot Springs, much to the delight of his nine amazed companions who found that the cutthroat "only needed a little salt to make them quite palatable."[9]

From its inception, fishing in Yellowstone was never just a men's club. Kids loved it, as evidenced by an article in the daily newspaper in Livingston, Montana, that proclaimed a 10-year-old boy "champion fisherman for the season of 1896" after he caught 76 cutthroats in less than an hour from a creek south of Yellowstone Lake.[10] Women were in on the fun, too. In 1897 Mary T. Townsend wrote a magazine article titled "A Woman's Trout Fishing in Yellowstone Park." In it she calls the cutthroat trout "a brave and dashing fighter" and poetically notes, "The pleasantest angling is to see the fish cut with her golden oars the silver stream."[11]

In 1938 Howard Back published the park's first stream-by-stream fishing guide, called *The Waters of Yellowstone with Rod and Fly.* In it he wrote, "I know of nowhere in the world where a man may, for so little money, enjoy so many miles of first-class trout fishing in such beautiful surroundings."[12]

Back's would be the first of many books loaded with superlatives about fishing in Yellowstone. Volumes by heralded trout writers like Ernie Schweibert and Ray Bergman added to Yellowstone's mystique as America's greatest trout sanctuary.

But behind the raves and below the waves, a very different drama was playing out in Yellowstone's waters, a drama that continues today.

Westslope cutthroats, like this one from High Lake in Yellowstone, are native to the Madison and Gallatin Rivers in the park, plus all their feeder streams. PHOTO BY NATE SCHWEBER

2 Lewis River, Lewis Falls to Lewis Lake

Don Daughenbaugh

During his decades as a ranger, Don Daughenbaugh was the Park Service's go-to guy to take visiting VIPs fishing, because he always knew where to catch the best trout in Yellowstone.

But he kept one spot mostly to himself. A spot that is thick with moose and thicker with big brown trout that attack dry flies with gusto. It is the Lewis River between its showstopping falls and its namesake lake.

"You have to hit it just right, but when you do—oh my God—the fish in there," said Daughenbaugh, 84.

For nearly 30 years, Daughenbaugh worked as a summertime ranger in Grand Teton National Park and lived in a cabin near Yellowstone's South Gate. Many springs, when other anglers struggled to find fishable water,

---

Trout: Browns and lakers averaging 12 to 20 inches.

Bugs: Mahogany Duns in the spring; also Green and Gray Drakes and Golden Stoneflies.

Suggested fly box: Parachute Adamses size 14; Mahogany Duns size 14; black, tan, and olive Woolly Buggers size 4 to 8; Marabou Muddlers and Zonkers size 2 to 6.

Key techniques: Match the hatch, or search water with an attractor dry fly, nymph, or streamer.

Best times: June after the runoff; also September and October.

Directions: Park at the pullout for Lewis Falls and bushwhack up, or hike to the river from the Lewis Lake Campground.

Special rules: Limit of two brown trout, only one over 20 inches.

The headwaters of the Lewis River, where it pours out of Lewis Lake and runs about two miles before plunging over its namesake falls, is a great, early season spot to target brown trout. PHOTO BY NATE SCHWEBER

Daughenbaugh took the quick ride to the spot where the Lewis River flows out of Lewis Lake. He would park at the Lewis Lake Campground and then walk down the east side of the lake and fish the river.

Daughenbaugh said that the brown trout that live in the lake run down into the Lewis River and then follow the receding runoff back up around mid-June or later in heavy snow years.

"I'd say the average fish is between 14 and 18 inches, just gorgeous fish," Daughenbaugh said. "I don't think I've fished for a stronger fish than in there."

Daughenbaugh said the top of the Lewis River offers fantastic early season dry-fly fishing, particularly with size 14 parachute Mahogany Duns. He said, "I remember some mayfly hatches being so dazzling that I couldn't see my own fly on the water because of all the naturals."

"I often tell the story that one time I was fishing in there and the trout were taking a parachute fly with a rusty, brown body, which is a Mahogany Dun," he said. "I ran out of flies with a brown body, so I tied this other parachute on there that was more or less a Light Cahill. I threw that fly out there, and by darned they come and take. It didn't make much difference. I just hammered them."

Though Lewis Falls is the most famous waterfall on the Lewis River, upstream there are beautiful runs and chutes, plus wildflowers and thermal areas. PHOTO BY NATE SCHWEBER

He added, "It was a good experience to remember things like that."

Though the river holds most of its big brown trout through mid-June, a few keep residences in the stream all summer long. This section of river is all rushing chutes of water and an expanse of unfathomable blue at the outlet of Lewis Lake. When Daughenbaugh fished here in July, he always made sure to wade across the 100-foot river and try the west shore of Lewis Lake about 200 yards from the river outlet. "A lot of those fish congregate where the water funnels down and you get a lot of insects scattering together," he said. Daughenbaugh added that his best luck in that area was with wet flies and nymphs.

Sometimes Daughenbaugh caught fugitive lake trout that followed the browns down into the river, though he considered them better as dinner than as a sport fish. Catching a lake trout, Daughenbaugh said, is "like reeling up a sucker."

I took Daughenbaugh's advice and fished his stretch of river. I saw new falls, brilliant wildflowers, unseen hot springs, and an up-close marmot.

Daughenbaugh had warned me of another animal to be mindful of.

"One of the things I remember about fishing in that area is almost always I'd hear some splashing around behind me, and there would be about a 900-pound moose 10 feet from me," he said. "There always seemed to be a lot of moose up in there."

Daughenbaugh, who is now retired and lives in Montoursville, Pennsylvania, earned a reputation in his ranger days as the best guy to take visiting politicians fishing. "It just so happened that I caught every fish out there about four times," he said.

He tells a funny story about one-upping the First Doctor by painlessly removing a size 14 Yellow Humpy that President Jimmy Carter accidentally hooked in his left cheek while fishing with Daughenbaugh on the Snake River in 1979. Carter thanked Daughenbaugh by inviting him to the White House and serving for dinner cutthroat they had caught together on Yellowstone Lake.

I learned about Daughenbaugh during a conversation with former Vice President Dick Cheney, who had me hold the line while he looked up Daughenbaugh's number.

"They are two totally different people, but they are both dedicated fishermen," Daughenbaugh said. "And we never talked about politics; we were always too busy catching fish."

3 DeLacy Creek

Chris Hunt

Chris Hunt thought he was showing off to the big cow moose that chewed its grass about 30 feet away from where he plucked one wildly colored little brook trout after another out of DeLacy Creek.

Then he turned around and almost stepped on her calf, which was sleeping in the grass by the banks of this parking-space-wide creek.

"It was one of those heart-in-your-throat moments when you're not sure what's going to happen because mama moose tend to be ornery," said Hunt, who works for Trout Unlimited in Idaho Falls.

DeLacy Creek is a babbling little mountain stream that teems with hungry brookies from the spot where it passes under Grand Loop Road to

---

Trout: Brookies averaging 4 to 8 inches, with a few slightly bigger brown trout by the creek's mouth at Shoshone Lake.

Bugs: Terrestrials, mayflies, and caddis.

Suggested fly box: Size 14 attractor dry flies, including Royal Wulffs, Humpies, Elk Hair Caddis, and Parachute Adamses. Also, Dave's Hoppers size 6 to 14; crickets size 8 to 14; Parachute and Chernobyl Ant patterns size 14 to 18; foam beetles size 14.

Key techniques: Almost any dry fly tossed on the water here stands a good chance of catching a brook trout.

Best times: Anytime after spring runoff.

Directions: Park at the DeLacy Creek Trailhead, about nine miles south of Old Faithful or nine miles north of West Thumb. The trail parallels the creek down to Shoshone Lake.

About as wide as a parking spot, DeLacy Creek is easy to access from a pullout on the Grand Loop Road via a trail that follows the stream about three miles down to where it pours into Shoshone Lake. PHOTO BY NATE SCHWEBER

where it trickles into Shoshone Lake, three miles away. Hunt became curious about the little stream, which he calls "beautiful by anyone's barometer," after he saw it from the road. He researched it by "following the blue line" on a Yellowstone map. He fished it and discovered it was filled with his favorite backcountry delicacy: brook trout.

"In my opinion, the brook trout is the most underrated salmonoid in North America. They're feisty, they've got incredible survival skills, and for the record, they are the tastiest," said Hunt, who writes a conservation blog called Eat More Brook Trout, which recognizes the importance of lemon pepper in helping eradicate nonnative fish.

DeLacy Creek gurgles through stretches of pine forest and lush, green meadows that turn brown and bug-free by autumn. It was named for explorer Walter Washington DeLacy, who led a prospecting expedition from Jackson Hole up into southwest Yellowstone in 1863.[1] In the fall, a few brown trout run up into the lower parts of DeLacy Creek from Shoshone Lake. The browns can stretch a foot or more; they are veritable whales compared to DeLacy's resident population of 4-inch to 6-inch brook trout.

Hunt fishes for these brookies with an ultralight 2-weight or a Tenkara rod. Tenkara rods, originally from Japan, feature a fixed length of line attached to a long rod with no reel. The angler just daps the fly on the water's surface.

"Occasionally, you'll catch a pig that goes 9 inches," he said. "On a 2-weight rod you'll think you're fighting Moby Dick after a day of catching 6-inchers."

Eager brook trout fill DeLacy Creek, and a few slightly larger brown trout from Shoshone Lake can occasionally be found in the lower part of the stream. One day the park service may try to stock this stream with cutthroats, which are native to Yellowstone. PHOTO BY CHRIS HUNT

Hunt's favorite DeLacy Creek patterns include Parachute Adamses, Elk Hair Caddis, small Stimulators, and Royal Coachmans "if I'm in a colorful mood."

"They're not real picky," Hunt said. "It's a pretty austere environment, so when they see food, they go eat."

I visited DeLacy Creek twice. The first time, the creek was flushed with muddy runoff and I couldn't buy a strike. I also got caught in a hailstorm that felt like ice buckshot. The second time I visited, I couldn't keep count of the brookies I caught.

On the June day that Hunt met the moose, he was enjoying a quick afternoon fishing session while his wife and two kids rode bikes nearby. He noticed the moose staring at him when he was "close enough to hit her with a pine cone."

His initial pang of shock subsided fast when the moose acted nonchalant. Standing on the precipice of a fishy-looking hole, Hunt figured that being fixed in the glare of a 600-pound ungulate was no reason not to try to catch a few pretty fish. He plucked forest green, orange-bellied brook trout with white-edged fins and red spots practically from underneath that moose's hooves.

"That's Yellowstone right there," Hunt said, "one of the most unique experiences you can have as a fly fisherman anywhere."

When he finished, Hunt took two steps up the bank, and his nostrils filled with "that wet cow smell." Suddenly, a moose calf, around 150 pounds, leapt up from its bed in the streamside grass and bounded through DeLacy Creek toward its mother. Hunt's pulse thundered. The two moose sauntered off "without a care in the world," leaving Hunt to ponder why the encounter hadn't been more confrontational.

"In hindsight, that's nothing I would ever recommend; I damn near stepped on her calf," Hunt said. "Thankfully she didn't get pissed off and come after me."

Despite his deep love for DeLacy Creek and all her nifty brookies, Hunt supports a Park Service plan to poison out the creek's nonnative fish and stock it with Yellowstone cutthroats.[2]

"We've done a pretty good number on the natural order of things out here. Exotic brookies are everywhere in Yellowstone National Park, and introduced lake trout have absolutely decimated the native cutthroat fishery in Yellowstone Lake," Hunt said. "Anywhere we can do the right thing on behalf of native fish, I'm in favor of it. I probably won't get to see much of it, because it'll take years of work; but my kids will, and my grandkids will, and that makes me smile."

4 Crawfish Creek

Marty Meyer

Fast-clearing streams are a precious resource in the Yellowstone spring-time. Hordes flock to the fabled Firehole each season opener, as most of the park's other famous rivers rage with runoff.

Few crowd Crawfish Creek, which pours into the Lewis River after tumbling over Moose Falls near the southern border of the park. Marty Meyer, a ranger at the National Elk Refuge in Wyoming, has gone to fish the little stream in June, when it bubbles like 7 Up while other rivers still churn like chocolate milk.

"Early season fishing is scarce, and this is a stream that drops out and clears up pretty quick," said Meyer. He added that he fishes only a couple streams in Yellowstone with any regularity, and Crawfish Creek is one.

Meyer's most vivid memory of the creek is watching a fishing buddy beat him to their favorite hole and then act giddy for a half hour as each cast rose another cutthroat trout.

Trout: Cutthroat trout averaging 6 to 12 inches.

Bugs: Mayflies, caddisflies, and terrestrials.

Suggested fly box: Size 14 attractor dry flies, including Royal Wulffs, Humpies, Elk Hair Caddis, and Parachute Adamses.

Key techniques: Search the water with a bushy dry fly.

Best times: June and July.

Directions: Park at the pullout for Moose Falls right by the bridge over Crawfish Creek on South Entrance Road 1½ miles north of the south entrance of the park.

Special rules: Catch-and-release for cutthroats.

Deadfall clutters both banks of Crawfish Creek and the creek itself. While this can make for tough wading and hiking, it makes for plenty of lies for cutthroat trout.

PHOTO BY NATE SCHWEBER

"He caught fish cast after cast after cast for as long as he could take it and stood there giggling the whole time," Meyer said. "He was trying to rub it in. I just had to stand there and watch."

That the honey hole wasn't big enough for two underscores this stream's bite size. Its fish are appropriately proportioned. The first time Meyer came here, having gone exploring with his fly rod on the advice of a friend, he caught a Crawfish Creek lunker—almost 13 whole inches.

"That was a monster," Meyer said.

Most of the other Crawfish Creek cutthroats are around half as long, he said. And they attack just about any attractor dry fly—Royal Wulffs, Humpies, Elk Hair Caddis, Parachute Adamses. These trout strike with a ferocity that is energizing and joyous. They porpoise when they strike, or they breach completely and flip.

"You could spit in the water, and they'd eat," he said. "Any old dry fly will do."

About 1^1/$_2$ miles up Crawfish Creek, there is a meadow with a few hot springs where locals have been known to bathe. The warm water from the springs makes the creek hospitable to many of its namesake crawfish, and this stream boasts Yellowstone's biggest population of the crustacean.[1] It's also home to New Zealand mudsnails, an exotic, introduced species. Anglers and hikers need to take special care to clean and rinse their wading gear before getting near any other body of water.

While the average Crawfish Creek cutthroat is small, these fish slash at bushy dry flies, often porpoising and vaulting into the air. PHOTO BY NATE SCHWEBER

Moose Falls is a popular tourist attraction on Crawfish Creek, just upstream from where it pours into the Lewis River. Few anglers venture upstream, even though this stream often runs clear in the early season. PHOTO BY NATE SCHWEBER

Taking Meyer's advice, I fished Crawfish early in the summer, when other streams were still too high. Sure enough, I caught my fill of beautiful Yellowstone cutthroat trout on simple, bushy dry flies. One of them may have even been as big as Meyer's trophy. There is no trail that parallels Crawfish Creek, and there's plenty of downfall both in and out of the stream. Meyer calls wading versus hiking "six of one, half-dozen of the other."

Small trout and tough going keep Crawfish Creek a nonstarter in most anglers' minds. That is precisely what Meyer loves about it.

"There will be a handful who fish it in a given season," he said. "It doesn't attract many people."

5 Fawn Lake

Don Williams, James Woodhall

Don Williams's quest for the biggest brook trout he could catch brought him to Fawn Lake in northwest Yellowstone some 30 years ago.

A quest for his sack lunch brought the biggest grizzly bear he'd ever seen there, too.

Five-acre Fawn Lake lies in the Swan Lake Flats underneath Electric Peak, a five-mile hike up the Glenn Creek and Fawn Pass trails. Formerly part of the Mammoth water supply, the lake has been open to fishing for only about 40 years. Fawn Lake lies in rolling hills dotted by timber. "It's pretty open country," Williams said, "and it's not a difficult hike."

Brook trout grow big in Fawn Lake. Williams, who worked for a half century as a guide and outfitter out of Livingston, once caught a "big, heavy, fat"

Trout: Brook trout averaging about a foot, but with some trophies rumored to still swim there as well.

Bugs: Damselflies, scuds, and terrestrials.

Suggested fly box: Black, tan, and olive Woolly Buggers size 6 to 10 and size 14; tan scuds size 14; damsel nymphs size 8 to 12; Hare's Ear nymphs size 14, Parachute Hoppers size 8 to 12; Parachute Ants size 16 to 18.

Key techniques: Strip Woolly Buggers, scuds, and damselfly patterns.

Best times: Early and late in the season, with fishing slowing during mid-summer.

Getting there: Start at the Glen Creek Trailhead just south of Mammoth Hot Springs. Continue for two miles and then hike three miles on the Fawn Pass Trail. Fawn Lake will be unmarked to your left.

Sky-high Electric Peak peeks down at Fawn Lake, a brook trout fishery hidden in thick grizzly country a beautiful hike up the Fawn Pass Trail. PHOTO BY NATE SCHWEBER

Until about 40 years ago, Fawn Lake was closed to fishing because it was a water supply for guest services at Mammoth Hot Springs. It gained a reputation as trophy brook trout water, and though today's average fish measure about a foot, rumors of lunkers still abound. PHOTO BY NATE SCHWEBER

brook trout on Fawn Lake that he estimates stretched 20 inches and weighed four pounds.

"I thought, 'That's the biggest one I ever caught,'" Williams, 74, remembered. "I have a thing about catching a big trout of each species."

It's a gorgeous hike with breathtaking vistas of the bulky Gallatin Mountains to reach Fawn Lake. In midsummer the trail winds up through meadows blanketed with yellow arnica and lavender lupine. The first time I tried to go there, the trail was closed for a family of grizzlies. When I finally was able to go, I saw a big cow moose. I also sunk to my waist in muck when I tried to wade into Fawn Lake, but a brook trout with bodacious colors made it worthwhile.

Williams had a simple method for fishing Fawn Lake. He'd hike in with a light pair of waders and a sack lunch, which he'd stash up in a tree to keep it away from bears. He said he would wade out on the mucky lake bottom until the water was at his waist. Then he would cast out over the drop-off that parallels the shore. "The fish congregate there," Williams said. In the fall, when the biting bugs are mostly gone, the brookies "really color up" and spawn in Fawn Lake's feeder streams, which I noted in the summertime were filled with huge numbers of tadpoles.

Williams had his best luck stripping small Woolly Buggers, damselfly nymphs, and scud patterns.

"The size of the brookies seems to have dropped in the last few decades," Williams said, "but not by much. The lake still has plenty of two- and three-pound brook trout, and a big four-pounder isn't beyond the pale."

"There's still a lot of good ones, a lot of two-pounders, which for this country is a pretty good brookie," Williams said. "I've always had a thing for brookies, they're a beautiful fish."

Don't forget, it's also pretty good griz country. Williams learned that lesson well one day with his friend James Woodhall, a Forest Service firefighter and middle school teacher.

Williams and Woodhall, nicknamed "Woody," hiked into Fawn Lake with their usual gear—waders and sack lunches of sandwiches and fruit. When they got to the lake, they put on their waders and then hung the lunches in a tree inside a backpack.

Williams was waist deep, casting out toward the cruising brook trout when he felt a premonition to turn around. On shore, about 200 yards away, he saw a big grizzly bear walk out from behind a couple trees and head straight toward the dangling backpack.

Williams joked to his buddy, "Hey Woody, you want to share your lunch?"

"Woody said, 'What?'" Williams laughed. "I said, 'Look behind you.'"

Woodhall whirled around and saw the griz prowling toward the pack. The two fishermen shouted and whistled at the bear.

"This big ol' grizzly bear rears up on its hind feet and sniffs the air," Williams remembered. "It must've been seven feet tall."

Woodhall, 74, called it a "close encounter" that was "a little intense for a few minutes."

"But it was a wild bear," he said by phone from his home in Livingston. "He recognized human voices."

The bear dropped back down to all fours and "moseyed away," Williams said.

"I was glad to see him leave," Williams said. "And we went back to fishing."

6 Gibbon River

Shelton Johnson

Ranger Shelton Johnson and his young son Langston caught golden brown trout on that chilly summer day when they first fished the Gibbon River together.

The way Johnson looks at it, the fish caught them.

"For me that was a very powerful experience because it was my only son in a place I love more than any other place on the planet," Johnson said.

Johnson was one of the standout speakers in Ken Burns's 2010 series *The National Parks: America's Best Idea*, which aired on PBS. Born in Detroit, Johnson came to Yellowstone in 1987 and went through, in his own words, "a period of transformation."

"Yellowstone reveals who you are," he said. "Your best self comes out."

The Gibbon River, named for General John Gibbon,[1] has three distinct sections as it flows its entire length through Yellowstone Park. It begins at Grebe and Wolf Lakes, reservoirs of the rare arctic grayling. Sometimes these fish wash down into the river itself. Above Virginia Cascades, a lovely waterfall, the upper Gibbon teems with little, colorful brook trout that slash size 14 attractor dry flies and don't get many visits from anglers. The upper Gibbon has been eyeballed by park biologists as a possible place to try reintroducing westslope cutthroat trout, which are native to the drainage.

In its middle section, the Gibbon courses easily through broad meadows filled with bison and elk. Here big, wary brown trout hang under overcut banks and in deep pools. Catching them often requires technical match-the-hatch fly selection and extreme stealth. A simple tip I heard from a guide is that these trout will occasionally mash a simple olive Woolly Bugger drifting past them.

Below the meadows, the Gibbon turns into more of a freestone stream with riffles, pocketwater, and rainbow trout. Fish the pocketwater sections with attractor dry flies and nymphs and don't neglect unobvious places.

Some Gibbon trout have been known to hang out in unusually shallow water. Below the fantastic Gibbon Falls, which kept the upper portions of this stream historically fishless until it was stocked, whitefish show up, as do big fall browns that run up from Hebgen Lake.

Yellowstone was the first place that Johnson ever hiked in a National Park, climbed a mountaintop, camped in the backcountry, and surprised a grizzly bear. He said it is a place where the idea of being wild "isn't philosophical. You breathe it in; it makes your heart beat faster; you feel it against your skin."

Yellowstone was also the first place Johnson ever went fishing. It was on a fall day on the Gallatin River with his late friend Takayuki Kawakami, a fellow ranger and avid fly fisherwoman.

Johnson was eager to share the experience with his son.

Trout: Small brookies in the upper reaches that mix with some big browns up to 20 inches long in the meadow sections. Rainbows averaging 8 to 14 inches increase in density farther downstream. There are also whitefish below Gibbon Falls and an outside chance of a grayling washed down from Grebe Lake.

Bugs: Mayflies, including Brown Drakes, Pale Evening Duns, and *Baetis*; caddis; stoneflies; and terrestrials.

Suggested fly box: Royal Wulffs, Royal Coachman Trudes, Elk Hair Caddis, and yellow Stimulators size 14 to 18; Parachute Adamses size 14 to 20; Brown Drakes size 8 to 12; Hare's Ear and Prince nymphs size 14 to 20. Also, black, tan, and olive Woolly Buggers size 4 to 6.

Key techniques: Match the hatch; search pocketwater with attractor drys; stalk big fish carefully in the slow-moving meadow sections. Swinging soft-hackle wet flies can also be very effective on this river.

Best times: Just after runoff subsides through the summer on the main part of the river; through the first Sunday in November, for big brown spawners run up from Hebgen Lake below Gibbon Falls.

Directions: From its headwaters at Grebe Lake almost to Ice Lake, the Wolf Lake Trail roughly parallels the upper Gibbon. Then the river flows along Norris Canyon Road to the Norris Campground, where Grand Loop Road follows the river all the way to its junction with the Firehole at the headwaters of the Madison River.

Special rules: Catch-and-release for all species of trout, except brook trout.

Dramatic Gibbon Falls kept trout out of the upper reaches of this river until park officials stocked those waters with rainbow, brown, and brook trout plus grayling.
PHOTO BY NATE SCHWEBER

"I wanted him to feel he was a part of something bigger than he was," Johnson said. "When you have that line in the water, you're connected to something bigger than you."

Having grown up in urban Michigan, Johnson never had that experience as a child. In his capacity as a national parks advocate, Johnson has worked hard to bring more minorities into the parks, particularly those who live in inner cities. As an African-American who is also part Cherokee and part Seminole, Johnson espouses the message that the national parks are part of every American's heritage, regardless of color, background, income, or home-town.

Taking his son to fish at the Gibbon River was Johnson's way of person-alizing his philosophy.

"An African-American father bonding with his son on the edge of a trout stream in Wyoming is not a typical kind of bonding experience for many African-Americans in this country," Johnson said. "But it was an experience I wanted to pass along from one generation to the next."

He chose the Gibbon River because it was easy to get to from Grand Loop Road. "What I remember most about that day is my son and my wife, being together with my family beside the river, and just having a great time," he said.

Today, Johnson works in Yosemite National Park in California. He spent seven years working in Yellowstone and still visits annually.

A fishing line remains one way that Johnson stays connected to the national parks, to his family, and to the earth.

"There's an electricity you feel coming up the line when a fish strikes, kind of like the electricity Ben Franklin felt in the string attached to his kite in the thunderclouds," he said.

He added, "Fishing is illumination without electrocution. Hopefully."

7 Seven Mile Hole

*Tom McGuane, John Bailey,
Rachel Andras*

Author Tom McGuane first trekked to the bottom of the Grand Canyon of the Yellowstone in the late 1960s, shortly after he moved to Montana. Thinking back on his trips to Seven Mile Hole, the acclaimed writer said that the trout seemed to be not of this continent and the scenery not of this earth.

"The cutthroats were more colorful than African parrots," McGuane, author of more than a dozen novels, said from his home in Montana's Boul-

> **Trout:** Native Yellowstone cutthroats averaging 12 to 18 inches. In recent years, anglers have reported catching a few brook trout that have probably been migrating upstream.
>
> **Bugs:** Stoneflies, especially Golden Stones and Giant Salmonflies, plus mayflies, caddis, and terrestrials.
>
> **Suggested fly box:** Salmonfly patterns size 2 to 6; yellows Stimulators size 6 to 12; tan Elk Hair Caddis, Humpies, and Royal Wulffs size 14; Parachute Adamses size 14 to 18; Dave's Hoppers size 6 to 14; crickets size 8 to 14; Parachute and Chernobyl Ant patterns size 14 to 18; foam beetles size 14 to 16; black, tan, and olive Woolly Buggers size 4 to 8.
>
> **Key techniques:** Search the surface with dry flies.
>
> **Best times:** High summer, particularly during the Salmonfly hatch in late June, July, and early August.
>
> **Directions:** Start at the Glacier Boulder Trailhead on Inspiration Point Road near the canyon; take the Seven Mile Hole Trail about five miles, way down to the bottom.
>
> **Special rules:** Catch-and-release for all cutthroats.

It's only about five miles, not seven, to the bottom of Seven Mile Hole. But it's 1,300 feet down, and then 1,300 steep feet back up. PHOTO BY NATE SCHWEBER

der River valley. "And the landscape is almost like a science fiction setting. It's not reassuring; it's just a big crack in the stone in the middle of nowhere with a phenomenal fishery at the bottom of it."

The path to Seven Mile Hole, ominously nicknamed "The Goat Trail," is one of the only spots where the Yellowstone River is accessible inside its iconic canyon. The hike isn't actually seven miles; it's only about five. The spot takes its name because it lies seven miles downstream from the awesome, 300-foot falls that the Yellowstone River plunges over before it runs through this great gash of yellow rock.

The length of the trail is little consolation when considered against its contours. It's 1,300 feet down to the Yellowstone River and then 1,300 feet back up. Despite the difficulty, many veteran anglers call this trail essential. The path winds through jagged, chiseled stone that radiates with yellows, oranges, reds, and powdery, white rhyolite. It's a geologist's dream—a place of stone, steam, water, and wind; the very gears inside the clock of Yellowstone time.

"It's such an unusual landscape down there," McGuane said. "It's like a lightning fissure, like nothing you've ever seen before in your life."

McGuane said he was just as dazzled by the trout. He said Seven Mile Hole offered "crazy good fishing for big Yellowstone cutthroats." He remembers hooking them on old, classic attractor flies like Sofa Pillows and Picket Pins—patterns, he said, he hasn't seen in years.

Many veteran Yellowstone anglers make an annual pilgrimage to the bottom of the Grand Canyon, where the big river rushes through a great gash and cutthroats abound. The scenery here is unsurpassed. PHOTO BY CHRIS STETLER

"The cutthroat were so driven in their spawning activity they didn't even notice we were there; it was like being in a herd of caribou," McGuane said. "There would be these rivulets of water coming down out of the walls of the canyon with bathtub-sized puddles, and the fish would be climbing up the side of the rock. It was fishing for four-pound cutthroat at eye-level 10 feet away."

McGuane said that for many years he made annual treks to Seven Mile Hole. He called himself "young and adventurous then" and had caught "an absurd number of trout."

"But being young and adventurous doesn't do you any good," he said. "As you're fishing you're thinking, 'Now how am I going to get out of here?' You look up at the towering rock walls and see the shadows going down, and you think, 'I've got to get going;' but there's no point in rushing because it's so steep you can't go very fast."

Still, he came back year after year.

"It was like a ceremony," McGuane said.

Another man who made yearly pilgrimages to the spot is John Bailey, whose father Dan Bailey was the one who had told McGuane about Seven

Mile Hole. John said he would pick a day every spring to rise at four o'clock and make the long drive to the Seven Mile Hole Trailhead and the even longer hike to the bottom. John Bailey now runs Dan Bailey's Fly Shop, the family business that his old man founded in Livingston, Montana, in 1938.

"When you live in Livingston, you have to drive by an awful lot of good water to fish the park, so you might not do it that often," Bailey said. "But Seven Mile Hole is just so unique you have to go there; it's the kind of place you never forget."

Bailey said that the way the light bounces off the rocks at Seven Mile Hole; the way the water hue changes as the sun arcs over the sky; and the way eagles, ospreys, and ouzels swoop down below the canyon lips make it so no two visits are alike. They are always different in detail, but always constant in wonder.

"You can't help but look down from the rim of the Grand Canyon of the Yellowstone and think, 'What's it like down there?'" he said.

Then there's the fishing. Bailey described it as "just sensational."

"You tie on a fly, drop it in the water, and catch a fish," he said.

Rachel Andras caught her first Yellowstone cutthroat at the bottom of Seven Mile Hole after reminding herself to say "God save the Queen" between the moment she saw the trout rise and the moment she set the hook. PHOTO COURTESY OF RACHEL ANDRAS

Vivid reds, oranges, and yellows color the walls of the Grand Canyon of the Yellowstone at the bottom of Seven Mile Hole, while the river rushes big and turquoise. No two visits to this place are exactly the same. PHOTO BY JEFF REED

I made that long hike down to Seven Mile Hole on a day when the air was filled with Salmonflies. I moved a cutthroat trout with every cast, all of them seeming to glow in the jade water rushing over burnt sienna rock. I fished from shore in my hiking boots rather than dare dip a toe in the brawny, hemmed-in Yellowstone River. The catching was as good as anything I've experienced, at least once I figured out how to time my hook set.

Rachel Andras, founder of a women's fly-fishing club in Redding, California, also learned about the nerve-testing timing it takes to hook a Yellowstone cutthroat at the bottom of Seven Mile Hole. In 2004 she made her first visit to the spot with her husband and two friends. She quickly rose—and missed—a succession of big cutthroat trout with a size 18 Parachute Adams. "My companions jeered me from the bank, really giving me the business," she said.

Andras remembered she once heard a tip: Say "God save the Queen" between the moment you see a Yellowstone cutthroat rise and the moment you set the hook. That made all the difference.

"You know how painfully slow cutties are to eat a dry fly," she said. "It took me a few to get my groove on, to really start feeling it."

Soon she brought to hand her first Yellowstone cutthroat, all golden and brown with rose-colored cheeks and obsidian speckles.

"It was another feather in my hat; I always dreamed of catching a Yellowstone cutthroat in the heart of the park, where I heard how all the fish were strong and healthy and eager to eat a dry fly," she said. "And they were. It was just fly-fishing heaven."

8 Madison River at Elk Meadows

Craig Mathews

The top of the Madison River, which flows through Elk Meadows, is fly-fishing expert Craig Mathews's favorite spot because of a big brown trout that still makes him proud and a grizzly bear that still makes him laugh.

The first time Mathews fished Elk Meadows was in the fall of 1970 as a visitor. Three years later he would move to West Yellowstone to work as chief of police and open his shop, Blue Ribbon Flies. He would also go on to author books on fishing in Yellowstone, and the Madison River specifically. But on that first day he fished the river, Mathews learned an important lesson about the Mad's bad browns and bruiser bows.

"We were fishing big stonefly nymphs and stripping streamers," he said. "In the early afternoon, a snow squall came through and *Baetis* started popping, little Blue-Winged Olives, and the big fish started coming up."

The Madison, named after Secretary of State James Madison,[1] has an enormous variety of insect life, and in any hour of any given day, the trout might feed on mayflies, caddisflies, stoneflies, or even midges. Anglers must pay extremely close attention to figure out which ones the trout are eating, Mathews said.

"You have to be observant; you have to know the time to change flies," he said. "You might be there in the morning when there's a spinnerfall, and then 20 minutes later there's a hatch of White Millers, a caddisfly that's become a major hatch over the past few years because of the warming water."

Elk Meadows gets plenty of angling pressure, as West Entrance Road parallels the Madison for most of its 14-mile run out of the park. I was never alone when I fished here. But Mathews says most people drive out without a trout.

Prodigious weeds, the result of water that infuses the Madison from Yellowstone's geysers, create tricky currents that make drag-free drifts a wicked challenge. Plus the water is gin-clear, like a spring creek. Mathews recommends extralong leaders and hair-thin tippets.

"It's not a place for beginners," Mathews said. "You really have to be on your toes and on top of your game to fish it effectively and catch the bigger fish."

But, oh, what bigger fish those are. The Madison is famous for fall runs of hook-jawed golden brown submarines from Hebgen Lake, a trout factory just outside the western boundary of the park. Springtime brings the jet-powered rainbows. In July and August, the big fish have mostly migrated back down to the lake.

The biggest brown that Mathews caught in Elk Meadows, maybe the biggest brown he ever caught on a dry fly, typifies the mix of skill, persistence, and luck that goes into a successful day on the Madison. One June, Matthews saw a massive flash of gold against the far bank. He tried for that trout every day for a week, inching closer and closer until the river water lapped at the top of his waders. The brown was holding behind a stump that created the most bedeviling current, one that made it next to impossible to float a dry fly down without drag.

Trout: Resident rainbows and browns averaging 8 to 14 inches as well as spring and fall runners from Hebgen Lake that average 16 to 20 inches, with a fair number of even bigger fish. Also plenty of whitefish and even a remote chance of catching a grayling washed down from Grebe Lake.

Bugs: Mayflies, including *Baetis*, Pale Morning Duns, Gray Drakes, and Tricos; caddisflies; stoneflies, including Salmonflies and little yellow stones; and terrestrials, including hoppers, ants, and beetles.

Suggested fly box: Pale Morning Duns size 16 to 18; *Baetis* size 18 to 22; Gray Drakes size 10 to 12; Tricos size 20 to 22; X-Caddis and Elk Hair Caddis size 14 to 16; big Salmonfly patterns and yellow Stimulators size 10 to 14; Dave's Hoppers size 6 to 14; crickets size 8 to 14; Parachute and Chernobyl Ant patterns size 14 to 18; foam beetles size 14 to 16; Marabou Muddlers and Zonkers size 2 to 6.

Key techniques: Match the hatch; search with nymphs and streamers. Swinging soft-hackle wet flies can also be productive.

Best times: May and June; also September and October.

Directions: West Entrance Road parallels the Madison from its headwaters almost down to the border of Yellowstone.

Special rules: Catch-and-release for all species of trout, except brook trout.

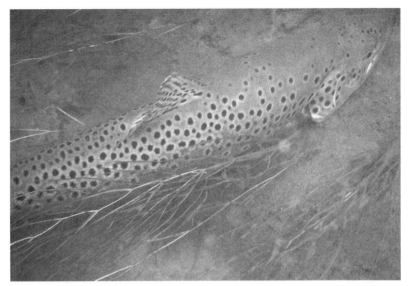

It takes skill, patience, and luck to catch a big brown trout like this one in the Elk Meadows section of the Madison River. Make sure to watch the water closely to determine exactly what kind of insect fish are feeding on. Keep an eye out for wildlife too.

He tried for that fish too many times to count. Then, as a last resort, he threw a pile cast with a size 16 Sparkle Dun at the end of his 6X tippet. Miraculously, the fly drifted without drag for all of two feet. "Up he took," Mathews said.

That brown trout measured more than 23 inches.

Mathews noted ruefully that the only audience to his triumph was a herd of bison. This is a fine illustration as to just how good the wildlife watching is in Elk Meadows, which lies in the shadow of National Park Mountain. A lot of anglers ought to watch the wildlife a bit more closely, as Mathews's good friend Paul Studebaker learned one day.

Studebaker was fishing on the far side of the river, opposite Mathews. A big griz came sauntering toward Studebaker, who didn't see it because he was casting to a pod of rising, splashing trout.

"I yelled, 'Hey Paul, you have a griz coming at you,'" Mathews said.

Studebaker didn't believe him.

"He yelled back, 'Yeah, right,'" Mathews said.

Kay Studebaker, Paul's wife, said from her home in Minnesota that both her husband and Mathews are "kidders."

"So it makes sense that Paul would think Craig was pulling his leg," she said.

Moments later, Studebaker saw the bruin come around the bend. The griz was less than 50 feet away and wasn't about to stop. Studebaker was boxed in between a sheer rock wall to his back and a river in front. The water was over his head.

"Paul yelled, 'What do I do?'" Mathews said. "'I said, 'You've got to swim for it.'"

Studebaker leapt in the river—with waders, vest, and all—and paddled to the other side.

"When he told me that story," his wife said, "I thought it was just par for the course."

Studebaker passed away in December 2006. Mathews said he always thinks about his friend when he fishes Elk Meadow. Kay Studebaker said for her late husband, "Yellowstone was his heaven on earth." Mathews hung a framed picture of Studebaker on the wall at Blue Ribbon Flies. The bear story still cracks him up.

"You can draw the same correlation between Paul failing to see the bear because he was concentrating on rising trout," Mathews said, "and fishermen concentrating so hard on stripping streamers that they fail to see the rises going on around them."

9 Minaret Creek

Mike Loebl

It's not being coy to say that the greatest fishing Mike Loebl ever had in Yellowstone was on Minaret Creek, even though you won't find that name on any park map.

Calling this gem of a stream by its original name, albeit a very short-lived one, reminds us of one of the funnier scenes in Yellowstone's early history.

Loebl, a guide, first fished Minaret Creek one June day with his buddy Jamie Crane, a screwball trout bum who drove a run-down, sticker-covered Ford Explorer with Connecticut plates and more trout flies stuck to the roof than any other vehicle on the road, save for maybe Loebl's Subaru.

Trout: Native Yellowstone cutthroat trout averaging 12 to 15 inches, plus brook trout and rainbow trout averaging 8 to 11 inches.

Bugs: Salmonflies, terrestrials, caddis, and mayflies.

Suggested fly box: Salmonflies size 2 to 8; yellow Stimulators size 6 to 14; Royal Wulffs, Elk Hair Caddis, Humpies, and Parachute Adamses, size 14; Beadhead Prince, Hare's Ear, and Pheasant Tail nymphs size 14; Dave's Hopper size 6 to 14; crickets size 8 to 14; Parachute and Chernobyl Ant patterns size 14 to 18; foam beetles size 14 to 16.

Key techniques: Cast bushy dry flies upstream into pools, behind rocks in current seams, and into pocketwater.

Best times: June through September.

Directions: Park by the Tower Campground in the lot by the general store and follow the trail down to the Yellowstone River near the mouth of Tower Creek.

Special rules: Catch-and-release for cutthroats.

The rock spires at the top of this beautiful waterfall inspired early park explorer Walter Trumbull to name it "Minaret Falls." The name was short-lived. PHOTO BY NATE SCHWEBER

This stream charges hard and fast to the Yellowstone River below its falls, and nice Yellowstone cutthroats can often be seen leaping into the air to get from one pool to the next. PHOTO BY NATE SCHWEBER

"I honestly don't know how that thing could run," Loebl said. (I tried hard via email to set up an interview with Crane, who now lives in Australia. It never worked out.)

Before their drive to the park's fishy northeast corner, where Minaret Creek swan-dives over Minaret Falls before its sprint to the Yellowstone River, Crane helped himself to breakfast.

"He pulled out some disgusting pasta dish in a pan that he kept underneath his car seat," said Loebl. "Then when he was full he put the pan back under his seat to eat later."

The dudes started fishing Minaret Creek right where it pours into the Yellowstone River. By the second pool, they realized they were in the middle of something extraordinary.

"It was some of the best fishing I've ever experienced," Loebl said. "Every spot you thought there would be trout, there were trout; and when you put your fly there, they would eat it like it was the first fly they'd ever seen in their lives."

Minaret Creek finishes strong to the Yellowstone River. Below its majestic, 132-foot falls, the creek sloughs off hundreds of feet of elevation, making for plunge pools and miniwaterfalls that I watched leaping cutthroats try to scale. "Every single pool had a bunch of cutthroats in it coming off the spawn," Loebl said. He said the foot-long to15-inch-long cutthroats, and a smattering of 8-inch brook trout, would "eat pretty much any size-14 dry fly you had a halfway decent drift with."

In particular, Loebl loved that each Minaret Creek cutthroat was pristine and perfect. "They weren't all hook-scarred like every fish you ever catch in Slough Creek," he said.

And he adored the way they ate dry flies.

"They'd eat it with a ridiculous, stupid innocence that was just wonderful," he said. "Native Yellowstone cutthroat come up slowly to a fly like they're trying to cherish it, like a little girl eating an ice cream cone, like it's the greatest thing in the world."

Just a short distance up the creek, Loebl and Crane looked at each other and said the same thing.

"We were both just like, 'Dude! The fishing is ridiculous!'" Loebl said.

The guys had to scamper up some boulders to get from the Yellowstone River up to the falls. At times, Loebl and Crane had to strategize as to the best route to scramble, and they had to pass their fly rods back and forth.

Then they reached awesome Minaret Falls. Craning their necks to gaze up at the cascading water, Loebl said he was stunned at "just how pretty" it was.

He said he also felt disappointed.

"Before we realized it," he said, "we had gone through all the water."

Actually, Minaret Creek above the falls offers nifty fishing, too, as Pennsylvania resident Greg Glitzer found out one fall day when rains blew out all the other streams around. He and a buddy had a ball on the upper creek juking out little brook trout and rare, genetically pure rainbows[1] that looked like they'd been rolled in pepper.

"For someone from upper Pennsylvania, pool-hopping in these little brookie streams was a very natural thing to do," he said. "And once you start, you can't stop."

But Loebl and Crane did stop, and reluctantly they hiked back to Crane's beat-up SUV with dinner waiting underneath the driver's seat. They drove away from Minaret Creek.

Only, it wasn't really Minaret Creek.

In 1870 an explorer named Walter Trumbull, son of Illinois Senator Lyman Trumbull, joined an expedition led by Henry Washburn, Montana's surveyor general, into Yellowstone. The group's job was to map the region that would become the first national park and name its geographical features. A rival of Trumbull's named Samuel T. Hauser was also a member of the expedition. The men in the group had made a gentleman's agreement not to name landmarks after family and friends.

Trumbull came to that majestic waterfall that one day a pair of awestruck fishing buddies would stand beneath. Trumbull thought that the spire-like rock formations around the falls resembled minarets. He suggested calling the cascade "Minaret Falls" and the stream "Minaret Creek." The other men in the expedition accepted the idea.

That night Hauser spread a rumor around camp. Trumbull, Hauser said, had a girlfriend in St. Louis named "Minnie Rhett." He named the falls after her in a blatant ploy for her affections and in flagrant disregard of the group's agreement.

Angered, the other expedition members scratched the name "Minaret" and let Hauser choose what to call the stream and the falls.

He dubbed them "Tower Creek" and "Tower Falls."[2]

Later Trumbull heard that Hauser—who would go on to be governor of Montana—had a girlfriend in St. Louis himself. Her name was "Miss Tower."[3]

So it was that Loebl and Crane didn't fish Minaret Creek; they fished Tower Creek.

Whatever the name, Loebl said there's only one word for the fishing: excellent.

"That day was one of the top memories I have in the park; the scenery was mind-blowing, and I was in a state of awe as to how good the fishing was," said Loebl, 34, who moved to West Yellowstone in 2001 from his home state of Michigan.

He added, "If there was a way for me to go back to that feeling, I would pay money for that."

10 Lower Gardner River

Yoshi Neff

For decades, park employee Yoshi Neff has loved fishing the lower Gardner River from the towering bridge near Mammoth down to the beer halls on Second Street in Gardiner because the river offers a Yellowstone grand slam: rainbow, brown, brook, and native Yellowstone cutthroat trout, plus whitefish.

These days he gives a little more respect to the cow elk he sees along the way.

"The Gardner is my favorite small stream to fish in the park because it has got it all," said Neff, a park employee since 1985. "It brings back the little boy in you again."

The lower Gardner is a ribbon of diversity: riffles, seams, undercut banks, side channels, tiny islands, and pockets behind boulders like the one where Neff caught a 20-inch rainbow one spring. During the brown trout spawning run in the fall, those same boulders harbor big

A giant Salmonfly clings to a blade of grass near the lower Gardner River. One of the most exciting hatches in the West, Salmonflies can be found on Yellowstone's waters from June through August. PHOTO BY NATE SCHWEBER

57

browns from the Yellowstone River—"just waiting to take a shot up through the next riffle," Neff said.

Neff began fishing the tumbling river soon after he started working in the park in Mammoth Hot Springs. He would park his ride just east of Mammoth, near the High Bridge over the river, and fish downstream to the park boundary. There he would grab a rinse or four in the Blue Goose or Two Bit Saloon in Gardiner before hitchhiking back home to Mammoth.

"It's a great day's fishing trip," Neff said. "But it's not for the faint of heart."

(The town of Gardiner is spelled with an extra "i" due to an early discrepancy about the correct spelling for Johnson Gardner, an 1830s-era mountain man for whom both the river and the town are named.)[1]

The trout are diverse. The riffles hold rainbows, and the deeper channels and runs harbor brown trout and cutthroats. Gardner River brook trout, which Neff calls "ferocious little fighting fish," are also sprinkled throughout, particularly just upstream from the Boiling River, a natural hot springs favored by bathers, where scalding runoff from the Mammoth Terrace drains into the river.

Trout: Browns, rainbows, brookies, native Yellowstone cutthroats, cuttbows, and whitefish.

Bugs: Stoneflies, including Salmonflies, caddis, mayflies, and terrestrials.

Suggested fly box: Salmonflies size 2 to 8; yellow Stimulators size 6 to 14; Royal Wulffs, Elk Hair Caddis, Humpies, and Parachute Adamses size 14; Beadhead Prince, Hare's Ear, and Pheasant Tail nymphs size 14; Dave's Hopper size 6 to 14; crickets size 8 to 14; Parachute and Chernobyl Ant patterns size 14 to 18; foam beetles size 14 to 16; black, tan, and olive Woolly Buggers size 4 to 8. In the autumn, Marabou Muddlers and Zonkers size 2 to 6; Montana and Bitch Creek nymphs size 2 to 6.

Key techniques: Fish the soft spots behind rocks, beside banks, and along current seams; in the autumn, dead-drift big nymphs and strip big streamers.

Best times: June through November.

Directions: Northwest Entrance Road roughly follows the Gardner River from the High Bridge just east of Mammoth almost down to the park border and the river's confluence with the Yellowstone River. Access it midway via the Lava Creek Trail.

Special rules: Catch-and-release for cutthroats and whitefish.

The lower Gardner River is an excellent, easy-to-navigate, and often-overlooked stream that holds cutthroat, brown, rainbow, and brook trout plus mountain whitefish. The Mammoth Road parallels this river from the Northeast Entrance up to Mammoth Hot Springs. PHOTO BY NATE SCHWEBER

"After a while you know the different types of strikes; you notice a subtle slurp of a cutthroat or the slash, smash of a brook trout," Neff said. "That's what makes it exciting; it's like, 'Oh look, I got a brookie; oh look, I got another cutthroat!'"

The lower Gardner River's banks range from sagebrush flats to cottonwood forests to cliffs filled with bighorn sheep.

Neff's favorite flies depend on the time of year. In June and July, he loves fishing the Salmonflies, which, he said, create clouds so thick along Mammoth Road that "if you're riding a motorcycle on that road, you're a man." Neff likes to match the Salmonfly hatch with a big Stimulator. In midsummer the bug-du-jour is the caddisfly, which Neff likes to imitate with an X-Caddis, a Prince nymph, or a caddis pupa dropper.

Late summer is grasshopper time, Neff said. In the canyon section, he particularly likes to aim his hopper pattern at the rock walls so the fly will ricochet off and "cause a splash that excites fish to eat."

In the cold, short days of the fall, Neff drifts big, gaudy, rubber-legged stonefly nymphs like Girdle Bugs, Bitch Creeks, and Montana nymphs for the spawning brown trout.

Neff said the fishing is great in the Gardner from the time it clears of spring runoff in June until the park fishing season closes in November. He added that it's a good stream for beginners because most of its length offers

Prickly pear cactus blooms on the banks of the lower Gardner River and is one of many wildflowers that add color to the overall experience of fishing in Yellowstone. PHOTO BY NATE SCHWEBER

plenty of room for casting, shallow water for wading, few crowds, and trout that aren't so wary that fishermen need to "put the sneak on."

I caught a frisky brown trout on my first cast in the Gardner River and then a chunky native cutthroat after that. Salmonflies and Golden Stoneflies clunked against my head, and some fell down my T-shirt. I stopped to look at resplendent, blooming lavender iris and yellow prickly pear cacti. I snapped off a couple big browns. I really did feel a little like I was 11 years old again, learning to fish on a stream filled with friendly trout.

One June day, Neff went out in his work clothes in the middle of a split shift to fish the Salmonfly hatch on the Gardner River near the swinging footbridge that is part of the Lava Creek Trail. In a meadow, he saw a cow elk munching on grass about 60 yards away. Neff watched his yellow Stimulator bob down a riffle, and when he looked up, "that cow elk was about 10 inches from me."

Neff, who hails from Pocatello, Idaho, said he grew up around wildlife and wasn't concerned. The next thing he knew the "Gol-darn elk" was on its hind feet throwing punches at him with its front hooves. Neff said he was backed up to the river in his work clothes thinking, "I'm not going in the river for you, bitch!" He shouted at the elk and got her to back off enough for him to turn around and try to beat a retreat. The cow rammed him in the back with her head.

A harem of cow elk and their calves tromp the banks of the lower Gardner River. Mother elk can act aggressive when protecting their young. PHOTO BY NATE SCHWEBER

"Next thing I know she jumped up and bit me on the shoulder," Neff said. "Left a good little bruise; it was just like getting chomped by a horse."

Neff whirled around and bopped the elk in the nose with the butt of his fly rod.

At that moment, just three feet away, a spotted baby elk—small, wobbly-legged, and shaking—emerged from its hiding spot underneath a bush and ran away. Its mother followed. Suddenly, Neff knew exactly why he'd been attacked.

"The calf was lying right next to me and didn't make a noise or nothing," Neff said. "If I'd have kept fishing, I probably would've stepped on her."

Neff said the elk bite only added to his love of fishing the lower Gardner River.

"It really does have a little bit of everything," he said. "That's why it's fun."

11 Grebe Lake

Molly Semenik, Jimmy Carter

Molly Semenik came to Grebe Lake chasing a ghost—the gray ghost. That is a nickname for one of the most rare, native salmonids in the continental United States—the arctic grayling, a silver fish with a sail-like dorsal fin that shines with colors more brilliant than gemstones.

Grebe Lake is the best place in Yellowstone to catch the gray ghost, and anglers like Semenik speak about them in a way that makes it almost seem like they are haunted by this fish.

"Catching a grayling," Semenik said, as she and I hiked to Grebe Lake one gray afternoon, "is like catching a little bit of history."

Stream-dwelling arctic grayling once swam the Madison River and all its feeder streams inside Yellowstone Park, including the lower Gibbon and Firehole Rivers and, appropriately, Grayling Creek. They also ran the Gallatin River. Once this fish flourished in Montana's Beaverhead, Jefferson, Smith, and Missouri Rivers,[1] as well as the Au Sable River in Michigan, for which the streamside town of Grayling, Michigan, was named.

Trout: Arctic grayling and rainbow trout.

Bugs: *Callibaetis*, scuds, and damselflies.

Suggested fly box: Attractor drys, including Royal Wulffs and Parachute Adamses size 14 to 16; Prince and Hare's Ear nymphs size 14 to 18.

Key techniques: Fish near drop-offs in the lake; chase after rising fish.

Best times: June through September.

Directions: Park at the Grebe Lake Trailhead, about $3^1/2$ miles west of Canyon Junction.

Special rules: Catch-and-release for all grayling.

Grebe Lake, the headwaters of the Gibbon River, has long attracted anglers hoping to catch a rare grayling. PHOTO BY NATE SCHWEBER

By the end of the twentieth century, native, stream-dwelling grayling, or *fluvial* grayling, went extinct everywhere but for a tiny population in Montana's upper Big Hole River.[2] Only in the Big Hole does this ultrasensitive, native fish hold its final stand against the killer forces of drought, dewatering, pollution, introduced species, and climate change. Attempts to restock them in their native streams have had minor to zero success.[3]

In 2002 Semenik was guiding on the upper Madison River just outside the park when her client caught an amazing, 16-inch grayling. Amber Steed, a fisheries biologist with Montana Fish, Wildlife, and Parks, said this grayling most likely washed down from Grebe Lake, the headwaters of the Gibbon River, which upon joining the Firehole River becomes the Madison. "There aren't huge numbers, but there are consistent grayling coming down from Grebe Lake, which has a pretty robust grayling population," Steed said.

Semenik remembers being spellbound by the sight of her first gray ghost.

"It was spectacularly beautiful," she said.

Semenik decided that day that she wanted to catch her own. She purchased and poured through volumes about fishing Yellowstone. She discovered Grebe Lake.

Biologists stocked Grebe Lake in 1921 with grayling eggs taken from Montana's Georgetown Lake,[4] which were introduced there from grayling eggs harvested from Upper Red Rock Lake in Montana in 1898 and Ennis

Grayling are distinguished by their large, sail-like dorsal fins, which shine with iridescent greens and blues. Grebe Lake sports a thriving population of this fish, which is nearly extinct in all its native rivers in the lower 48. This one was caught on a *Callibaetis* imitation. PHOTO BY NATE SCHWEBER

Lake on the Madison River in 1908. Grayling flourished so well in Grebe Lake that in 1931 the Park Service built a fish hatchery on the shore and raised hundreds of millions of eggs and used them to stock waters in 14 states before the hatchery was shuttered in 1956. Because Grebe Lake sits above Gibbon Falls, a natural fish barrier, it was fishless until 1907 when biologists stocked it with Yellowstone cutthroat trout, which were replaced by rainbow trout that were stocked in 1912 and today coexist with the grayling.[5]

Semenik first visited Grebe Lake in June 2002, arriving at the water's edge around eleven o'clock in the morning. Already the surface was pocked with grayling lips. She tied a size 16 Royal Wulff to a 5X tippet at the end of a 9-foot leader and waved her 4-weight wand. The ghost appeared.

"The grayling came up; his head came out of the water. He ate the Royal Wulff and swam off," Semenik said. "I slowly reeled him in, reached down with my hemostats, and took the hook right out of his mouth. I didn't even touch him."

The next time she caught a grayling, Semenik gently lifted up the foot-long fish's dorsal fin with her fingertips. She gazed like it was a silk tapestry.

"It was blue and iridescent green," she said. "Spectacularly beautiful, exquisitely beautiful!"

For Semenik, who has fished for 40 years, these first grayling made a vivid memory.

"It was really special to hold this native fish, this really special fish that is having a hard time surviving," she said.

Semenik is one of many who have made the grayling pilgrimage to Grebe Lake. In 1981 President Jimmy Carter and his wife Rosalynn came here, a trip he chronicled in his 1988 book *An Outdoor Journal.* "This crystal-clear body of water is one of the few places in the lower 48 states where native grayling have survived," Carter wrote. The first couple watched seagulls, osprey, and otters, and "caught and released several dozen grayling."[6]

Remembering back on his Yellowstone visits, President Carter told me in 2011, "It's good to realize that, if love and peace can prevail on earth, and if we can teach our children to honor nature's gifts, the joys and beauties of places like Grebe Lake will be here forever."

Almost a half century earlier, in 1933, seminal fishing writer Ray Bergman also traveled far for Grebe Lake grayling, which he described in his book *The Trout Fisherman's Bible* as "graceful, racy and colorful."

"When you looked at them in the water preparatory to landing them," Bergman wrote, "they looked like fish-shaped, animated purple flowers."[7]

I visited Grebe Lake with Semenik in the summer of 2011 and stood in a blizzard of mosquitoes under threatening skies while we cast toward the grayling rises just beyond a drop-off in the water. Within minutes, Semenik got one on a Parachute Adams that imitated the copious *Callibaetis* mayflies rising all around.

The fish was beautiful—incandescent.

Then lightning streaked the sky. We let the grayling go, reeled in, and headed back, lest we get caught in an electric storm. Hustling, Semenik said she loves the trail to Grebe Lake, which winds through groves of dead pines burned in the fires of 1988. For Semenik it's one of the best places in the park to hear her favorite woodsy sound, the cello-like creaking and percussive snaps of burnt pines in the wind.

They make a fitting soundtrack for a Grebe Lake ghost story.

"Anywhere I go I want to educate myself and be aware of the native landscape," Semenik said. "Grebe Lake gives me a sense of history."

12 South Arm of Yellowstone Lake

Dick Crysdale

For decades Dick Crysdale came to the South Arm of Yellowstone Lake to hear what he calls "the symphony of nature," trumpeter swans sounding, moose sloshing in the shallows, scores of geese thundering, and the percussive slurp of cutthroat trout rising.

"That symphony is gone now," Crysdale said, and its final notes have echoed through his ears down to his heart.

"Nineteen ninety-nine was the last year that Yellowstone Lake was itself," he said. "That year, I took a friend to the South Arm, and on a red and white daredevil spoon he caught 60 cutthroats in a row; good sized, two pounds and up."

The last time Crysdale visited the South Arm, in 2003, it took him and two friends nearly two hours to catch a single cutthroat trout.

"That's the contrast," he said.

From 1957 through 1960, Crysdale, 73, put himself through college by guiding two parties a day, six days a week to the South Arm of Yellowstone Lake. He called it, "always my fail-safe area."

"Where else in the world could you do that? Only on Yellowstone Lake," said Crysdale, who went on to work as a park ranger from 1961 to 1964.

Crysdale's fondest memory from this remote, backcountry part of the lake, accessible only by boaters and to the most intrepid hikers, was the time his then nine-year-old daughter CrisAnn accidentally caught a cutthroat while walking through a forest. Yellowstone Park sits above a massive caldera, a volcano from which the park's iconic geysers get their heat. Because of seismic shifts deep underground, the north end of Yellowstone Lake is rising bit by bit, making the water incrementally deeper on the south end, he said.[1]

In the early 1970s, CrisAnn sloshed through a pine forest on the bank of the South Arm that was covered with about eight inches of water, the result of both the lake's geologic tilt and the remnants of spring runoff. She slung her spinning rod over her shoulder and walked on, not knowing that her Mepps spinner dangled in the water behind her. Suddenly, a 15-inch cutthroat trout tugged back.

"She started laughing," Crysdale said. "She said, 'This is crazy.'"

Things got crazier a few years later when Crysdale and his wife paddled a canoe into a marshy cove where a giant bull moose munched on underwater muck. Crysdale wanted to ease up close and snap a good picture. He also figured it would be a good time to try and call the moose using a technique he said he learned from his friend Fred Garlow, grandson of William Frederick "Buffalo Bill" Cody.

Gliding right up close in the canoe, Crysdale, "gave it the moose call."

"I don't know what I said to it, but I must've pissed it off because it started charging," Crysdale said. "We took off in that canoe so fast you could've water-skied behind us."

Later, as Crysdale and his family shared ghost stories around a glowing campfire on the edge of the lake, they heard sloshing footsteps coming out of the water. They gaped as a behemoth bull moose, bathed in orange firelight, strode right through their camp and disappeared into the forest.

Trout: Yellowstone cutthroat trout averaging 15 to 20 inches and lake trout.

Bugs: Mayflies, including *Callibaetis*, Pale Morning Duns, and Gray Drakes; caddisflies; terrestrials; scuds; and leeches.

Suggested fly box: Black, tan, and olive Woolly Buggers size 4 to 8; Parachute Adamses size 12 to 18; Elk Hair Caddis size 14 to 16; Prince and Hare's Ear nymphs size 14 to 18; scuds size 14; Parachute Hoppers size 6 to 14; crickets size 8 to 14; Parachute and Chernobyl Ant patterns size 14 to 18; foam beetles size 14 and 16.

Key techniques: Strip Woolly Buggers from shore; fish near drop-offs; watch for rising trout.

Best times: June through September.

Directions: Reach the South Arm of Yellowstone Lake by parking at the Heart Lake Trailhead on South Entrance Road and hike approximately 22 miles on the Heart Lake Trail, the Heart River Trail, and the Trail Creek Trail. Or go the long way: park at the Nine Mile Trailhead on East Entrance Road and hike approximately 30 miles, taking the Thorofare Trail to the Trail Creek Trail.

Special rules: Season opens June 15. Mandatory kill for all lake trout; if you don't wish to keep the fish, puncture its air bladder and throw it back in the lake. Catch-and-release for cutthroats.

"We just sat still and watched it," Crysdale said. "That was something."

For years Crysdale brought his family back into Yellowstone Lake's South Arm each summer for backcountry camping, wildlife watching, and fishing. "The spot was a rhapsody," he said.

Today it's still gorgeous on the South Arm of Yellowstone Lake. The cerulean waters and jagged, snowcapped, backcountry mountains still inspire the eyes; and the few cutthroats that remain are big, strong, and perfect enough that it is worth all the effort it takes to catch them.

But for backcountry lovers like Crysdale who once heard Yellowstone Lake's orchestra, the silence aches. Forty-two species of animals, from pelicans to grizzly bears, depended on Yellowstone Lake's cutthroat trout for food. They now seem as few and far between as the cutthroats themselves.

"Bald eagles, trumpeter swans, osprey, pelicans, bunches of geese, loons—oh, man, the loons were something else," Crysdale said.

Despite Crysdale's sadness about losing what he calls "the true wilderness experience" on the South Arm of Yellowstone Lake, he is optimistic that one day the cutthroats can rebound. But only if humans stay committed to killing those illegally planted, nonnative lake trout. To that end, Crysdale wrote a book called *Yellowstone, Cutthroats, and Me: A Fishing Guide's Autobiography*, and he is donating all the proceeds to the East Yellowstone Chapter of Trout Unlimited to boost efforts to kill the lake trout. For a copy of the book, send $35 plus $6 shipping to Dick Crysdale, 4268 West Lake Circle South, Littleton, CO 80123, call 303-795-9148, email cutthroats@dickcrysdale.com, or visit http://dickcrysdale.com. So far, Crysdale has donated more than $5,000.

"I'm optimistic that we can bring the cutthroat trout back," Crysdale said. "However, it's going to take a major effort to keep the lake trout population under control."

Alien Invasion

liens invaded Yellowstone in the late 1800s. Horse-drawn wagons filled with fingerlings from a Michigan hatchery allowed park officials to stock the first nonnative fish in 1889. They planted brook trout, originally from the Northeast, in the upper Firehole River and rainbow trout, originally from the West Coast, in the upper Gibbon River.[1] In 1890 they put a load of red-spotted, Von Behr brown trout, originally from Germany, into Nez Perce Creek.[2]

These were the first fish to arrive in Yellowstone not of their own gumption, but of early stewards' desire to "improve" the fishery. With the invention

In the late 1960s and early 1970s, park managers set strict creel limits in order to boost flagging populations of Yellowstone Lake cutthroats. The result was an incredible trout resurgence, as seen by this cluster of cutthroats near LeHardy Rapids on the upper Yellowstone River; a common sight in the 1970s, 1980s, and early 1990s.

Between the mid-1970s and mid-1990s, this was the scene each spring on streams that poured into Yellowstone Lake. Millions and millions of cutthroats returned to the places they were born to spawn.

Rainbow trout, which can crossbreed with cutthroats, were first stocked in Yellowstone in the late 1800s. They contributed to the near wipeout of westslope cutthroats in the park as well as the decimation of many pure populations of Yellowstone cutthroats.

of the car, more tourists flocked to the park expecting to catch fish. By the 1920s, park managers figured that stocking was just the way to fill their creels.[3]

The floodgates opened. Historically, almost 40 percent of lakes and streams in Yellowstone were fishless,[4] most of them lying above waterfalls that acted as natural barriers. Park officials built three fish hatcheries in Yellowstone, at Trout Lake, Grebe Lake, and Yellowstone Lake.[5] They stocked grayling in the headwaters of the Gibbon River around 1921 and then rainbow trout in the Little Firehole River in 1922. Brown trout were stocked in the Madison in the park in 1929 and rainbows the following year, augmenting the population that had already been stocked in the river outside the park.[6] The new browns and rainbows were buoyed by the 1915 completion of the Hebgen Dam, which flooded crucial grayling spawning areas and impeded their migrations,[7] but created a giant reservoir for rainbows and browns to grow fat.

In the 1930s, park managers also stocked rainbow trout in the Lamar River, giving the native cutthroats, for the first time, a second sport fish with which to compete. As both species of fish spawn in the springtime, the 1930s also marked the first time the Lamar River ever saw a third kind of trout, a hybrid between a cutthroat and a rainbow known as a cuttbow.[8]

Sunset over the backcountry of giant Yellowstone Lake, where many species of animals have been hurt by the decline of the cutthroat trout. PHOTO BY NATE SCHWEBER

Park managers even tried stocking Yellowstone Lake with rainbow trout, Atlantic Salmon, and whitefish. Fortunately, none of these took hold.[9] It seemed as if no sport fish could survive in Yellowstone Lake but its scores upon scores of cutthroats.

Just a few miles from Yellowstone Lake, in historically fishless Lewis and Shoshone Lakes, a lake trout population took hold. Around 1890, famous zoologist David Star Jordan hatched the plan to stock Lewis Lake with 40,000 lake trout from Lake Michigan and, to feed the lake trout, thousands of Loch Levan brown trout from Scotland plus Von Behr browns (Loch Levan brown trout have almost entirely black spots while Von Behr browns may have a few red spots. The two species have mixed in America). Workers brought the fingerlings to Lewis Lake in milk cans hauled on mules and packhorses.

Soon Jordan raved that "every place they put the lake trout, it did well." In a quote that reads like Dr. Frankenstein in retrospect, Jordan said that inside Yellowstone's waters the lake trout was the "king of beasts."[10]

Native fish numbers began to drop almost immediately. Nowhere was this more pronounced than on the west side of the park. By the late 1930s, all the westslope cutthroats in the Madison River were gone, followed shortly by the grayling.[11] The same thing happened in the Gallatin River. In many other streams in Yellowstone, introduced brook trout outcompeted and wiped out native Yellowstone cutthroats. In 1936 the Park Service realized what was happening, and they banned the stocking of exotic fish species anywhere in Yellowstone.[12] But the damage was done, and it reverberates to this day.

By the 1950s, even mighty Yellowstone Lake was in trouble. Decades of early tourists catching cutthroats by the mule-loads ripped out a huge chunk of the population, as did anglers plucking cutthroats out of the prime spawning habitat below Fishing Bridge. Biologists sounded the alarm in 1954 when the weir at Clear Creek, built in 1945, counted only 3,161 spawning cutthroats,[13] down precipitously from more than 20,000 just a few years earlier.

Yellowstone's stock as a trout dreamland plummeted. Historian John Byorth wrote in 2002 that by the 1950s, fishing in Yellowstone "stunk."[14] A May 1985 *Field & Stream* article said fishing in the park "reached an all-time low in the 1960s" and added, "By 1970, fishing was so poor that few visitors who thought of themselves as experienced anglers even bothered to fish."[15]

Park officials took decisive steps to turn things around. In the late 1960s, they imposed the strictest creel limits yet on cutthroats caught in Yellowstone Lake. In 1973 they outlawed fishing from Fishing Bridge. And in 1975 they instituted a rule that Yellowstone Lake cutthroat could only be kept if they were less than 13 inches, thereby saving the big spawners.[16]

The result was a trout renaissance. Freed from the pressures of overharvest, the Yellowstone Lake cutthroats came roaring back. From the late 1970s to the early 1990s, the weir at Clear Creek counted on *average* more than 43,000 spawning cutthroat each spring. The count spiked to an incredible 70,105 spawning cutthroats in 1978.[17] Birds and otters thrived. Grizzlies fished for cutthroats in Yellowstone Lake's feeder streams like brown bears in Alaska fished for salmon. The Park Service proclaimed that the Yellowstone Lake had returned to a state of "ecological bliss."[18]

Anglers fell in love with Yellowstone all over again, and they told their fish stories with the same exuberance as their predecessors a century earlier.

In that giddy cutthroat year of 1978, fly-fishing Hall of Famer Lee Wulff raved about the resurgent park in *Sports Afield*, saying, "I have seen the fishing of the future. It is superb."[19] In a new introduction for a reprint of Howard Back's book *The Waters of Yellowstone with Rod and Fly*, Craig Mathews wrote, "The fishing here is as good, and in many cases better, than when Back wrote his book in 1938. We *are* living in the 'good ol' days.'"[20]

Legendary park angler Charles E. Brooks gushed in his 1984 book *Fishing Yellowstone Waters*, "This is the greatest trout-fishing paradise anywhere on this earth and its future is brighter today than it was ten years ago."

He added, fatefully, "Ten years from now it will be better still."[21]

He never predicted the disaster coming a decade down the line.

13 Heart Lake

Boots Allen

Ever since he was a boy, Boots Allen knew that trophy fish came out of the deep backcountry waters of Heart Lake.

In 1983 when Allen was just 11 years old, his father Joe Allen had his picture in the *Jackson Hole News* for leading an expedition into Heart Lake with rubber rafts that dredged up several lake trout that weighed between 35 and 40 pounds.

Trout: Yellowstone cutthroat trout and lake trout averaging 15 to 20 inches, some considerably larger.

Bugs: Mayflies, including *Callibaetis*, Pale Morning Duns, and Gray Drakes; caddisflies; terrestrials; scuds; and leeches.

Suggested fly box: Black, tan, and olive Woolly Buggers size 4 to 8; Clouser Minnows, JJ Specials, and Tequeelys size 2 to 6; Parachute Adamses size 12 to 18; Elk Hair Caddis size 14 to 16; Prince and Hare's Ear nymphs size 14 to 18; scuds size 14.

Key techniques: Strip streamers and Woolly Buggers from shore; fish near drop-offs; watch for rising trout.

Best times: July; again in September.

Directions: Park at the Heart Lake Trailhead on the left side of South Entrance Road just before Lewis Lake comes into view on the right. It's a moderately strenuous eight-mile hike to Heart Lake, which features several backcountry camp spots.

Special rules: No limit for lake trout; if you don't wish to eat the fish, puncture its air bladder and throw it back in the lake. Catch-and-release for cutthroats.

The stunning view of massive Heart Lake from the Heart Lake Trail with steaming thermal vents in the foreground and snowcapped mountains in the background.
PHOTO BY NATE SCHWEBER

"He had very big guys along on that trip, and they strung the big lake trout across one of the oars of the boat," Allen said. "It took three guys to lift five of those fish."

Despite its fishery, which some veteran anglers have dared call the best for inland cutthroats in the country, Heart Lake remains a seldom-visited treasure that is protected by threat and toil. Named for Hart Hunny, an early hunter,[1] Heart is wholly a backcountry lake, almost an eight-mile hike from the nearest trailhead. Grizzlies abound on its shores, and their tendency to hunt fish on Heart Lake's feeder streams in the spring prompted park managers to close the lake until July 1. The trail to Heart Lake winds past ominous geysers and through veritable walls of bloodsucking bugs.

Hearty anglers are rewarded with the opportunity to catch an eight-pound native Yellowstone cutthroat blooming with color, or maybe even a lake trout that weighs as much as a newborn horse. Seeing pictures of his dad's monster macks "really set me off," Allen said.

"Some say the next record lake trout is going to come out of Heart Lake," said Allen, 39, who has in his life had but three fish mounted, all of them Heart Lake mackinaws. The biggest fish ever caught in Yellowstone, a 42-pound mackinaw harvested in 1931, came from Heart Lake. Today that fish is mounted above the help desk in the ranger station at the Bridge Bay Marina near Yellowstone Lake. It is the size of a reef shark.

Heart Lake is home to an incredible native cutthroat trout fishery, despite having been invaded by lake trout that were stocked in Lewis Lake in 1890. Excellent cutthroats like this are commonplace, and anglers are allowed to kill any and every lake trout caught here. PHOTO BY NATE SCHWEBER

Historically, Heart Lake, like all of Yellowstone's waters, had no lake trout. They swam here after they were introduced to Lewis Lake in the 1890s.[2] Heart Lake is now also home to other species of nongamefish, including suckers, chubs, and possibly predatory brown trout, biologists say. That diversity of fish species might be the answer as to why cutthroats and lake trout can coexist in Heart Lake, but not in less-diverse Yellowstone Lake. Park fisheries biologist Pat Bigelow said lake trout in Heart Lake could feed on the abundance of suckers and chubs and not almost exclusively eat cutthroats, as happens in Yellowstone Lake. Still, Bigelow said it's worth imagining Heart Lake without lake trout. At one time, giant, fish-eating cutthroats swam here, sometimes reaching the sizes of some of today's lake trout, she said.

"Those big, piscivorous cutthroats aren't there anymore," she said, "but it's worth remembering they used to be."

The cutthroats are what Allen comes to Heart Lake to catch. He calls them "classic lake cutthroat" that are "girthy and fat" and "have that serious heaviness to them." Allen said he's caught cutthroats upwards of ten pounds in Heart Lake, fish specimens at least five years old that are fully mature so "they've got these achingly beautiful colors."

"They have that buttery yellow that goes along with the rosy, almost crimson gill plates and the deep, dark, red cuts under their jaw," he said. "They might be the most beautiful trout in the world."

While fishing for a Heart Lake cutthroat, Allen has never minded hooking a memorable lake trout.

Around 2000 Allen took his customary days-long excursion into Heart Lake with a friend. "It's a long hike, so once you're in there you want to stay for a bit," he said. One evening at dusk he went to fish the flat in the northeast bay, not far from the source of the Heart River. He waded out to his chest and threw long, sweeping casts into the encroaching darkness. He caught a few beautiful cutthroats on an olive-over-white Clouser Minnow. Then he got snagged. Or so he thought.

"I was thinking, 'Did I hit bottom?' And then this thing began to move with a nose-down, bulldog-type movement, like a redfish," he said.

The tug was so strong and the movement so exaggerated that for several minutes Allen thought he foul-hooked a big trout and was fighting to pull it in by the tail. He strained his eyes through the darkness and could tell when the fish sliced the surface that it wasn't foul-hooked. Soon he dragged the fish to within 10 feet of him and saw its "gray-on-white, white-on-gray" coloration and knew he was fighting a leviathan lake trout. Finally, his friend was able to grab the fish by its tail and haul it onto the shore.

"I think that's the largest freshwater fish I've ever caught on my own," Allen said. "I'd caught big lake trout trolling down deep with my dad, but this one I did on my own way the hell out in the back of nowhere, and I was pretty damn happy about it."

Today that mackinaw swims on Allen's wall, over his fly-tying desk.

For both cutthroats and lake trout, Allen strips streamers that look like suckers and chubs. He likes to use JJ Specials or Tequeelys on sinking-tip lines. He fishes them around drop-offs, shelves, and points that he approaches by wading from the shore. Allen also likes to fish near the mouths of Heart Lake's feeder streams, particularly early in the season when cutthroat congregate to feed on eggs from spawning suckers that wash down the creeks. Cutthroats, chubs, and the suckers themselves then become snacks for big macks.

Even when he sees trout rising, Allen prefers to cast streamers rather than switch to dry flies. He believes that by stripping a streamer past a rising trout, he can prompt a territorial strike.

"It gets hit less as food and more out of aggression," Allen said. "If you strip a streamer through rising trout, you'll get hit a lot."

I was amazed by the fishing at Heart Lake. After a healthy hike in spent marveling at geysers and the snowcapped mountains in back of Heart Lake's big blue, I waded out and stripped Woolly Buggers. I caught a two-foot cutthroat and several more that topped 20 inches—thick, olive-backed submarines that cranked my reel backward while I braced the butt of my fly rod against my forearm for support. I didn't catch any lake trout. At night a group of friends visiting from Monterey, California, and Washington, D.C., invited me to their camp and gave me their last splash of Scotch. In the course of conversation, a 14-year-old named Duncan, who fished beside me much of the afternoon, told a story about getting a canoe ride in Heart Lake with a kind ranger who had tied his own Woolly Buggers with black bear hair. Duncan said he had used one and caught an 18-inch cutthroat.

Allen got the name Boots from his grandfather Leonard Raymond Allen, who stopped in the town of Moran, Wyoming, in 1927 to help finish the Jackson Lake Dam and stayed to catch for the town's baseball team (he was the only one with the right mitt). He got his nickname one night before a big Jackson Hole dance when he pulled on a cowboy boot only to discover that someone had punk'd him by filling it with cow flop. In 1935 Leonard "Boots" Allen became just the second outfitter in the town of Jackson Hole. He passed the family business on to his sons.

Leonard's grandson, Joseph Boots Allen, first visited Heart Lake with his father when he was 10 years old. He's kept coming back for the trout and the solitude. "You walk a mile or two into the backcountry and people disappear; they melt away," he said. "When there's no moon, the amount of stars you see is magnified tenfold and you see that wispiness in the night sky, whatever it is up in space that gives it the name Milky Way."

On one seven-day trip, Allen remembers seeing just two rangers and one pack-horse expedition.

"And that was crowded," he said.

14 Cascade Creek

Allen "Flysoup" Crise

Allen "Flysoup" Crise tells a story about getting one of his biggest thrills, and biggest chills, on Yellowstone's tiny Cascade Creek.

After he retired from his career as an electrical engineer, Crise, who lived, built rods, and taught fly casting in Glen Rose, Texas, visited Yellowstone each summer in an RV. He came with his wife Nola Crise and a list of fish that he wanted to catch in his lifetime.

One of them was the Yellowstone cutthroat trout.

Trout: Yellowstone cutthroat trout averaging 6 to 11 inches, with an outside shot of a bigger cutthroat or an arctic grayling washed down from Cascade Lake.

Bugs: Mayflies, caddisflies, and terrestrials.

Suggested fly box: Size 14 attractor dry flies, including Royal Wulffs, Humpies, Elk Hair Caddis, and Parachute Adamses; Dave's Hoppers size 6 to 14; crickets size 8 to 14; Parachute and Chernobyl Ant patterns size 14 to 18; foam beetles size 14 to 16.

Key techniques: Search the water with attractor dry flies.

Best times: June through October.

Directions: Park at the Cascade Lake Trailhead a half mile west of Canyon Junction. You will pass right over Cascade Creek. Follow the stream up.

Special rules: Catch-and-release for cutthroats. Make sure all gear used in any other water has been cleaned and dried in order to protect against the spread of invasive species, such as whirling disease and the New Zealand mudsnail. Barbless hooks only. Check the most current regulations.

Easy to manage, and filled with colorful cutthroats, Cascade Creek has kept many anglers fishing for longer than they intended.

The Crises parked their RV within sight of where little Cascade Creek trickles underneath Grand Loop Road not far from Canyon Campground. Ol' Al, as many called him, headed out with a day pack, his waders, and his four-piece, 3-weight custom rod kitted out with Concept single-foot guides and a Fly Logic reel loaded with DT-4F line.

"I felt that I would want to make short casts and quickly load the rod with a short line," he wrote. "I had glanced at the creek the night before as we returned from a West Yellowstone shopping trip. There were no overhead trees to worry about, just low brush in the valley."

Before he fell asleep on the eve of his fishing trip to Cascade Creek, Crise read a book with details about its fish. He was excited to learn that the length of the creek held his quarry, the Yellowstone cutthroat, along with possibly a few grayling washed down from Cascade Lake.

Crise walked down to the stream that early July morning, whistling a tune. Puffs of vapor hung in the air after each breath. He saw birds and ground squirrels and even a yellow-bellied marmot that dove into its burrow. Nola watched from the porch of their RV until he was out of sight.

"He went off as carefree as all get-out," she said.

Crise maneuvered his way to the stream over spongy ground and through tall brush that left him soaked with morning dew. Direct sunlight made the rocks on the bottom of the creek look like rainbows. The creek was only about three feet wide. He noticed tiny mayflies caught in spiderwebs and tied on a size 16 Pale Morning Dun. He cast upstream where the glassy water was dimpled with rises, and he looked for lies that might hold Yellowstone cutthroat, the trout that would allow him to put one more check on his lifetime list.

Fifteen minutes later, he got one.

"She was a fighter, about eight inches long," he wrote. "Not what you would call big or even a large trout. What it was to me was a big step in my fly-fishing life. Yellowstone cutts were one of the things I wanted to mark off this year."

By 8:30 in the morning, he'd caught and released about a dozen earnest little cutthroats, the biggest one stretching to about 11 inches. Sometimes he saw a splash at the end of his line and took so long to set the hook that he was sure the trout spat his fly out. More than once he found that the determined little cutthroat kept that Light Cahill clenched in its jaws long enough for Crise to hook it, net it, and release it. He took a picture of one of his catches sparkling in his net.

A little farther upstream, Crise spotted two moose at the far end of a wide meadow.

"They were belly-deep in the rich summer grass," he wrote.

Crise cast to another cutthroat. He waded about 50 feet upstream. Then he looked up again to check on the moose. They had been about 200 yards from him. Now one of the moose was about three-quarters that distance and coming at him with hilarious, but alarming, determination.

"I have seen some funny-looking things in my time," Crise wrote. "The moose was like a young foal trying to run the first day, or a camel racing across the desert."

Crise quickly realized that he was alone in wild country with nothing more to fend off the moose or, God forbid, bears than the smile on his face. He turned back toward the road, checking over his shoulder for an angry, awkward animal with a big snoot.

"When he saw that moose coming at him, he decided that wasn't really a good place for him to be right then," Nola said.

Like Crise I found Cascade Creek so easy to navigate, and its cutthroat so pretty and friendly, that I unknowingly ventured far farther upstream than I intended to go.

Crise heaved a sigh of relief when he finally saw the road. Near where the creek tumbled beneath it, he cast to a few more cutthroat trout. He enjoyed how fishing relaxed him again.

Just then a gray wolf came into view along the edge of a nearby valley.

"He was just trotting along as if it was his very own backyard," Crise wrote. "As well it was."

When he got back to his RV and told his wife about his adventures with the moose and the wolf, she was livid.

"I really got onto him about going down there all by himself," she said. "I was always the worrywart."

Despite her admonishments, she couldn't take the smile off her husband's face. He had a list to find, and it needed another check mark.

Crise passed away on Valentine's Day 2010 after a battle with throat cancer. He had been vice president of education for the Southern Council of the Federation of Fly Fishers. He also worked with Casting for Recovery, Reel Recovery, and Project Healing Waters to help cancer survivors and wounded veterans fly-fish. Perhaps his most lasting legacy is the scores of youngsters whom he taught to fly-cast.

"He poured his soul into teaching kids to fly-fish," said his friend Ken Morrow.

Allen Crise shared his Cascade Creek adventure on an Internet fly-fishing forum. Nola spoke about her late husband from her home near Dallas.

She said she's working on a book about her husband's remarkable life—a life that, thanks to Cascade Creek, included Yellowstone cutthroat trout.

15 Trout Lake

Jeff Hull

Author and journalist Jeff Hull once brought a dozen students enrolled in his nature-writing class to Trout Lake for a lesson about observing the natural world.

Hull then observed scores of big cutthroats and a few jaw-dropping rainbows cruising the looking-glass waters of Trout Lake.

Trout: Cutthroat trout averaging 14 to 22 inches; rainbow trout up to 10 pounds.

Bugs: Pale Morning Duns, Blue-Winged Olives, caddis, midges, damselflies, and scuds.

Suggested fly box: Copper John, Hare's Ear, and Prince nymphs size 18 to 20; damselfly nymphs, including Skinny Buggers, size 6 to 12; Egg-Sucking Leeches size 4 to 8; tan scuds size 14; tan Elk Hair Caddis size 14 to 16. Also egg patterns.

Key techniques: Sight cast to cruising trout.

Best times: Early in the season. In the late summer, weed growth on the lake bottom and fish used to seeing hooks make fishing more difficult.

Directions: There is a large pullout on the north side of Northeast Entrance Road 14.8 miles west of Cooke City or 18.3 miles east of Tower Junction. The hike to the lake is short, about 400 yards.

Special rules: Trout Lake opens June 15, but the area around the inlet stream is closed year-round. Catch-and-release for all cutthroats; limit of five rainbows. Park officials plan to rid this lake of rainbows soon to create a sanctuary for genetically pure westslope cutthroats.

"The cutthroat felt like you could almost pick them out of the water with your hands, and then, within 50 feet of them, I just noticed these huge rainbows," said Hull, author of the books *Pale Morning Done* and *Streams of Consciousness*.

Despite what he called the "Zen-like" essence of the writing assignment, which he taught for the Yellowstone Institute, the educational arm of the park-affiliated Yellowstone Foundation, Hull rigged up his rod to try for those big trout while his students scribbled in their notepads. They observed an exultant man lighting into some terrific fish.

The trick, Hull discovered, was that the rainbows gorged themselves on eggs from the spawning cutthroats. He tied on a neon egg pattern and quickly caught a few of those behemoth bows.

"I caught four 26- to 28-inch fish," he said. "I mean they were really big fish."

The cutthroats he caught were no slouches either, Hull said. They measured around 20 inches.

Besides just fishing, Trout Lake offers a fish-watching spectacle like no other in Yellowstone, particularly since Yellowstone cutthroat clusters in places like Fishing Bridge and LeHardy Rapids have been so diminished by lake trout. Standing on the lakeshore near the inlet stream, it's possible to see hundreds of big cutthroat trout milling about in the shallow water. Dozens more are visible in the little creek itself, thrashing the surface of the water with their tails as they churn upstream. It's been that way on Trout Lake for millennia. In 1871 prospector A. Bart Henderson, who named the lake, wrote, "This is the most beautiful little lake, and full of the finest trout, hence I gave it the name of Trout Lake."[1]

I spent most of my day at Trout Lake lying across the small, wooden footbridge over the inlet stream taking underwater video of cutthroats with my iPhone sealed in a waterproof bag.

From the 1920s to the 1950s, park officials ran a fish hatchery on the banks of Trout Lake, and during this time rainbow trout were reared here in addition to the native cutthroats. In 2010 park fisheries biologists released a plan to remove all the rainbows from Trout Lake in order to preserve the fishery as a reservoir for genetically pure Yellowstone cutthroat trout.[2]

Hull said he had learned the trick to catching the fish in this lake from a Blackfoot guide on the famous big-trout lakes just east of Glacier National Park in Northwestern Montana.

"Pick a cruising fish," Hull said. "And you want to plunk it on their nose."

Egg patterns work for the rainbows, and small nymphs—such as size 18 and 20 Copper John, Hare's Ear, and Prince nymphs—and midges bring the cutthroats. Small streamers, or a green Egg-Sucking Leech, are also good patterns, Hull said. Dry flies, not so much.

Big cutthroats swarm in amazing abundance near the inlet at Trout Lake. This scenic and popular northeast corner spot is also home to some massive rainbow trout, for now. PHOTO BY NATE SCHWEBER

Sight-fishing is the best technique here, as the water is clear and the size of flies prohibits them from making a big splash. Because of that water clarity, Hull recommends either fishing from shore or from a float tube, lest the muck on the bottom turn the water murky.

Early outlaws used to throw dynamite into Trout Lake to catch its fish.[3] As this lake lies a short hike from the road and is a popular angling destination for families, Hull recommends getting there before sunrise—making sure to hike in with bear spray at the ready. At dawn there is hardly any wind, and the lake is like a jewel.

"It's so peaceful and beautiful, like a little, round lens," Hull said.

Humans aren't the only competition for trout here. A family of otters lives by the inlet stream, and they can often be seen sliding, playing, and fishing. On one trip, Hull was able to get close enough to the otters that he could hear their jaws smack as they chewed on fresh-caught cutthroat.

"They have no trouble catching fish," Hull said. "But it's so fascinating to watch them swim; they're like the mirror image of a wave, like the otter becomes the water."

Perhaps the best thing about this little lake surrounded by Douglas fir and sage, is that there are enough of its namesake fish for everyone—angler and animal.

"There is a sense of abundance there," Hull said, "something so rare in this world that when you see it, it's just wonderful."

16 Yellowstone River at Sulphur Cauldron

Maggie Merriman

The buffalo that sent Maggie Merriman up a tree near the Sulphur Cauldron section of the Yellowstone River are still there.

But the cutthroat trout that Merriman chased are all but gone.

"I don't think it will come back in my lifetime," said Merriman, who turned 75 in 2011. "It breaks my heart."

Your ears are the first thing to notice Sulphur Cauldron. It sounds like a drive-through car wash deep within the ground. Then your eyes. Steam rises from the fumaroles like cups of coffee in the wintertime. Next is your nose. An eggy plume wafts from those turgid depths. Woe unto the person who ever touches the Sulphur Cauldron.

Behind the cauldron the Yellowstone River runs big, blue, and beautiful—as picture-perfect a western river as has ever flowed. For millennia the river's trout population matched its beauty with their size and concentrations. The Yellowstone River's magnificent fishery is what first drew Merriman here around 1980, when anglers stood shoulder-to-shoulder on the riverbanks and reeled in 18-inch cutthroats by the score.

"In its heyday you could stay there and have fish breaking the surface all day long," Merriman said. "You would just take your lunch and hang out all day fishing with friends in a beautiful part of the park."

In the early 1990s, Merriman began to suspect something was wrong. There seemed to be fewer cutthroats around Sulphur Cauldron. Bugs floated down the river unmolested by trout. Entire hatches went uneaten. It was almost as if there weren't any trout there anymore. Her friends noticed too.

"We said, 'Something's going on—what is it?'" Merriman said. "We talked to rangers and different people and weren't getting any answers."

An unthinkable rumor circulated: someone had planted lake trout, a voracious, cutthroat-scarfing predator, in Yellowstone Lake. Merriman said she and her friends felt "more and more suspicious," and in a frenzy for answers they researched lake trout to find out "what they do and how the hell they could've got there." She interviewed a fisheries biologist who told her that if lake trout had indeed been planted in Yellowstone Lake, the predators could decimate the cutthroats, which had evolved without competition in the lake's depths since the end of the last ice age.

In 1994 the Park Service confirmed the rumors. Someone had indeed stocked lake trout in Yellowstone Lake.

"We were all really mad for a long time," she said. "And we're still sad."

In just a few short years, Sulphur Cauldron, like the entire Yellowstone Lake fishery, went from one of ecstatic abundance to one of painful scarcity. "Just a complete 180," Merriman said.

But she did not stop fishing Sulphur Cauldron.

A hard day's fishing can still produce one or maybe even two commanding and beautiful Yellowstone cutthroats. Merriman calls them, "the survivors."

Trout: Native Yellowstone cutthroat trout averaging 18 to 24 inches.

Bugs: Stoneflies, including Salmonflies, around the time the river opens on July 15. Pale Morning Duns, Blue-Winged Olives, Green Drakes, and caddis.

Suggested fly box: Salmonflies size 2 to 6; Golden Stoneflies size 6 to 8; Adamses and Parachute Adamses size 8 to 18; Pale Morning Duns and Blue-Winged Olives size 16 to 20; tan Elk Hair Caddis size 14 to 18; Pheasant Tail, Hare's Ear, and Prince nymphs size 14 to 18; Stimulators size 14 to 16; Joe's, Dave's, Parachute, and Rubber-Leg Hoppers size 6 to 14; crickets size 8 to 14; Parachute and Chernobyl Ant patterns size 14 to 18; foam beetles size 14 to 16; black, tan, and olive Woolly Buggers size 4 to 8.

Key techniques: Sighting fish and casting to them. Watch for rises and, in clear water, watch for fish finning in the water.

Best times: Earlier in the season is better. By the late summer, many of the big cutthroat that come into this section to spawn have returned to Yellowstone Lake.

Directions: Grand Loop Road parallels the Yellowstone in this section. Look for the pullouts by Sulphur Canyon.

Special rules: Catch-and-release for all cutthroat; catch-and-kill for any lake trout; season opens July 15. Watch for signs indicating sections of the river that are closed for fishing to protect spawning trout.

Steam rises from the banks of the Yellowstone River near Sulphur Cauldron. These banks used to be packed with anglers, but the crowds have thinned now that the cutthroats have all but vanished. PHOTO BY NATE SCHWEBER

These fish can be 18, 19, or 20 inches or longer and broad as an airplane propeller blade.

"They have a beautiful orange stripe under their throat and a yellow and orange body with dark spots," Merriman said. "Just gorgeous."

Merriman said that today's Sulphur Cauldron angler must work every foot of water, casting six feet upstream and letting the fly drift down, then eight feet, then ten feet, and so on. It takes a tremendous amount of effort to catch the cutthroats.

"You look for an area where there's a drop-off, a run, a pool, places where fish used to hang out," she said. "You have to just pick an area and slowly cover the water and hope that it holds a fish. There's nothing else you can do."

The first thing to check for is a hatch, particularly the river's prolific hatches of Green Drakes and Pale Morning Duns, Merriman said. Barring that, she recommends searching with attractor patterns like size 14 and 16 Stimulators, size 14 and 16 Elk Hair Caddis, nymphs, and Woolly Buggers. "If the fish aren't up, you have to go down," Merriman said. July and August are months to try terrestrial patterns, particularly ants and beetles. Lucky is the angler who actually spots a fish rising.

"You're always looking for a rising fish," Merriman said. "And if you see one, fish to that fish."

I fished the Yellowstone River from Sulphur Cauldron upstream to Nez Perce Ford one afternoon. I didn't see a single trout.

Merriman cautions that it's also wise to keep an eye out for the wildlife that abounds around Sulphur Cauldron. On a late August day when Merriman was fishing Sulphur Cauldron with two friends, a herd of buffalo came tromping down the bank right at them. Alarmed, Merriman had one of her companions, a young man, boost her up into a pine tree where she climbed in her old rubber waders to a branch about 10 feet off the ground.

"I said, 'I know buffalo can't climb trees,'" Merriman said. "But it's not easy to climb a tree in your waders."

The guy who gave Merriman the boost scrambled up another pine. The third angler kept still in the middle of the river. Merriman clung to her perch for 40 minutes, "hardly breathing," while the buffalo passed underneath. When the coast was clear, she and her friend giggled, climbed down, and kept on fishing.

The fishing was easy then, but today it's even harder than tree-climbing in old rubber waders. But catching and releasing just one of the survivors is worth it. Merriman calls it "ecstasy, just pure ecstasy."

"It makes you feel good to be able to see one, touch one, and release one," she said.

An angler casts to cutthroats from the middle of the Yellowstone River near Sulphur Cauldron. A good day's fishing might still turn up one or two big cutthroats, fish that some anglers call "the survivors." PHOTO BY NATE SCHWEBER

17 Upper Gardner River at Sheepeater Canyon

Richard Parks

Richard Parks remembers the first time he visited the upper Gardner River where it cascades through Sheepeater Canyon, underneath chevrons of chiseled, volcanic cliffs.

He was 12 years old and alongside his father, Merton J. Parks, who founded Parks' Fly Shop. For more than half a century, Parks' Fly Shop has been a fount of advice, merchandise, and expert guides for Yellowstone and lies two short blocks from the park's front entrance in Gardiner, Montana.

Trout: Brookies and rainbows averaging 6 to 11 inches; brown trout, cutthroat trout, and mountain whitefish join the party below Osprey Falls.

Bugs: Mayflies, caddis, and terrestrials.

Suggested fly box: Royal Coachman Trudes size 12 to 14; Beadhead Prince nymphs size 14 to 16; Dave's Hoppers size 8; foam beetles size 14; Parachute Ants size 16.

Key techniques: Fish in pockets behind rocks and around structure.

Best times: After spring runoff subsides and before the late summer, when many of the brook trout leave to spawn.

Directions: The Sheepeater Picnic Area lies about 8 miles south of Mammoth or about 13^1/$_2$ miles north of Norris Junction. A trail leads down to the river. Reach Osprey Falls by parking at the Bunsen Peak Trailhead about 4 miles south of Mammoth and continuing to the Osprey Falls Trail.

Special rules: Creel limit is five nonnative trout per day, either brook trout or rainbow trout or a combination of both.

Sheepeater Canyon is the deepest gorge in the park, second only to the Grand Canyon of the Yellowstone. It is named for the Sheepeaters, a band of Shoshones who made their home here, even in the years just after Yellowstone was made a national park. PHOTO BY NATE SCHWEBER

Richard Parks said his old man told him, "Hey, we're going to go have some fun and catch some fish." Did they ever. Years later when he took over the family business, Parks, author of the book *Fishing Yellowstone National Park*, made the upper Gardner River his go-to spot to take beginning fly fishermen. With pocketwater packed with sparky brookies and frisky rainbows, it's the closest thing he knows to a sure-fire bet in Yellowstone.

"They're sort of fish with training wheels," Parks says. "Rookie fishermen need to be rewarded."

The six miles of river that flow through Sheepeater Canyon are best accessed from the Sheepeater Picnic Area. There anglers can park and follow a trail down to the water. From midspring through June, the river is a rushing torrent, generally unfishable. By September, many of the brook trout have gone to spawn. But in July and August, this section of river can provide a bounty.

The river starts near Electric Peak, which towers over the Mammoth area and, at 10,969 feet, is the second-highest mountain in the park. The river pours down three waterfalls in the Sheepeater Canyon section. Closest to the parking area is the 30-foot Sheepeater Cascades, more rapids than falls. Parks calls the 20-foot falls farthest upstream "Stairstep Falls," his own nickname.

Osprey Falls is the spot where the entire Gardner River crashes over a 150-foot cliff at the bottom of Sheepeater Canyon. In addition to this stunning vista, there is wonderful fishing around here. PHOTO BY CHRIS STETLER

Fun, fairly-easy-to-catch rainbow trout like this one abound in the upper Gardner River in Sheepeater Canyon. Try a big attractor fly, perhaps with a nymph dropper.
PHOTO BY NATE SCHWEBER

The name "Sheepeater Canyon" is in homage to the Sheepeaters, a band of Shoshones, who called this place home even years after Yellowstone was declared a national park. In 1879 Park Superintendent P. W. Norris trailed a wounded bighorn sheep through this canyon and discovered, to his astonishment, a recently evacuated Sheepeater campsite. He described it as "an enchanting dell; a wind and storm sheltered refuge for the feeble remnant of a fading race."[1]

On an early August day I hiked down into the terrific 900-foot-deep canyon with my best friend Chris Stetler to the base of Osprey Falls, the biggest falls in this canyon. We marveled at the entire Gardner River diving off a 150-foot cliff. I caught a trout nearly every cast, beautiful twisting rainbows and a surprise, handsome 13-inch brown right near the base of the cascade.

The trout were right where Parks said they would be: eddies behind rocks, riffles, little runs, and downed trees. Parks describes these trout as "enthusiastic," "numerous," and even "not too bright."

An experienced fisherman, Parks says, could easily net 60 in a day.

What these fish possess in willingness to bite, they compensate for in size. Few in Parks's memory have busted 12 inches on a tape measure. Most are somewhere north of 6 inches, but a few are "spectacularly smaller," he says.

But they do make for a simple fly box, he says. He suggests a size 12 Royal Coachman Trude with a size 16 Beadhead Prince nymph dropper. The trout usually grab one or the other, Parks says, and if not, well, that's a sign to enjoy the area's other attributes.

Fortunately, the canyon offers great scenery, as well as good wildlife watching. The most memorable wildlife sighting Parks ever saw happened here.

He was guiding a pair of newlyweds, both of whom were enjoying plucking little trout from the stream, when the groom yelled, "Duck!"

It was both a command and an observation. Parks whirled around and saw a young duck—it was moving too fast to identify—"hauling fanny." It was pursued by a swooping bald eagle. The birds whooshed just inches from the man's head.

The small duck streaked to safety in a nook underneath an old stump. The eagle? Contrary to its national image as a symbol of majesty and grace, Parks watched as the raptor "did a face plant" on the stream bank.

"It was the most spectacular bird wreck I ever saw," he says.

18 Southeast Arm of Yellowstone Lake

Dick Cheney

Toward the end of a conversation about fishing in Yellowstone National Park, Dick Cheney, the 46th vice president of the United States, interrupted in a gruff growl to speculate about how some other fly fishermen might perceive him.

"The Darth Vader of the administration?" chuckled Cheney, who served as vice president under George W. Bush from 2001 through 2009.

Trout: Yellowstone cutthroat trout and lake trout.

Bugs: Mayflies, including *Callibaetis*, Pale Morning Duns, and Gray Drakes; caddisflies; terrestrials; scuds; and leeches.

Suggested fly box: Black, tan, and olive Woolly Buggers size 4 to 8; Parachute Adamses size 12 to 18; tan Elk Hair Caddis size 14 to 16; Prince and Hare's Ear nymphs size 14 to 18; tan scuds size 14; Dave's, Parachute, and Rubber-Leg Hoppers size 6 to 14; crickets size 8 to 14; Parachute and Chernobyl Ant patterns size 14 to 18; beetles size 14 to 16.

Key techniques: Strip Woolly Buggers from shore; fish near drop-offs; watch for rising trout.

Best times: June through September.

Directions: Park at the Nine Mile Trailhead on the East Entrance Road, about nine miles from Fishing Bridge and about 20 miles from the park's east entrance. There are several backcountry campsites along the long hike down the Southeast Arm.

Special rules: Mandatory kill for all lake trout; if you don't wish to keep the fish, puncture its air bladder and throw it back in the lake. Catch-and-release for cutthroats. Season opens June 15.

The trail along the Southeast Arm of Yellowstone Lake offers some incredible vistas, almost like the California coast at Big Sur—only with the Grand Tetons looming in the distance. PHOTO BY NATE SCHWEBER

This same statesman who earned a reputation for ferociously guarding secrets, a bare-knuckled politician who was often reported to be bunkered down in an "undisclosed location," was as generous with his time as he was gracious with his memories when talking about places he loved to fish in Yellowstone. He even shared the secret of his favorite spot, the remote Southeast Arm of Yellowstone Lake.

"It is just magnificent back there," Cheney said. "Total wilderness."

Between 1979 and 1989, the years Cheney represented the state of Wyoming in Congress, he said he would often stay at the Lake Hotel for parts of the last half of July. He would charter a boat from the marina just west of the hotel and take the long ride across Yellowstone Lake to the Southeast Arm. There he would catch countless cutthroats by stripping purple, bead-head Woolly Buggers, flies he calls "goofy stuff."

"You weren't matching the hatch," he said.

He said that the trout, while very willing, tended to be "of uniform size," around 15 inches—smaller than the cutts at another one of his favorite park fishing spots, Nez Perce Ford (formerly Buffalo Ford) on the Yellowstone River below the lake.

One of the hardest parts about fishing the Southeast Arm was maneuvering around the downed timber on the shoreline, Cheney said. Sometimes, he said, he had to fish from the boat, casting back toward the cluttered shore.

During those trips, Cheney said, he had savored the park's natural beauty and basked in the respite from his hectic schedule in Washington, D.C. He even reveled in being so removed from crowds of tourists.

"It's Yellowstone; it's the middle of summer, the height of the season. The roads would be packed; there would be thousands of people going through the park," Cheney said. "But once you go over to the Southeast Arm, there wouldn't be anybody."

Sometimes big squalls blew in during the late afternoon, and Cheney gazed at their spectacle and then hunkered down for a bumpy trip back home.

"Occasionally you'd get a storm with high winds and a lot of thunder and lightning, and the lake could get pretty rough with whitecaps," Cheney said. "It was a rough ride back to the hotel."

Once off the lake, he enjoyed "thick steaks," "good whiskey," and "a comfortable bed at night." He also enjoyed camaraderie. Cheney would rendezvous at the Lake Hotel with around 15 or 20 friends, fishing buddies who introduced him to the Southeast Arm of Yellowstone Lake.

"You might not want to print this," Cheney said. "But there was a group of us, mostly connected to the oil industry. A lot of them like to fish too."

Whether villainized as an architect of wars, lionized as an uncompromising patriot, or lampooned for a quail hunting accident in which he shot his friend in the face (the friend made a full recovery), Cheney's zest for fishing is undisputed. Famously, his Secret Service nicknamed him "Angler."

While Cheney's love of fly fishing has never been challenged, many sportsmen have railed against the energy policies he advocated while in power. In 2009 some anglers protested a speech that Cheney gave at the American Museum of Fly Fishing in Vermont, on the grounds that his work on behalf of companies that extract fossil fuels could have devastating long-term consequences for trout in the forms of pollution and climate change. Cheney, unbothered, said that he learned long ago that like fishhooks, his political enemies use barbs.

"It goes with the turf," he said. "If you've been vice president for eight years, you'd better be used to being on the receiving end of criticism and part of Jay Leno's monologue a couple times each week."

In a statement that could make even his predecessor Al Gore applaud, Cheney said that during his 11-year tenure in the House of Representatives, he was most proud of sponsoring the 1984 Wyoming Wilderness Act, which permanently preserved 1.1 million acres of the state's scenic backcountry.

"I felt it was the most important piece of legislation I sponsored," Cheney said.

For years Cheney made annual forays into Wyoming's backcountry, until his job as vice president "really cut into my hunting and fishing time." He

Wolf tracks, interspersed with elk tracks, are a common sight on the long trail down the Southeast Arm of Yellowstone Lake. PHOTO BY NATE SCHWEBER

said he followed the news about the demise of the cutthroat fishery at his favorite Yellowstone spot, and he sounded glum when talking about the illegally introduced lake trout.

"It's a shame," he said.

Cheney talked fondly about a trek he took deep into the Wind River Range with his friend, former secretary of state James Baker, and also about a 100-mile pack trip he took into the Thorofare region of the Bridger-Teton National Forest, just outside the boundary of Yellowstone. Cheney called wilderness "a magnificent resource" and said, "It's very important it be protected." He said he sees visiting wilderness areas as both something that brings him joy and also part of his duty.

"In Congress we had a lot of so-called experts, but they were from New York City or Los Angeles or someplace, and they'd never really spent any time in the wilderness to appreciate it the way you would have expected," he said. "It was a very special part of my responsibility."

So it is left to scholars and historians, trout and trees to ultimately adjudicate Cheney's lasting legacy. Did he go above and beyond in protecting the wilderness that he so loves to visit? Or did the deals he made with friends in the oil industry jeopardize the very trout that, ironically, they both chased together? Cheney, who spoke by phone from a restricted number and keeps a home in Jackson Hole, Wyoming, said he would prefer to go fishing than worry about such things.

"I'll let my record speak for itself," he said.

19 Slough Creek, Upper Meadows

Marcia Woolman

Slough Creek ambles in its upper meadows through amber grass and minty willows and it teems with big cutthroats colored like Indian Paintbrush. Images of Slough Creek are like dream scenes. In one, a great horned owl swoops across the wagon trail near dark while you scout for the next morning's fishing spot. In another, a big bull moose stands at first light between you and the water. And then, just after the sun washes over the sky-scraping Absaroka Mountains, the scene is a bull buffalo stomping the lip of the far bank. It is close enough to pet with your rod; close enough that its reflection almost touches the spot where your thighs meet the creek water on your bones' anchoring plunge down to the pebble bottom.

The cutthroats, so gorgeously earnest, glow orange like sodium street-lights when they rise from this teal water. These fish seem less like quarry, and more like aquatic golden retrievers that splash at and fetch dry flies. There's a wonderland kind of mystique about Slough Creek.

Marcia Woolman, who lives in Virginia and spends her summers in Silver Gate, Montana, just outside Yellowstone's northeast entrance, has visited these upper meadows almost every year for close to two decades.

"Slough Creek is a very, very special place," she said.

Hikers reach the upper Slough Creek by parking at the trailhead next to the Slough Creek Campground and following the wagon road up into the meadows beyond. Horse-drawn carriages hauling tourists to the private Silvertip Ranch just over the park border, under special arrangement with the National Park Service, are a common sight along this trail.

Each of upper Slough Creek's three broad, beautiful meadows are segregated by short canyon sections featuring waterfalls. In the meadows, cut-throats regularly grow to between 18 and 22 inches, hovering in the gentle currents, sipping the bugs that flourish in the fields. George Anderson, who for more than three decades has owned Yellowstone Anglers, a fly shop in Livingston, describes upper Slough Creek's cutthroats as "pretty easy to catch." Woolman agrees. Mostly. She still recalls fish that prove Anderson wrong.

One was a burnt sienna, 17-inch cutthroat that held in an L-shaped eddy just below the canyon separating the second meadow from the first. The cutthroat followed each fly from the top of the eddy all the way down around the bend, sometimes even nudging it with its nose, as if checking for a hook. Woolman's husband, Hank Woolman, who builds bamboo rods, worked more than three hours to fool that fish. He finally did by sinking his tippet and using a Waterwisp fly pattern tied with the hook facing up.

"It wasn't the biggest fish," Woolman said. "But it was sure as heck the smartest one."

Other Slough Creek cutthroats are more accommodating. Woolman used to take people fishing in the upper meadows, and if any of them had an unlucky day, she had just the fish for them. Again in that canyon, in a pool beside a rock wall, lived a 19-inch cutthroat. Woolman said she would

Trout: Cutthroat trout and cuttbows that average 12 to 22 inches; also small rainbow trout.

Bugs: Mayflies, including Green Drakes, Pale Morning Duns, and *Baetis*; caddis; stoneflies, including Golden Stoneflies, little yellow stoneflies, and Salmonflies; and terrestrials, including hoppers, ants, beetles, and crickets.

Suggested fly box: Dave's Hoppers size 6 to 14; crickets size 8 to 14; Parachute and Chernobyl Ant patterns size 14 to 18; foam beetles size 14 to 16; Green Drakes size 8 to 12; Elk Hair and X-Caddis size 14 to 18; yellow Stimulators size 8 to 12; Parachute Adamses size 14 to 18; crane flies size 12 to 16; *Baetis* Sparkle and *Baetis* Thorax Duns size 20 to 22; Pheasant Tail, Prince, and Hare's Ear nymphs size 14 to 20; black, tan, and olive Woolly Buggers size 4 to 8; midges.

Key techniques: Sight and stalk specific fish; cast to rising trout; search water with a hopper/dropper rig; strip Woolly Buggers.

Best times: July through October.

Directions: Find the Slough Creek road about 6 miles east from Tower Junction or about 27 miles west from the northeast entrance along the Northeast Entrance Road. Drive up the dirt road and park at the campground. Follow the wagon trail up into the meadows.

Special rules: Catch-and-release for all cutthroats; consider harvesting any rainbow trout, particularly in the third meadow.

instruct her companion to literally cast the fly into the wall so that it would ricochet off into the water. The big cutthroat always took.

"It just made somebody's day," Woolman said. "I caught that fish once a year for three years."

Slough Creek got its name in the summer of 1867 when a prospector named Ansel Hubble scouted the stream and reported to his four companions, "'Twas but a slough." Jim Bridger probably called the stream "Beaver Creek," and trapper Osborne Russell likely harvested beaver here in the late 1830s.[1] Just outside the park border, above Silvertip Ranch, lies Frenchy's Meadow, named for Joseph B. "Frenchy" Duret. He was an alleged deserter from the French Army who built a cabin just north of the Yellowstone border and died in his namesake meadow in 1922, a mile and a half from the spot where a grizzly he trapped snapped its chain and savagely mauled him.[2]

Grizzlies roam all over the Slough Creek drainage. Once Woolman and a friend hiked in one day to find a black wolf feeding on a dead elk on the trail. By the time they hiked out, a griz was on the carcass. Despite her better judgment, Woolman dropped her rod, grabbed her camera, and tiptoed toward the bear, hoping for a good shot. Her companion tapped her on the shoulder, jolting her back to reality.

"I realized right then, 'Oh shit, I'm going to die,'" she said. "I used to laugh at tourists and wonder how in the world they could do these stupid things, but in that moment I had an epiphany; something just takes over your mind. It was very enlightening."

Woolman and her friend circled far enough around the feeding griz to avoid detection.

Slough Creek is famous for its dry-fly fishing, particularly with terrestrial patterns that imitate ants, beetles, crickets, and grasshoppers; the cutthroat culinaries that yellow strands of creek-side grass slough into the water all summer long. Caddis, *Baetis*, and even big Green Drakes hatch regularly in Slough Creek's upper meadows, but it's the terrestrials—and the ferocious strikes they entice—that most anglers come to throw in July, August, and September.

"What wins you over about these cutthroats," Woolman said, "is they are certainly the most likely to come to a dry fly."

On several occasions, Woolman said, she was blessed to have been a guest at Silvertip Ranch, whose wooden fence marks the northernmost border of Yellowstone Park. While stationed at the ranch, Woolman began sampling her fish for park biologists. In 2010 she made an awful discovery: in Slough Creek's third meadow, less than 200 yards from the northern border of Yellowstone Park, she caught a nine-inch, pure rainbow trout.

For decades the waterfalls separating Slough Creek's meadows acted as natural fish barriers that kept out nonnative rainbow trout, which were stocked in the Lamar Valley in the 1930s. Until recently, biologists thought that no rainbow trout could scale the waterfall between the second and third meadow, thereby keeping the big cutthroats at the top of Slough Creek genetically pure.

Woolman proved that's no longer true.

Todd Koel, Yellowstone's top fish biologist, said that in the drought years of the early 2000s, the water in Slough Creek dropped so low that rainbow trout were able to swim up the waterfalls which in years past had been too strong to pass. During these years, he said, the park's fisheries department was stretched so thin fighting illegally introduced lake trout in Yellowstone Lake—which were decimating that watershed's native cutthroats—that they simply couldn't spare the resources, like teams of biologists with electroshock equipment, to try and save the genetically pure cutthroats at the top of Slough Creek.

Thus, upper Slough Creek's pure cutthroats became another casualty from the clandestine stocking of lake trout in Yellowstone Lake.

Koel added that the cutthroats in Slough Creek above a waterfall upstream from Silvertip Ranch still test genetically pure, adding credence to the theory about rainbows migrating up the creek rather than possibly washing down from ponds on private property north of the park border.

Biologists encourage anglers to harvest any rainbow trout caught in upper Slough Creek, particularly in the third meadow.

Around 2005 Woolman remembers walking to the banks of Slough Creek's second meadow to fish right around dusk. She hooked onto a great trout, almost 20 inches; but when she brought it to shore, she was aghast. It was a rainbow, or rather probably a cuttbow with a tiny percentage of cutthroat genetics because it had just an orange freckle underneath its jaw. Remembering the park rule "if it has a slash, put it back," Woolman let the mongrel fish go.

"I've regretted it ever since," she said. "Today I wouldn't hesitate for a second to keep that fish, and I can go to the biologists and the game warden, and I can defend my position."

Slough Creek was the first place I visited in Yellowstone after being gone for almost 10 years, most of it in New York City. I went with my stepfather Bill Innes in both 2007 and 2008, and we camped there for three days at a time. Slough Creek made such an impression on me that I saw it in my dreams. I remember Bill gazing around those great meadows and commenting that he wished he could have gone with Major John Wesley Powell in the late 1860s when he explored parts of the Colorado and Green Rivers—back when the whole Rocky Mountain West looked more like Slough Creek and less like, say, Spokane.

Struggling to write a draft of this chapter, I emailed Bill asking how I could encapsulate a place as awesome as Slough Creek into just a few words. Here's what he wrote back:

> If expansive mountain meadows edged by rock walls and peaks, a slow meandering creek, trusting, exceptionally well-fed trout, and seclusion hold no appeal for you, then Slough Creek can be bypassed. On the chance that this describes a place that you would gladly backpack to, then you can park in the campground at the base of the trail.
>
> See you there, sir.

20 Beaverdam Creek

Pat Clayton

Pat Clayton catches trout differently than most. He uses a camera.

He's known by his nickname "FishEyeGuy," and his web site, fisheyeguy photography.com, features his astonishing underwater photographs of brilliantly colored trout swimming in their natural environment.

Some of his favorite spots in Yellowstone to photograph native cutthroat trout in their audacious spawning colors are the feeder streams on the Southeast Arm of Yellowstone Lake, particularly Beaverdam Creek.

"Spawning trout are second to none for subject matter," Clayton said. "If you find them in the right places at the right times, they don't even look real."

Clayton rows his kayak to Beaverdam Creek—"a long pain in the ass," he said—in search of the spawners. He said his key time to shoot them is when they turn deep crimson.

It's not easy to find these cutthroats anymore. I saw just one on remote Beaverdam Creek, which is at least a 34-mile round-trip hike from any trailhead.

"Twenty years ago that thing was like a salmon run," Clayton said. "But they're still in there; you'll find them in the creek if you poke around."

Clayton found his subjects hovering over gravel bars, spawning. Often, he said, he uses a fly rod to find fish on streams like Beaverdam.

Clayton lives in Bozeman and started taking underwater photos of trout years ago because he wanted to create a niche for himself as an outdoor photographer. To get his shots, Clayton will use a submerged camera with a shutter set to a remote control. Sometimes he'll don a dry suit and lie down in riffles with the fish. He said that for every good photo he takes, he puts in six to ten days of work.

"Nobody else is crazy enough to do what I do," he said.

To find the best trout action on Beaverdam Creek, Clayton gets there as soon after runoff subsides as possible. The lake and the streams don't open for fishing until July 15, to protect the spawning cutthroat. The fish spawn in waves, depending on snowpack, water levels, and temperature, Clayton said. Some cutthroats might still be spawning after July 15, so anglers need to be careful.

"Depending on the water, cutthroats will spawn until the last week of July. In the high country, they'll spawn until August," Clayton said. "But if you visit Beaverdam Creek in late August, they'll be gone back down to the lake."

With his photographer's eye, Clayton said, he's noticed that the trout up from the lake have more red coloring than their smaller, stream-dwelling counterparts, which are more golden.

"The lake fish are good-looking fish for sure," Clayton said. "They're colored up, and they're big too."

Trout: Native Yellowstone cutthroat trout, especially lake-run fish, averaging 15 to 20 inches.

Bugs: Stoneflies, including Salmonflies, around the time the stream opens on July 15. Pale Morning Duns, Blue-Winged Olives, and caddis. Also terrestrials, including hoppers, ants, and beetles.

Suggested fly box: Adamses and Parachute Adamses size 8 to 18; Pale Morning Duns and Blue-Winged Olives size 16 to 20; Yellow Humpies, Royal Wulffs, Royal Coachman Trudes, and yellow Stimulators size 14; tan Elk Hair Caddis size 14 to 18; Pheasant Tail, Hare's Ear, and Prince nymphs size 14 to 18; Dave's Hoppers size 6 to 14; crickets size 8 to 14; Parachute and Chernobyl Ant patterns size 14 to 18; foam beetles size 14 to 16; black, olive, and tan Woolly Buggers size 4 to 8.

Key techniques: Sight fish and cast to them. Watch for rises and, in clear water, watch for fish finning in the water.

Best times: Earlier in the season is better. By late summer, many of the big cutthroat in Beaverdam Creek have returned to Yellowstone Lake.

Directions: Park at the Nine Mile Trailhead on the East Entrance Road, about nine miles from Fishing Bridge and about 20 miles from the park's east entrance. It's about a 17-mile hike on the Thorofare Trail to Beaverdam Creek.

Special rules: Catch-and-release for all cutthroat; catch-and-kill for any lake trout; season opens July 15. Handle spawning trout delicately.

Remote Beaverdam Creek is a spawning stream for Yellowstone Lake cutthroats. The best time to fish here is as close to the July 15 season opener as possible; wait much longer, and the cutthroats will have migrated back to the lake.
PHOTO BY NATE SCHWEBER

Clayton said that in addition to the photo ops, he loves visiting Beaverdam Creek because of its remoteness. He's seen more grizzly bears there than people.

"It's wilderness, it's beautiful, and you'll love it," he said. "Go check it out, but make lots of noise."

21 Yellowstone River at Thorofare

Steve Hoovler

The Thorofare is a place where you don't hear wolf howls—you feel them. At 30 miles from any road—as a crow or a bald eagle would fly—it is a place where backcountry anglers double down on danger and on a chance to catch a trophy native cutthroat. At a glance the only thing to change about the Thorofare since trapper days is the number of Yellowstone tourists passing through. In the middle 1800s, almost all Yellowstone visitors crossed through the Thorofare. Today, almost none of them do.

The Thorofare draws people like Steve Hoovler for the fishing and keeps them coming back for the experience. It's as far into the wilderness as a human can get in the continental United States.

"That's the core concept of the Thorofare," said Hoovler, 33.

Early explorers traced the Yellowstone River from its headwaters near the slope of Yount's Peak in what is now the Teton Wilderness, across what would become the southeastern border of the world's first national park. They followed this river down through a broad, marshy valley that they called the "Thoroughfare,"[1] all the way to Yellowstone Lake. When the first carriage roads were built to Yellowstone, the Thorofare went from being the most direct route to the park, to the most remote.

Hoovler first backpacked into this region in the mid-1990s when he was 19 years old. He grew up in Pennsylvania reading stories about the mythical places on the far side of Yellowstone Lake, where the spring-run cutthroats filled the feeder streams like sardines in a can. "The classic walk-across-their-backs stories," Hoovler said. On that first visit, Hoovler found the fishing so incredible on those little creeks he couldn't pull himself away until he could no longer see. On one of those trips, he remembers having to hike through the grizzly darkness to his campsite and set up camp by moonlight. The cutthroats, trainloads of them, just wouldn't let him go.

"There were phenomenal numbers of fish," he said. "I'd just never seen anything like it."

H. A. Moore, 68, a veteran outfitter based in Gardiner, Montana, said that in the 1970s, the fishing was so incredible on the Yellowstone River in the Thorofare that he caught 20-inch cutthroats with his bare hands.

"It was awesome fishing; and nobody thought nothing of it, because it was commonplace," he said.

The fishing stayed that good through the late 1990s. But the year 2000 dawned differently in the Thorofare's streams. Those mighty swells of cutthroats started to thin as they never had during the previous 100 centuries. Then there was hardly a cutthroat to be found. Then the sardine can was empty.

The culprit, of course, was the illegally stocked lake trout that ravaged the native cutthroats in Yellowstone Lake like a virus multiplying inside a human

---

Trout: Native Yellowstone cutthroat trout averaging 15 to 20 inches.

Bugs: Stoneflies, including Salmonflies, around the time the river opens on July 15. Pale Morning Duns, Blue-Winged Olives, and caddis. Also terrestrials, including hoppers, ants, and beetles.

Suggested fly box: Adamses and Parachute Adamses size 8 to 18; Pale Morning Duns and Blue-Winged Olives size 16 to 20; Yellow Humpies size 14; tan Elk Hair Caddis size 14 to 18; Pheasant Tail, Hare's Ear, and Prince nymphs size 14 to 18; Stimulators size 8 to 14; Joe's and Dave's Hoppers size 6 to 14; crickets size 8 to 14; Parachute and Chernobyl Ant patterns size 14 to 18; foam beetles size 14 to 16.

Key techniques: Sight fish and cast to them. Watch for rises and, in clear water, watch for fish finning in the water.

Best times: Earlier in the season is better. By late summer, many of the big cutthroat that come into this section to spawn have returned to Yellowstone Lake.

Directions: Park at the Nine Mile Trailhead on the East Entrance Road, about nine miles from Fishing Bridge and about 20 miles from the park's east entrance. Hike approximately 30 miles along the Southeast Arm of Yellowstone Lake to the Thorofare section of the upper Yellowstone River. Or start at the South Boundary at the South Entrance Station near the Snake River and hike approximately 34 miles to the Yellowstone River.

Special rules: Catch-and-release for all cutthroat; catch-and-kill for any lake trout; season opens July 15. Handle spawning trout delicately.

The Thorofare region of Yellowstone National Park is farther from a road than any other spot in the continental United States; a full 30 miles in any direction. "That's the core concept," says guide Steve Hoovler. PHOTO BY STEVE HOOVLER

heart. Hoovler watched the sickness take hold. On a weeklong trip in 2002, he caught some fish. On a weeklong trip in 2003, he caught no fish.

"It was really, really bad," he said.

Hoovler stopped visiting the Thorofare. As a fishing guide, he just couldn't sell a bruising, weeklong, 70-mile backcountry trip with long odds that anybody would even see, much less catch, a cutthroat.

"I went out of my way to make sure I explained to anyone who expressed interest in going to the Thorofare that when I said there were no fish, I really meant there were truly no fish," he said. "I wasn't talking about a slow day where we would only catch one fish; I meant we would literally not see trout for days."

In 2010 two longtime clients told Hoovler they wanted to visit the Thorofare. Hoovler gave them the speech about the demise of the cutthroats. The men were unfazed. They wanted to see the country. After seven years away, Hoovler would return to the Thorofare.

"I was really excited," he said. "It was an area that I'd missed, an area that I'd wanted to get back to."

A visit to the Thorofare demands respect and care. The stakes are high. If the ankle snaps or the grizzly attacks, it's a long, long way for help. Hoovler pondered this in 2002 when he watched a giant grizzly rise up on its hind legs just across the Yellowstone River from his camp.

Tens of thousands of cutthroats used to run up the Yellowstone River into the Thorofare region each spring to spawn, but since the illegal introduction of lake trout into Yellowstone Lake, fishing in this remote region has more closely resembled big game hunts, guides say. PHOTO BY STEVE HOOVLER

Eight years later, during the first camp in the backcountry on the long ride into the Thorofare, Hoovler heard wolves howling in the night. He said he felt the vibrations in his chest, "like a car stereo with the bass cranked up too loud."

"It's a physical sound," he said. "When you're back there so far and you hear a wolf howl, it's like, 'It can't get any wilder than this.'"

The day the men approached the mountain-flanked Thorofare Valley, having circled around Two Ocean Plateau from South Entrance Road, Hoovler watched the landscape open up before him like great curtains. The country got more amazing with every step they took.

"The Thorofare Valley opens up more and more as it doglegs down," he said. "The more it opens up, the grander it gets, and it keeps pulling you in as it gets bigger, and you want to get a little farther and see what's around the next corner."

As ever, Hoovler said he was "just in awe of the scenery."

He was less in awe of the fishing. Hoovler and his clients spent a full day walking miles along the banks of the hurting Yellowstone River, scouring for cutthroats. They didn't see a single fish. They never even cast.

The next day dawned cold and gray. A few drops of rain fell down, and as if in compensation, *Baetis* mayflies and Mahogany Duns rose from the river. Even though the cutthroats are gone, their food remains.

Hoovler and his clients stalked the river's banks. In the distance, past a long gravel bar, they saw a disturbance in a pool not far from the confluence of Thorofare Creek. They quickened their steps.

"It was suspenseful," Hoovler said. "It was like, 'Holy cow, are those fish?' And then the closer we got, we said, 'Yeah those *are* fish!'"

Hoovler's heart ticked faster. He knew what he called the "bittersweet" truth of the Yellowstone River's post–lake trout fishery. The cutthroats today are scarce, but the ones left are huge.

The men arrived at the water's edge and found a rising pod of great cutthroats. One would pray that after trekking so far into the backcountry, and then searching miles of dead river, these lonely cutthroats would happily smash the first big Stimulator to float over their noses. No dice. These trout wouldn't take attractors. They wouldn't eat the Mahogany Duns that were hatching either. These long-odds cutthroats would only take size 20 Sparkle Duns tied to 6X tippets at the end of long leaders.

"You would think that when you're 30 miles into the backcountry, the fishing would be easy," Hoovler said. "But it's challenging fishing for these old cutthroats that have been around the block."

They were trophies, though. Hoovler called the scene "more like an elk hunt than a fishing trip."

Hoovler still saw no sign of the cutthroat fishery improving. The cutthroats from the summer of 2010 were "great to see," he said, but finding them where he hadn't in 2003 was "a matter of being in the right place at the right time," not evidence of a rebounding population. There still exists mile after sad mile of barren river in the Thorofare.

"Frankly, we still don't have a handle on the lake trout," Hoovler said.

But a visit to the Thorofare is still a bucket-list adventure that a cutthroat can only make more memorable.

"If you're there for the scenery, the experience, or the solitude, that's what you're going to remember," Hoovler said. "Because the experience of going to this part of the park and seeing this part of the world should be a higher priority than catching a number of fish."

22 Thorofare Creek

"Wild" Bill Schneider, Dave Hughes

Everybody knows that the fishing could be great in the most remote spot in the continental United States, says author, hiking expert, and fisherman "Wild" Bill Schneider.

But because visiting Thorofare Creek requires a 70-mile hike, precious few actually experience it.

"You've got to be pretty committed to fish Thorofare Creek," he said. "It doesn't get fished much; that's why it's my favorite."

Schneider, who wrote the guidebook *Hiking Yellowstone National Park*, says the Thorofare is the big daddy of all Yellowstone backcountry experiences.

"It's the hardest part in the lower 48 to get to," he said. "When you're at the Thorofare Ranger Station, it's 30 miles in any direction to get to a road."

The fishing, historically, was extraordinary. The last time Schneider visited Thorofare Creek, anglers were allowed to keep a cutthroat trout as long as it was under 13 inches. Schneider's backcountry menus included no trout.

"It was hard to catch one under 18 inches," he said.

Since lake trout were stocked illegally in Yellowstone Lake, Thorofare Creek, like all the waters in the Yellowstone Lake system, took an awful hit.

Thorofare Creek is the largest tributary to the Yellowstone River above Yellowstone Lake. It is a meadow stream with riffles, runs, pools, and braided channels. Spawning cutthroat trout from Yellowstone Lake run to Thorofare Creek every spring. To protect them, the fishing season doesn't open until July 15. Wait until too late in the year, and many will have migrated back to the lake.

But fish for them around the season opener, and you might get lucky, Schneider said.

"There are some big cutthroats in there," he said.

Fly-fishing author Dave Hughes fished Thorofare Creek years ago. He remembers seeing spawning cutthroats stacked up in the creek's pools on their flush back down to Yellowstone Lake. He caught slabs of them by swinging a black Woolly Bugger.

"They were schooled up like sockeye salmon, and they were very eager to take a Woolly Bugger," he said. "We just fished casually from camp, we had a beautiful camp right on the river, and we caught these great fish in this remote spot so far back."

Schneider, who visited Thorofare Creek three times spanning from the 1970s through the 1990s, said he only ever used three flies. He used an Adams Irresistible and a Royal Trude on the surface, and sometimes a Woolly Bugger wet.

"You could probably catch them on wet flies if you went that route," Schneider said. "But it's always more fun to catch them on drys."

Trout: Native Yellowstone cutthroat trout, especially lake-run fish averaging 18 to 22-inches.

Bugs: Stoneflies, including Salmonflies, around the time the stream opens on July 15. Pale Morning Duns, Blue-Winged Olives, and caddis. Also terrestrials, including hoppers, ants, and beetles.

Suggested fly box: Yellow Humpies, Royal Wulffs, Royal Coachman Trudes, tan Elk Hair Caddis, and yellow Stimulators size 14; Parachute Adamses size 8 to 18; Pale Morning Duns and Blue-Winged Olives size 16 to 20; Pheasant Tail, Hare's Ear, and Prince nymphs size 14 to 18; Dave's Hoppers size 6 to 14; crickets size 8 to 14; Parachute and Chernobyl Ant patterns size 14 to 18; foam beetles size 14 to 16; black, olive, and tan Woolly Buggers size 4 to 8.

Key techniques: Sight fish and cast to them. Watch for rises and, in clear water, watch for fish finning in the water.

Best times: Earlier in the season is better. By the late summer, many of the big cutthroat in Thorofare Creek have returned to Yellowstone Lake.

Directions: Park at the Nine Mile Trailhead on the East Entrance Road, about nine miles from Fishing Bridge and about 20 miles from the park's east entrance. Hike approximately 30 miles along the Southeast Arm of Yellowstone Lake and up the Yellowstone River to Thorofare Creek. Or start at the South Boundary at the South Entrance Station near the Snake River and hike approximately 34 miles to Thorofare Creek.

Special rules: Catch-and-release for all cutthroat; catch-and-kill for any lake trout; season opens July 15. Handle spawning trout delicately.

Beyond the campfire lies the Thorofare region of Yellowstone National Park. The junction of Thorofare Creek and the Yellowstone River is, as measured by distance to the closest road, the most remote spot in the continental United States.
PHOTO BY NATE SCHWEBER

What Schneider recalls most vividly from his Thorofare visits are the wildflowers. Vast sections of the trail leading to the Thorofare burned in the fires of 1988, and today those scorched sections are carpeted with lupine and balsamroot.

Schneider also saw scores of mariposa lilies, one of the rarest of wildflowers.

"You don't find the mariposa lily very many places in the park, and the Thorofare is pretty close to the best place to see them," Schneider said. "It's simply one of the best places in the park for wildflowers."

So on this trip of a lifetime, remember to literally stop and smell the flowers along the way.

23 Snake River

Terry Search

The Snake River is one of the West's most iconic trout streams, especially its course beside the epic Tetons on its four-state, 1,000-mile run down to the Columbia River.

At its headwaters in Yellowstone though, the Snake River is an enigma. It is shrouded in backcountry and difficult to reach, save for in its lowest stretch right next to the park's southern boundary.

Even its most sought-after fish, the Snake River finespotted cutthroat, is hard to define. Scientifically, the Snake River finespotted cutthroat is classified as just a Yellowstone cutthroat trout, not as its own subspecies, even though the two have distinctly different spotting patterns. Though the Snake River is home to mostly regular Yellowstone cutthroat trout, it's also the only place in the park where anglers have a chance to catch the elusive finespotted cutthroat.[1]

Terry Search, an outfitter with an apt name for seeking out finespotted cutthroats, has made loads of trips into the upper Snake River during his 15 years running Yellowstone Mountain Guides out of West Yellowstone. He calls the Snake River backcountry "one of my favorite haunts" and says its finespotted cutthroats are "bruisers"—spawners that run up from Jackson Lake and can stretch two feet or more.

"This is trophy fishing," he said. "I wouldn't say it's for the beginner as much as for somebody who is willing to put forth the effort to spot and stalk fish."

When it comes to catching a finespotted cutthroat in Yellowstone, timing is key, Search said. By late summer the big fish have migrated back down to Jackson Lake, in Grand Teton National Park just south of Yellowstone, but in early summer the Snake River is too flushed with runoff to access. The South Boundary Trail, which begins at the ranger station at the south entrance, starts with a ford of the big Snake River, goes past the mouth of the Lewis

River, and then follows the Snake up through miles of broad meadows, dense canopied forest, and burned areas to the Snake River Trail. That route follows the river past the mouth of the Heart River up a canyon to its headwaters south of the park border in the Teton Wilderness area. The Snake's headwaters are just across the Continental Divide from the Yellowstone's Thorofare region, to put its remoteness in perspective.

Search said much of the cobble-bottomed river looks like "classic rainbow water," with fast riffles. It's in the pools dotted up the river that he hunts for big finespotted cutthroats.

"I'm a cowboy fisherman," he said. "I hit a hole and run; if nothing takes in the first few casts, I keep moving."

Trout: Snake River finespotted cutthroat averaging 16 to 24 inches; Yellowstone cutthroat averaging 8 to 16 inches; brown trout averaging 10 to 12 inches with a shot at a big Jackson Lake spawner in the fall; also mountain whitefish and a few fugitive lake trout from Heart Lake or Jackson Lake.

Bugs: Stoneflies, including Salmonflies; Pale Morning Duns; Blue-Winged Olives; and caddis. Also terrestrials, including hoppers, ants, and beetles.

Suggested fly box: Salmonflies size 2 to 6; Golden Stoneflies size 6 to 8; Parachute Adamses size 8 to 18; Pale Morning Duns and Blue-Winged Olives size 16 to 20; tan Elk Hair Caddis size 14 to 18; Royal Wulffs, Royal Coachman Trudes, yellow Stimulators, and Yellow Humpies size 14 to 16; Hare's Ear, Prince, and Serendipity nymphs size 14 to 18; Golden Stonefly nymphs size 6 to 8; Dave's Hoppers size 6 to 14; crickets size 8 to 14; Parachute and Chernobyl Ant patterns size 14 to 18; foam beetles size 14 to 16; black, tan, and olive Woolly Buggers size 4 to 8; Muddler Minnows size 2 to 6.

Key techniques: Search deep pools and runs with attractor drys and hopper/dropper rigs.

Best times: Earlier in the season is better. By late summer many of the big cutthroat that come into the Snake River to spawn have returned to Jackson Lake.

Directions: The South Boundary Trail, which begins at the South Entrance Ranger Station, leads 2.7 miles to the Snake River Cutoff Trail, which goes 3.3 miles to the Snake River Trail, which follows the river in a huge curve around Big Game Ridge all the way to the southern border of Yellowstone Park.

Special rules: Catch-and-release for all cutthroat and whitefish. Handle spawning trout delicately.

The mighty Snake River in its upper reaches in Yellowstone National Park. These are some of the least-visited spots on this famous Western waterway. PHOTO BY NATE SCHWEBER

Search suggests working the water with attractor dry flies like Stimulators, hopper patterns, Royal Coachman Trudes, Royal Wulffs, and Parachute Adamses, plus some Blue-Winged Olives. He also suggests hopper/dropper rigs trailing Golden Stone, Prince, Hare's Ear, and Copper John nymphs, and Serendipities. He also suggests Muddler Minnows and black and olive Woolly Buggers; these can also be effective on the Snake River's small run of brown trout up from Jackson Lake in the fall.

Of his fly box selection, Search said, "I'd go in there loaded for bear because when you get that far away from the frontcountry, you can't just drive to the local fly shop and bone up on patterns."

The fishing, except on rare occasions, isn't fast here, but it can be furious. Search himself, and many folks he has taken up the Snake River, has been shocked to suddenly bolt on to a 24-inch finespotted cutthroat.

Historically Jackson Lake may have teemed with finespotted cutthroats, but the native trout took an enormous hit when lake trout migrated down and colonized the water after they were introduced upstream in Lewis Lake. Biologists then stocked Jackson Lake with hatchery cutthroats to prop up its wounded fishery.[2] Biologists today don't know whether it is remnants of Jackson Lake's native finespotted cutthroats, those descended from hatchery stocks, or a mix of both that run into the upper Snake.

The Snake River may be the only place in Yellowstone National Park to catch an elusive Snake River finespotted cutthroat, which is distinguished by having spots like ground pepper as opposed to a regular Yellowstone cutthroat, which has spots like peppercorns. Both kinds of cutthroat are present in the Snake River in Yellowstone, which can make identifying a finespotted cutthroat almost as tricky as finding one. PHOTO BY NATE SCHWEBER

Search compares the fishing for finespotteds on the upper Snake to trying to catch steelhead on dry flies in coastal streams.

"You might go on a four-day trip up there and never catch that fish," he said. "But if you did two or three of them consecutively, eventually you're going to rake into one of those big hogs."

I fished the Snake a short ways into the backcountry and caught a dozen or more little Yellowstone cutthroat trout plus one that stretched about 16 inches. In a run on a Prince nymph dropper, I hooked a brawny 18-inch cutthroat that pulled like a four-wheel-drive pickup. I had caught Yellowstone cutthroat trout in the park, plus genetically pure westslope cutthroat trout in High Lake; I wanted desperately for that diesel engine at the end of my line to have fine spots, so I could say I hit the grand slam for cutthroat in Yellowstone. I brought the red and gold prize to net and grinned. Its spots were tiny. I let the fish go but later wondered. Yes, the spots were small, but were they *fine*?

Such is part of what makes catching a Snake River finespotted cutthroat in Yellowstone so tricky.

There is other rare wildlife in the upper Snake country. Search said he's had a few "hello and good-bye" griz encounters back there, and he said he often grins to hear wolves howling around him. The scene he remembers best was drinking coffee with guests around a breakfast campfire one fall morning when two bull elk decided to lock antlers on the slope in front of them.

"We heard the clacking of horns, the bulls bugling at each other, and the crashing of one elk rolling down the hillside after it got shoved down," Search said. "It was a unique moment in my career as an outfitter, a little more icing on the cake on a neat fishing trip in Yellowstone where we get to see nature and wildlife at its best."

All of those elements draw Search back to the upper Snake River, along with many clients who come for their shot at one of those special finespotted cutthroats.

"When you get one, it's awesome," Search said. "It's one more notch for your gun belt."

24 Grayling Creek

James and Angie Marsh

The cobalt-blue pool sparkling with white bubbles along Highway 191 had to be loaded with trout, Angie Marsh thought. But she and her husband James Marsh kept driving past it en route to some of Yellowstone's marquee rivers, like the Gallatin and the Madison.

Finally, Angie convinced James to pull over to try fishing Grayling Creek just once. That was 10 years ago, and neither James nor Angie has passed up a chance to fish it since.

"There's a whole flock of fish in there, and you wouldn't even know it," Angie said.

James said the first time he and Angie tried medium-sized, tumbling Grayling Creek, he caught around 40 bright 10-inch cuttbows in three hours.

Trout: Rainbow trout and cuttbows averaging 8 to 11 inches.

Bugs: Mayflies, caddisflies, and terrestrials.

Suggested fly box: Size 14 attractor dry flies, including Royal Wulffs, Humpies, Elk Hair Caddis, and Parachute Adamses; Pheasant Tail, Hare's Ear, and Prince nymphs size 14 to 18; Dave's Hoppers size 6 to 14; crickets size 8 to 14; Parachute and Chernobyl Ant patterns size 14 to 18; foam beetles size 14 to 16.

Key techniques: Search the water with attractor dry flies.

Best times: June through October.

Directions: Highway 191 parallels this creek for several miles north of West Yellowstone.

Special rules: Catch-and-release for cutthroats.

Often overlooked by trophy-seeking anglers, Grayling Creek is easy to reach and filled with eager little trout that readily take dry flies. PHOTO BY NATE SCHWEBER

He also caught a few brown and rainbow trout. Some of the fish might have even pushed 14 inches on a tape measure, he said. Angie remembers how she felt after fishing out that pool she noticed from the road.

"Ooh, my arm was hurting," she said. "That was an armful."

Highway 191 parallels Grayling Creek for about six miles and crosses over it twice on the stream's run from trail-less backcountry, across the park border, and down to Hebgen Lake. It sports excellent hatches of Green Drakes, Pale Morning Duns, caddisflies, and Golden Stoneflies. James said he's always done just fine with basic dry attractors like Parachute Adamses and Elk Hair Caddis.

"In Grayling Creek it doesn't matter what's hatching or what's not hatching," James said. "Attractors catch a whole lot of fish."

James's preferred way to fish Grayling is to simply pull over to the side of Highway 191 beside one trouty-looking spot. He'll fish for a while; then he'll find another spot a little up the road. Grayling Creek is often an excellent stream to warm up on, before pushing on to what Angie calls "name-brand rivers" like the Gallatin and the Madison.

Despite its easy access, James said he has always been amazed by how few people fish Grayling Creek, while the nearby name brands stay packed with anglers.

"There's never anyone there," he said. "You also hear it ignored in West Yellowstone, even though it's very close; it's just not talked about."

Grayling Creek trout hide in the likeliest of spots: behind rocks, along current seams, underneath overhanging banks, and in the various runs and pools. Drag-free drifts with high-floating dry flies are an excellent way to get the trout splashing the surface.

James said that he and Angie have also seen some memorable wildlife along Grayling Creek, including otters, two young bull moose, and three wolves up close. But the animal James saw that impressed him the most, the image that stays frozen in his mind, is that of the biggest buck mule deer he ever saw.

"Its horns were big enough to be an elk; I mean just Boone and Crockett Club," James said. "I couldn't think for a minute. I was like, is this real?"

As soon as he reached for his camera, the deer bolted into the forest.

James worked as a saltwater fishing guide in Panama City, Florida, before moving with Angie in the 1990s to Pigeon Forge, Tennessee, just five miles from the border of Great Smoky Mountain National Park and, Angie noted, home of the Dolly Parton theme park Dollywood. In summer time, the couple tries to spend a month or two in Yellowstone. Over the course of eight years, they shot an instructional DVD series on fishing the park that showcases more than a dozen Yellowstone streams.

Grayling Creek has been tapped by park biologists as a possible site to remove nonnative trout and reintroduce native westslope cutthroat and grayling.[1]

Angie calls Grayling Creek "fun" and "always an adventure." James said he and his wife still laugh about all the people who pass it by.

"I run into all these guys who have flown up to Yellowstone, and they're there a week, and all they talk about is, 'Well, I caught a few today on the Madison,'" James said. "It gets funny to Angie and me because we know we can just pull off at Grayling Creek and in an hour or two catch 30 or 40 trout."

25 Obsidian Creek

Mark D. Williams

It wasn't the willows, the water, or the wild brook trout—"fat as Churchill cigars"—that made little Obsidian Creek a favorite for Mark Williams.

It was the company he kept. He visited Obsidian Creek with his brother-in-law Kenny and his two 12-year-old nephews Chase and Bryan.

"It sounds corny, but Obsidian Creek was about what we wanted to pass on to the boys about the wildness of being in Yellowstone," said Mark, 50, a high school teacher in Amarillo, Texas, who has written more than a dozen books about fishing.

The two men brought the boys to Yellowstone for the first time in the early 1990s. Mark said he found Obsidian Creek by studying topographic

---

Trout: Brook trout averaging 6 to 11 inches.

Bugs: Stoneflies, mayflies, caddisflies, and terrestrials.

Suggested fly box: Size 14 attractor dry flies, including Royal Wulffs, Humpies, Elk Hair Caddis, and Parachute Adamses; Pheasant Tail, Hare's Ear, and Prince nymphs size 14 to 18; Dave's Hoppers size 6 to 14; crickets size 8 to 14; Parachute and Chernobyl Ant patterns size 14 to 18; foam beetles size 14 to 16.

Key techniques: Almost any dry fly tossed on the water here stands a good chance of catching a brook trout.

Best times: Anytime after spring runoff.

Directions: Grand Loop Road north of the Norris Campground and south of Mammoth Hot Springs parallels Obsidian Creek for several miles.

Special rules: Limit of five brook trout per day.

Obsidian Creek is filled with slashing brook trout and is one of a few streams in Yellowstone where youngsters are allowed to fish with bait. It offers plenty of fun and memorable moments for experienced anglers too. PHOTO BY NATE SCHWEBER

maps of the park. He wasn't fazed when he read in the park's regulations that Obsidian is one of just a few places in Yellowstone where kids under the age of 11 are allowed to fish with worms.

"I saw it on a map and read that it's for children, and I thought, 'I can walk those children out of the way no problem,'" Mark said. "There are aggressive, wild fish if you snake back in there, and that's what I wanted to turn my kids on to."

Obsidian is a small creek, pouring into the Gardner River near the Indian Creek Campground seven miles south of Mammoth Hot Springs. Mark described it as a stream that "meanders and snakes" through plenty of "dips and dives" and that, the farther upstream you get, "the darker and more primeval it gets."

"It's in a meadow, but there are trees everywhere; it has amazingly deep holes in places," he said. "If you can jump halfway decent, you can jump across it."

Even though it is often overlooked by trophy-hunting anglers, Mark said he loved Obsidian Creek.

"We didn't see another angler," he said. "We went from pool to pool; it was guerilla fishing."

Mark and Kenny brought Chase and Bryan to Obsidian at the beginning of their two-week Yellowstone visit. The boys' grandfather Fred, who passed away in 1992, had taught them to fish when they were just four years old, and they had honed those skills on a small creek near the family's cabin in Colorado. But this was their first time fishing in a wilderness as vast as Yellowstone. They had plenty to learn.

"A place like that is the kind of a place you want to take your sons to," Kenny, who is Chase's father, said from his home in Amarillo, Texas. "It's getting back to the way things should be."

On Obsidian Creek, Mark and Kenny taught the boys about stealth. They taught them to creep along the bank and not let their shadows fall across the fishy-looking holes. They watched as the boys hid behind trees and rocks and dapped from their knees.

The boys fished with Royal Wulffs, Stimulators, and Goddard Caddis patterns. "We tried to stay away from things the boys could sink," Mark said. Later, he and Kenny taught the boys to high-stick nymphs and swing wet flies under Obsidian Creek's undercut banks for its biggest brookies, some stretching nearly a foot.

"If you got a halfway decent drift, these wild brookies were slashers," Mark said. "They were aggressive."

Obsidian's woody banks meant the boys couldn't simply backpedal to pull their fish out of the water. They had to learn to use their reels and play the trout.

The boys had to learn lessons about being in the wilderness, too. At that age, Mark remembers the boys being "just absolutely fearless," often scurrying ahead without a thought about bears, hot pools, or God knows what else. Mark and Kenny decided to teach them a lesson. The two men snuck up ahead of the boys and then came running at them "screaming like banshees."

"That scared some sense into them," Mark said.

The men also passed along a hard-won lesson about one of Yellowstone's more overlooked hazards, something Mark calls "Kenny sticks," his nickname for the sharp, broken-off branches that jut up from the fallen trees that litter the ground all over Yellowstone. The little, downed daggers got their nickname one day when Mark and Kenny fished the Lewis River. Kenny saw a big brown trout rise and went hustling up toward it. He leapt over a downed tree but landed on a Kenny stick that jabbed deep into his calf. "He's a tough guy, but he was hurting," Mark remembers.

Mark ran to give aid to his brother-in-law. But then he saw that big trout, too. So Mark left Kenny bleeding and went and caught the 20-inch brown.

"Boy, that fish was big. What was I going to do?" Mark said. "Kenny still has a scar and he still gives me a hard time about it."

"I didn't say much at the time, just 'Hey, nice fish,'" Kenny recalls. "But I was thinking, *'It might be your last fish!'*"

The four fishermen chased Obsidian Creek brook trout for two hours up and two hours back for a few days early in that visit to Yellowstone. They fished other spots in the park, too, and made sure to do plenty of wildlife and geyser watching. On their last day, the boys asked to come back to Obsidian Creek. They said they loved it almost as much as the candy stores in the town of West Yellowstone.

"They wanted to go back to where they knew it would be a slam dunk," Mark said.

Hiking out of Obsidian Creek on their last day, Mark called it a "Leave-it-to-Beaver moment."

"We were the proud dads—male bonding with the boys, walking away whistling like Andy Griffith," he said.

Someone else was on everybody's mind: Grandpa Fred.

"We thought, wow, wouldn't Fred have loved this?" Mark said.

The boys are grown now. Bryan lives in China, and Chase just took a job at a law firm in Fort Worth, Texas. He still thinks back to Obsidian Creek and how catching wilderness trout with his dad and uncle helped him mature.

"I remember feeling after that trip like I'd accomplished something," he said. "I remember feeling a little older, a little more grown up—a step closer to manhood."

26 Fall River

Nathan Bennett

Like poet Robert Frost at his famous crossroads in the Yellow Woods, the path less traveled made all the difference for Nathan Bennett. It led him to the Fall River.

This hidden stream, which pours over spectacular waterfalls as it drains Yellowstone's remote and aptly named Cascade Corner, is Bennett's kind of spot.

"Everybody comes out here and asks about fishing the big rivers," said Bennett, 29, who owns Teton Fly Fishing in Jackson Hole. "But . . . if you get off the beaten path, that's where the magic is."

The Fall River is best known for the stunning Cave Falls, a broad and awesome double waterfall a ways up a dirt road from the park's seldom-traversed

---

Trout: Cutthroat trout, rainbow trout, and cuttbows averaging 6 to 12 inches.

Bugs: Mayflies, caddisflies, and terrestrials.

Suggested fly box: Size 14 attractor dry flies, including Royal Wulffs, Humpies, Elk Hair Caddis, and Parachute Adamses; Pheasant Tail, Hare's Ear, and Prince nymphs size 14 to 18; Dave's Hoppers size 6 to 14; crickets size 8 to 14; Parachute and Chernobyl Ant patterns size 14 to 18; foam beetles size 14 to 16.

Key techniques: Search the water with attractor dry flies.

Best times: June through October.

Directions: Grassy Lake Road runs roughly parallel to the Fall River just below Yellowstone Park above Grand Teton National Park. Use a topographical map to find the best routes to the river.

Special rules: Catch-and-release for cutthroats.

The Fall River was named for the many waterfalls along its length as it drains the aptly-named Cascade Corner of Yellowstone. It's an excellent place to explore for rainbow and cutthroat trout, and to enjoy wilderness solitude. PHOTO BY NATE SCHWEBER

southwest entrance. The Fall River runs somewhat parallel to the southern boundary of Yellowstone from its headwaters at Beula Lake. Grassy Lake Road, the type of dirt road that makes you thank your lucky stars for four-wheel-drive, parallels the park boundary on the south side in between Yellowstone and Grand Teton National Parks. Bennett decided one day to bushwhack from that dirt road into the Fall River. The stream was originally named "Falls River" for its numerous waterfalls, but the "s" was officially dropped in 1998.[1]

That July morning, he parked along Grassy Lake Road and followed his topographical map north to the Fall River. En route he crossed tiny Calf Creek and stopped to whisk out a few 6-inch rainbows. When he reached the Fall River, the streambed was made of flat rocks that made for riffle stretches that every so often would give way to pools. Bennett said he cast with "standard western" flies, Stimulators, Parachute Adamses, and Chernobyl Ants. "Nothing technical," he said. He plucked out some foot-long cutthroats and some half that length.

Bennett worked his way down the river to an area where it broadened and glided through a marshy meadow with banks covered in thick willows and fir trees. He had to push and weave his way through the tall growth, and he made plenty of noise. After all, this is the grizzly's home.

He came around a bend and suddenly heard rustling and twigs snapping, as if a big animal just stood up on the sprint. Bennett's heart jolted, and he pictured a griz and thought, *Here we go.*

Instead he saw a giant bull moose crash out of the willows and splash across the Fall River. It disappeared on the far side.

"It turned out to be uneventful," Bennett said, "which is a good thing."

The river changed character here. The water bounced over riffles and then smoothed into 15-foot-long pools with willows hanging over each bank. The pools looked so fishy that Bennett thought catching trout in them would be a slam dunk. "Usually when you're fishing the more remote waters around here, your first cast brings up a fish," Bennett said. Not so here.

He cast a Chernobyl Ant into a run of water with an eddy on the side, "One of those spots where you'd bet your wife that a fish would come up," Bennett said—but nothing. Then on the twelfth cast—something.

"A big, pretty rainbow came up and went running down the water, fighting, jumping, surrounded by willow trees and fir trees," Bennett said. "In a setting like that, it's so cool."

The Fall River near Ashton, Idaho, gets bigger and so do its fish, Bennett said. Still, he far prefers to fish the upper river. "Nobody talks about fishing it in the woods," he said.

"It's the difference between being able to go fish somewhere with a 5-weight rod and one box of flies, or you've got to get your vest with eight different fly boxes and you're struggling to find the turnout and fight for space," Bennett said. "With the Fall River in the park, you can just grab the bare necessities and go, and see a part of the country that most people don't see."

Bennett calls the upper Fall River "true wilderness" with fascinating burn areas, old growth fir trees, and geysers.

"It's beautiful in there; but no one goes, because it's not connected to the main part of the park," he said.

Bennett moved to Jackson Hole in 2003. He grew up in the middle of Pennsylvania's Amish country and studied art at college in Vermont, but he said, "The fish were the top priority." On summer vacations, he fished the Tetons with his grandfather and got to know several of the region's longtime guides. "I fell in love with the place and decided I just wanted to pursue trout," he said.

Today he loves nothing more than to explore backcountry spots, like the drainages in the Cascade Corner. He's fished several of them and looks forward to more.

"You could stand elbow to elbow in the Firehole, or you could fish this kind of stuff," he said. "I don't think any magazine would make a profile of it; but there's enough fish to keep it interesting, and it's wild country. Once you fish one, you want to see what's next."

27 Fan Creek

Steve Tureikas, Bob Jackson

Steve Tureikas was unnerved on his first hike into the fishy meadows of Fan Creek by the grizzly bear claw marks, some of them stretching 12 feet high, on seemingly every spruce tree just past the stock bridge over the Gallatin River along the Fawn Pass Trail.

He also wondered if a creature that some say is even scarier than a grizzly bear lurked somewhere in that basin.

"First these bear claw marks," Tureikas said, "and then you've got bigfoot in the back of your mind, too."

Tureikas, 53, a Princeton University engineer who studies nuclear fusion, first visited Yellowstone in 1990 and has returned to the Rockies every year

---

Trout: Cutthroat trout, rainbow trout, cuttbows, and brown trout averaging 8 to 13 inches.

Bugs: Mayflies, caddisflies, and terrestrials.

Suggested fly box: Size 14 attractor dry flies, including Royal Wulffs, Humpies, and Elk Hair Caddis; Parachute Adamses size 10 to 18; Pheasant Tail, Hare's Ear, and Prince nymphs size 14 to 18; Dave's Hoppers size 6 to 14; crickets size 8 to 14; Parachute and Chernobyl Ant patterns size 14 to 18; foam beetles size 14 to 16.

Key techniques: Search the water with attractor dry flies.

Best times: June through October.

Directions: Park at the Fawn Pass Trailhead along Highway 191 along the stretch where the highway parallels the Gallatin River. Take the trail up into the Fan Creek meadows.

Special rules: Catch-and-release for cutthroats.

Fan Creek pours through some of the loveliest mountain meadows in all of Yellowstone. Rivulets of water in its headwaters are shaped like veins in an aspen leaf, or spokes in a handheld fan, earning this creek its name. Many anglers swear the name is short for "fantastic." PHOTO BY NATE SCHWEBER

since. Sometime in the mid-1990s, he overheard Craig Mathews at Blue Ribbon Flies in West Yellowstone rave about Fan Creek, named for the shape of the valley at its headwaters.[1] Tureikas's sense of wanderlust was piqued. He studied a topographical map and headed out for this stream that pours into the Gallatin River.

"I thought I'd died and gone to heaven," said Tureikas, who is also an avid nature photographer. "I fell in love with it at first sight."

In its picturesque mountain meadows, about a mile and a half past the trailhead, Fan Creek runs about 20 feet wide and has classic riffles and pools, crystal-clear water, a pebble bottom, and "more S-turns than you can count," Tureikas said.

On that first visit, Tureikas turned over river rocks and found caddisfly larvae, Pale Morning Dun nymphs, and *Baetis* nymphs. He watched some big Green Drakes hatch. "For such a small stream, it's very fertile," he said.

Over the course of several visits, Tureikas has had great success casting Pale Morning Duns, Elk Hair Caddis, and Parachute Hopper imitations. The best technique for catching fish is simply casting dry flies upstream.

"Nothing more technical than that," he said.

Despite its small size, Fan Creek is home to some surprisingly large and hard-fighting trout, particularly cuttbows, rainbows, and a few brown trout that run up from the Gallatin River. PHOTO BY STEVE TUREIKAS

Because it's high and cold, Fan Creek doesn't usually fish well until the water warms in late morning, Tureikas said. This makes the stream perfect for a hike in after breakfast with a picnic lunch packed.

The trout in Fan Creek are predominantly cuttbows—hybrids of introduced rainbows and Yellowstone cutthroats with a remnant population of westslope cutthroat trout. There are also a few browns in Fan Creek, visitors from the Gallatin River. Most of the trout run 10 inches or a foot, but some grow bigger, a real treat in a backcountry stream like Fan Creek.

Tureikas said he was most impressed by Fan Creek's westslope cutthroat/rainbow hybrids, which, he said, were "full of piss and vinegar." He remembers one 14-inch cuttbow nailing a hopper and then tearing line out of his 9-foot, 5-weight rod until it wrapped around a root clump under an overhanging bank and busted off.

"It was like being hooked to a little piece of dynamite," Tureikas said. "My jaw just dropped to have that kind of fishing in such a small stream."

Tureikas's jaw isn't the only one to have dropped on Fan Creek. In the 1970s, Bob Jackson, a backcountry ranger who earned honors for busting elk hunters using illegal salt licks in Yellowstone's Thorofare region, was riding his horse near a tributary that pours into Fan Creek. A sound "like a thousand elk going to their death" cut through the countryside, he said. The sound went on louder and longer than anything he'd ever heard in the backcountry before.

Weeks later, in a subalpine fir meadow 11 miles up Fan Creek, Jackson watched a deer grazing on the edge of a thicket. Suddenly, a shaggy, 6-foot-tall creature ran toward the deer on two legs, upright, just like a man.

"I related back to that sound I'd heard," Jackson said from a bison ranch he runs today in Iowa. "I'd say it was the same thing."

Jackson was about 50 yards away from the creature when it turned and looked at him. Black hair hung down from its long arms and covered its face. The thing ran away from Jackson, zigzagging from bush to bush, sprinting and hiding.

"This thing was smart," he said. "I've never seen an animal trying to pick up protection as it fled."

Jackson, who worked as a Yellowstone ranger for 30 years, still isn't sure what he saw.

"Some say it was bigfoot," he said.

Tureikas had read about Jackson's tale before he visited Fan Creek.

"Considering this report came from one of the head rangers in Yellowstone National Park," Tureikas said, "it was hard to dismiss."

Functionally Extinct

On the breezy afternoon of Saturday, July 30, 1994, a ranger brought a nightmare into the main fisheries office near the banks of Yellowstone Lake. Biologist Robert Gresswell, who had worked in the park for 17 years and left feeling most proud of the role he played in the resurrection of Yellowstone Lake's magnificent cutthroat fishery, just happened to be visiting a former colleague while on break from his PhD program in Oregon. Gresswell saw the ranger walk in with a fat, healthy, 19-inch lake trout that a fishing guide had turned in. A client had just pulled it out of Yellowstone Lake.

"When I saw that fish," Gresswell said, "it was like somebody hit me in the gut."

Dan Carty, a fish biologist working in Yellowstone at the time, was called down from his office in Mammoth to come take a look at the specimen, which was stored in a freezer. Carty noted that the 19-inch lake trout "kinda just looked like a 19-inch lake trout." The cold, dead fish was unspectacular in every way but for the chaos it foretold.

For several seasons, rangers had heard rumors that anglers occasionally caught lake trout in Yellowstone Lake. Used to tourists misidentifying their catches, and having no proof that the giant, voracious, predator could have somehow gotten loose in Yellowstone Lake, park workers treated the stories as just that—talk.

Nobody in that office could deny the cobalt slab of toothy trouble staring back at them.

"You can't see a lake trout and know that it's been introduced to a place like Yellowstone Lake and think it could be anything but bad," Gresswell said, "which is exactly what it was."

An adult lake trout can devour between 40 and 60 Yellowstone cutthroat trout annually, and they can live for 40 years. The world record lake trout weighed more than 100 pounds. Because they will feed on insects and even each other, lake trout can completely eradicate native species and still survive, biologists say. They are the largest freshwater salmonid species in North America, and relative to their body size, they also have the biggest mouths. All the better to eat you with, my dear.

A bull elk stands silhouetted by the waters of Yellowstone Lake. Since illegally stocked lake trout decimated the cutthroats, hungry grizzly bears around Yellowstone Lake have turned to eating elk calves for their springtime protein. PHOTO BY NATE SCHWEBER

Technically a char, lake trout, or *mackinaw*, are native to deep waters across the northern United States, including the Great Lakes, as well as Canada and parts of Alaska. Prized by some boat fishermen for their size, lake trout were stocked in the early twentieth century in lakes all over the west, including Tahoe in Nevada, Flathead in Montana, and Pend Oreille and Coeur d' Alene in Idaho.[1] In each place, the lake trout decimated native species, particularly cutthroats.

Suddenly, Yellowstone fisheries managers were confronted with the chilling reality that while they were able to bring Yellowstone Lake's cutthroats back by changing the rules for humans, now they were dealing with a devastating deepwater foe over which they had no jurisdiction. Some scientists estimated that if they didn't take action, lake trout would extirpate cutthroats from Yellowstone Lake by 2033.[2]

Yellowstone Lake's cutthroats evolved with no underwater predators and developed a life cycle that, in hindsight, seems tailor-made for a lake trout smorgasbord. Baby cutthroats hatch in their spawning streams and then migrate down to Yellowstone Lake where they swim out to deep, open water

A fisherman in the late 2000s who set out to catch a cutthroat trout in Yellowstone Lake displays some of the lake trout he caught instead. PHOTO COURTESY OF RICK McCOURT

to grow into adults. Since the clandestine introduction of lake trout, probably in the 1980s, millions of little Yellowstone Lake cutthroats have followed their natural instincts down to what had once been their pelagic nursery, a nursery that now teems with teeth.

In 1998 John D. Varley, the former chief of research for Yellowstone Park, and fisheries historian Paul Schullery wrote ominously of the burgeoning lake trout epidemic in their book *Yellowstone Fishes.*

"In our combined 50 years of personal involvement in Yellowstone issues, and in our long study of the park's history, we've rarely come across a scarier situation," they wrote.[3]

Speaking in 2011 from his home in Bozeman, Varley said that given what happened in the decade after he wrote the book, he was wrong.

"The lake trout situation turned out to be even scarier than we feared back then," he said. "It makes me sick to my stomach."

Historically, scientists estimate that Yellowstone Lake held as many as four million cutthroats, but in the two decades after lake trout were introduced, the cutthroat numbers plummeted by *99 percent*.[4] It's worth noting that to date, lake trout in Yellowstone Lake have eaten more Yellowstone cutthroats than are currently living in Idaho, Utah, and Nevada *combined*.[5]

Nowhere was the cutthroat free fall measured more acutely than at the Clear Creek fish weir where in 2008 biologists counted only 241 cutthroat before the weir washed out. The year before, the last full count, there were just 538 cutthroats.[6] These were by far the smallest cutthroat counts in the more than 60-year history of the weir, and a horrific drop from the more than 70,000 cutthroats tallied 30 years earlier.

Scientists don't know how many lake trout there are in Yellowstone Lake, but annual harvest counts speak to their almost exponential growth. In 1999 workers netted more than 15,000 lake trout. By 2005 they hauled up more than 35,000. In 2008 the number jumped to more than 75,000,[7] and in 2010 parks crews, augmented by a private fishing company, caught almost 150,000 lake trout. Big ones were sliced open, and biologists watched as

That same fisherman displays the only Yellowstone cutthroat he was able to catch after a full day's fishing on Yellowstone Lake. PHOTO COURTESY OF RICK McCOURT

handfuls of pale, dead cutthroats spilled out of their bellies. Scientists estimate that the diet of adult lake trout in Yellowstone Lake is 99 percent cutthroat trout.[8]

If the Park Service's efforts didn't seem adequate to combat the problem, they were hardly buoyed by the voices of many sportsmen. In March 1996 *Field & Stream*'s "Conservation," columnist George Reiger criticized the nascent lake trout control plan as the Park Service trying to "spend other people's money" on "problems that may not even exist."

"How can biologists be so sure that Yellowstone lake trout will prove to be an ecologic disaster," he wrote. "Yellowstone cutthroat and lake trout will probably achieve some level of coexistence without the Park Service lifting a finger."[9]

The cutthroats buckled around 2000, when the population of lake trout was such that netters, with smaller crews working fewer days than they would in the coming years, caught between 15,000 and 20,000, said Todd Koel, the top fisheries biologist in Yellowstone. With today's lake trout population such that crews are catching almost *ten times* as many lake trout as they did in 1999, there is little hope of the cutthroat fishery pulling out of its flat spin.

"There are more lake trout out there now than would have caused the cutthroat's initial decline back in 2000," Koel said. "We should not expect the cutthroat to come back until we drive the lake trout population back down."

Animals tell another part of this story. In 1987 alone pairs of osprey around Yellowstone Lake raised 44 fledglings, said park ornithologist Douglas W. Smith. From 2008 to 2010, they raised none. Meanwhile, the number of baby bald eagles dropped by half, he said. Otters all but vanished from the creeks and streams pouring into Yellowstone Lake, where they used to catch cutthroat in the springtime to feed their pups just emerging from their dens, said otter biologist Jamie R. Crait. Terry McEneaney, a former park ornithologist, said, "There just aren't enough cutthroats in Yellowstone Lake anymore to support the birds and the animals; Yellowstone Lake is dying."

Many feared for the survival of the great grizzly because by 2000 biologists counted close to 100 grizzlies catching cutthroats in Yellowstone Lake tributaries. Surprisingly, the grizzly population seems not to have been affected at all, said Kerry Gunther, bear management biologist for the park. But in a stark illustration of nature's intertwined web, it is elk that have suffered terribly because of the lake trout. Grizzlies used to fish for spawning cutthroat after emerging from their dens. Now with the cutthroats gone, the bears have turned to eating elk calves for their springtime protein, he said. Human hunting and predation by wolves reduced elk numbers in the northern Yellowstone region, as well as around Jackson Hole and in other parts of Wyoming, but the predation by grizzlies in the calving grounds around Yellowstone Lake is contributing to the herd's not bouncing back, he said.

Lake trout do not fill the cutthroat's role in the ecosystem. Adult cutthroats cruise Yellowstone Lake's shallows and migrate into creeks each spring to spawn. In the process, they become food for more than 40 species of animals, including bears, otters, eagles, and pelicans.[10] Lake trout live and spawn in the deep, out of reach. They provide next to no sustenance for hungry bears, otters, or birds, and few anglers can catch them without a boat.

Cutthroat anglers watched from the front line of the decline. In 2000, just six years after the lake trout discovery, anglers venturing to the most remote parts of Yellowstone Lake and her feeder streams caught some cutthroat trout, down significantly from the plethora they caught just a few years before. Over the next two years, the situation got worse. Backcountry anglers caught only a few cutthroats in 2001 and 2002, and by 2003 they caught almost none. These anglers' observations are in sync with data from fisheries biologists that show the plummet of the cutthroat population. "In '99 the Thorofare was still fishing pretty good, but around 2000 we watched it just fall off to nothing," said Terry Chase, outfitter and founder of Yellowstone Mountain Guides.

Thus, the introduced lake trout destroyed Yellowstone Lake's awesome cutthroat fishery, once the greatest on earth. It was a fishery that seemed infinite to early explorers and was hailed by generations of anglers as the last big, pure, unspoiled cutthroat oasis in America. The Yellowstone Lake cutthroats, mule loads of them, delighted throngs of tourists and nourished scores of animals.

It took less than a generation for them to vanish; for the pulse of Yellowstone Lake to flatline. A 2010 Park Service report described the status of Yellowstone Lake's cutthroats using just two words: "functionally extinct."[11]

A woman casts to rainbow and brown trout on the Firehole River just downstream from Muleshoe Bend as thermal steam rises in the background. PHOTO BY DR. GUY R. MUTO

Anglers can cast to trout in some of the strangest and most beautiful scenery on earth in Yellowstone Park, like here at Biscuit Basin on the Firehole River. PHOTO BY DR. GUY R. MUTO

Indian paintbrush color the banks of Duck Creek, a spot visited mostly by local anglers and a lot of grizzlies on the far west side of Yellowstone Park. PHOTO BY DR. GUY R. MUTO

The Yellowstone Plateau sits at an average of 7,000 feet above sea level.
PHOTO BY JOHN JURACEK

Below: Native Yellowstone cutthroat trout are the marquee fish of the world's first national park. Incredibly beautiful, with hues of gold and crimson and speckled with obsidian, this fish has suffered a terrible decline in recent decades due to hybridization with rainbow trout, drought, disease, and an illegal stocking of lake trout in Yellowstone Lake, this cutthroat's stronghold. PHOTO BY PAT CLAYTON

The Gibbon River is scenic and provides plenty of easy access for opportunities to cast to its rainbow, brown, and brook trout, plus a rare grayling that washes down from the river's headwaters at Grebe Lake. PHOTO BY DR. GUY R. MUTO

The Madison River at one of many beautiful sections not far from West Entrance Road. PHOTO BY DR. GUY R. MUTO

Snow dusts the Gneiss Creek Trail just downstream of Seven Mile Bridge, which crosses the Madison River along West Entrance Road. When the streambanks look like this, the river is often filled with spawning brown trout running up from Hebgen Lake. PHOTO BY DR. GUY R. MUTO

Fan Creek pours through some of the most beautiful mountain meadows in the park. This drainage is home to some almost genetically pure westslope cutthroats, grizzly bears, and maybe even bigfoot. PHOTO BY JOHN JURACEK

The Firehole River near Midway Geyser Basin. PHOTO BY JOHN JURACEK

A fisherman casts into the Madison River as seen from Riverside Drive, a side road off West Entrance Road that routes close to the river's southern bank. Generally the water here runs about two feet deep, but West Yellowstone anglers know of slicks and holes that are deeper and hold higher concentrations of trout. PHOTO BY DR. GUY R. MUTO

Above: Trout don't live in ugly places. PHOTO BY JOHN JURACEK

Right: Shades of blue run the gamut in Yellowstone, such as this thermal pool near the bank of the Firehole River. PHOTO BY JOHN JURACEK

Above: An angler lands a survivor, one of the few, giant Yellowstone cutthroat trout that still swim in the upper Yellowstone River since the illegal introduction of lake trout into Yellowstone Lake. The Yellowstone River remains one of the most iconic places to fish in the park. PHOTO BY JOHN JURACEK

Below: Trout Lake can be a great place to catch cutthroat trout and an even better place to watch schools of them preparing to spawn in the springtime. PHOTO BY JOHN JURACEK

Mount Haynes looms above the Madison River, where it takes skill, luck, and patience to land big rainbow and brown trout. PHOTO BY JOHN JURACEK

Above: Nez Perce Creek has fantastic fishing and an incredible history. PHOTO BY JOHN JURACEK

Right: Scalding water from a Yellowstone geyser pours into the Gibbon River as an angler casts to brown, rainbow, and brook trout. PHOTO BY JOHN JURACEK

Soda Butte Creek in Yellowstone's northeast corner features impressive mountain vistas and great wildlife viewing opportunities. PHOTO BY JOHN JURACEK

Above: The scenery in the Yellowstone's grand Lamar Valley is unmatched. PHOTO BY JOHN JURACEK

Left: The stuff of angler's dreams—Slough Creek, where big Yellowstone cutthroat swim. PHOTO BY JOHN JURACEK

28 Bechler River at Bechler Meadows

Mike Atwell

The story of how Mike Atwell discovered the Bechler Meadows reads more like a detective novel than a fish story. Call it *Yellowstone Noir*.

It's been 30 years since Atwell met the Bechler. The river is home to secrets, mystery, and 10-pound rainbows. When Atwell first asked about the Bechler, his boss at the fly shop dropped what he was doing like a priest drops his Bible when Madonna walks into a confession booth.

"How did you hear about the Bechler River?"

Atwell got wise to the river on the sly during a gig as a guide at a secret cabin that belongs to an old, exclusive fly-fishing club. The nineteenth-century

---

Trout: Rainbows, many over 20 inches.

Bugs: Mayflies, caddisflies, and terrestrials.

Suggested fly box: Parachute Adamses size 10 to 18; Pale Morning Duns and Blue-Winged Olives size 16 to 20; tan Elk Hair Caddis size 14 to 18; Royal Wulffs, Royal Coachman Trudes, yellow Stimulators, and Yellow Humpies size 14 and 16; Pheasant Tail, Hare's Ear, Prince, and Serendipity nymphs size 14 to 18; Dave's Hoppers size 6 to 14; crickets size 8 to 14; Parachute and Chernobyl Ant patterns size 14 to 18; foam beetles size 14 to 16; black, tan, and olive Woolly Buggers size 4 to 8; Muddler Minnows and Zonkers size 2 to 6.

Key techniques: Stalk these ultraspooky trout carefully.

Best times: August and September.

Directions: Take the Bechler River Trail or the Bechler Meadows Trail from the Bechler Ranger Station, located about 10 miles up a dirt road from Ashton, Idaho.

Behind the dark side of the Grand Tetons lies a river that knows how to keep its secrets. Visit the Bechler River, and you might be driven mad by its enormous rainbows. PHOTO BY NATE SCHWEBER

lodge is hidden in thick pines on the dark side of the Tetons. It lies way up a rotten road in Park Island, Idaho. The clientele were all legacies, rich ones.

"All older people," Atwell noted. "Except the wives."

During the members' afternoon siesta, Atwell took a snoop around the joint. On a table in the foyer, he found a three-foot by two-foot leather-bound book from the early 1900s. Its pages were made of brittle rice paper. Each one showed the tracing of a giant trout. Trout traces on rice paper were the Polaroid pictures of their day.

Page after page, underneath outlines of some of the biggest rainbows, Atwell saw the words "Bechler River."

"I was like, 'Whoa, where is this Bechler place?'" he said.

Nobody from this club returned any of my calls. Nobody wanted to talk much to Atwell about the Bechler River either. It's a mysterious stream named after a cantankerous, old mapmaker[1] tucked away in the seldom-visited southwest part of Yellowstone called the Cascade Corner. Once Atwell visited the Bechler, he was told to keep his mouth shut, or else.

"Thirty years ago, it was quite unusual for anyone who wasn't a local resident to ask about the Bechler," said Mike Lawson, Atwell's former boss at Henry's Fork Anglers, whose father fished the Bechler in the 1930s.

Atwell visited the Bechler River that autumn. He drove the dirt road from Ashton, Idaho, to the Bechler Ranger Station and followed a flat trail five miles along the Fall River to its confluence with the Bechler River. Just upstream, Boundary Creek joined the Bechler, and above that spread the Bechler Meadows. Here the Bechler River smoothes glassy and clear like a spring creek with secrets to hide.

"The Bechler River is probably the closest thing we have to New Zealand in terms of huge rainbows in deep pools that will take dry flies," Atwell said.

Baetis mayflies began hatching like little, doomed angels. Atwell crept his way upriver. He caught more than a half-dozen rainbow trout that busted 20 inches.

"It was just unbelievable," Atwell said. "I was like, 'This is it! This is the place from the book.'"

Atwell found the deepest pool in the river. Up against the far bank swam a rainbow trout longer than a tommy gun. He tried a cast, but the suspicious rainbow "just backed down like a log into the big hole," he said.

Atwell could still see the beast through the glassy water. It lay in moss like a fat gangster in a bed of money. Night was coming on like a hooker, but Atwell wanted one more shot at the prize.

He tied on a streamer. He figured the big rainbow might be excited to murder by a baby trout imitation ripped past its nose. He tied on an extra-long leader and weighed it down with lead. He cast far upstream to give his fly time to sink. When the fly approached the big guy, Atwell yanked on his line, bringing the streamer to life.

"Bang!" Atwell said. "He eats it."

The fight was on. The big trout powered to the dark bottom of the pool. It held so hard that for a time, Atwell thought he wrapped around a drowned tree. Fifteen minutes later, Atwell fought the fish to within just four feet of him. "I was like, '*Oh my God,*'" he said.

Then the line went slack. The "big-shouldered rainbow," Atwell said, "just came unbuttoned."

A couple years later, in the late 1980s, a friend of Atwell's named Jeff Currier whispered that he planned to visit the Bechler. Atwell shared the secret of the pool with the huge rainbow. When they met again that fall, Currier told Atwell he had something to show. He reached into his backpack and pulled out a Polaroid picture. Polaroid pictures were the rice paper tracings of their day.

"He threw it down on the table and said, 'Twenty-eight inches. I caught it on a size 14 Dave's Hopper. That fish was exactly where you told me it would be,'" Atwell said. "It was a monster. We figured 10 pounds."

"It fought like a steelhead," Currier said. "Just unbelievable, out of control."

Currier sent me the photo of him cradling that rainbow. If I'd been holding a Bible, I would've dropped it.

You can look down into the scrubbed-glass clear water of the Bechler River and see rainbow trout that seem as long as your legs. Most of the time, they see you, too. Good luck catching one. PHOTO BY NATE SCHWEBER

Big Bechler bows may gobble dry flies like a mobster on a plate of grandma's spaghetti, but they require the stealth of a private dick to catch. In the Bechler Meadows, where the big money swims, fishermen have to spot trout and stalk them like bounty hunters. It can be a powerful rush, Atwell said, to watch a big rainbow rise eight feet up from the bottom of a pool to massacre a dry fly. It can also break your heart to watch those big fish spook like criminals in a police raid.

The buggy Bechler banks make terrestrials like hoppers, beetles, and ants as tempting to trout as another hit to a blackjack junkie holding 11. Other attractor patterns work, too, like that old standby, the Royal Wulff. Make sure you use a light tippet, Atwell said. You don't want to get made by a trout.

The Bechler Meadows are so boggy and filled with mosquitoes that, Atwell said, if you visit too soon, you could have the blood sucked out of you, or be driven to madness, or both. There's a lot of griz there, too. So watch out you don't get killed.

Wanted trout ain't the Bechler River's only secret. In the early 1980s, Atwell went into the meadows one morning. He saw a herd of around 20 elk, some 200 yards away, hanging by the forest near the far side. Apart from them stood a lone dame elk. She was obviously sick.

Atwell felt the hair on his neck stand up when he saw what happened next.

Two canines "as black as oil" that "looked like German shepherds" and were "easily twice the size of coyotes" started stalking and circling that cow, Atwell said.

"I knew they were wolves," he said. "They were big and black as night."

Remember, Atwell saw this drama more than a decade before wolves were reintroduced to Yellowstone National Park in 1995. Prior to the reintroduction, wolves were widely believed to have been hunted, trapped, and poisoned to extinction throughout all the continental United States, save a small remnant population in upper Michigan and a few that would straggle down from Canada into Glacier National Park in Montana. The reintroduction of wolves remains one of the most contentious issues in the West today, pitting some ranchers against wildlife watchers and some hunters against the Endangered Species Act.

Now Atwell wonders, how could wolves have been reintroduced if they were there all along?

Douglas W. Smith, leader of the Yellowstone Wolf Project, said that prior to reintroduction, there were unverified reports of wolves in the park, but no permanent packs.

"Likely there were wolves passing through," he said. "But we are sure there was no wolf population and this was the criteria upon which our decision to reintroduce was based."

Atwell, now 51, remembers the strange thrill he felt on that Bechler trip. In his young mind, it was as though he saw the land exactly as it was intended, with all of nature's elusive and magnificent beasts playing out the same roles as they had done since time eternal. He contacted a friend, a lady whose name he won't reveal. She worked for the park, and Atwell thought she would be excited to hear about the phantom wolves. He never anticipated her reaction.

"She said, 'You shouldn't be talking about this,' and she was someone of prominence and significance," Atwell said. "She said, 'Yep, there are wolves back there; but they are protected, and there are ranchers outside the park who want them dead, so just keep it under your hat.'"

Years later, Atwell felt the cold flash of déjà vu when he saw a pack of wolves in the Slough Creek Valley. They looked exactly the same as the shadowy creatures he saw as a young man by the Bechler River.

"Back then I didn't think of the controversy of it," he said. "I guess I was pretty naive."

29 Lamar River at Lamar Valley

Alice Owsley

Northeast Yellowstone's sweeping and wild Lamar Valley is the spot where Alice Owsley took her father to catch a big Yellowstone cutthroat in the river that slithers through the broad valley floor.

It's also where a grizzly bear almost caught her.

"The Lamar Valley is one of those spots that people should experience," she said. "It's just amazing."

The Lamar River sashays through this wildlife-rich valley nicknamed "The Serengeti of North America." Perhaps the most remarkable thing about the Lamar Valley is it is one of the last keyholes through which the bygone, pristine American West can still be glimpsed, where people can still see all

> **Trout:** Cutthroat trout, cuttbows, and rainbow trout averaging 12 to 20 inches.
>
> **Bugs:** Terrestrials, mayflies, and caddisflies.
>
> **Suggested fly box:** Dave's Hoppers size 6 to 14; crickets size 8 to 14; Parachute and Chernobyl Ant patterns size 14 to 18; foam beetles size 14 to 16; size 14 attractor dry flies, including Royal Wulffs, Humpies, Elk Hair Caddis, and Parachute Adamses; Pheasant Tail, Hare's Ear, and Prince nymphs size 14 to 18; black, tan, and olive Woolly Buggers size 4 to 8.
>
> **Key techniques:** Stalk the bank, watching for rising trout, and fish to them.
>
> **Best times:** August and September.
>
> **Directions:** Northeast Entrance Road follows the Lamar River for most of its length through the Lamar Valley.
>
> **Special rules:** Catch-and-release for all cutthroats.

A gray, female, alpha wolf stands on the bank of the Lamar River. Scenes like this, fantastic as they seem, happen frequently in this wildlife-packed valley, which has been nicknamed "the Serengeti of North America." PHOTO BY NATE SCHWEBER

the big, wild American animals that people like Lewis, Clark, Major John Wesley Powell, and countless Native Americans saw in their day. Herds of buffalo call this valley home, as do some of the park's most visible wolves, which draw big roadside crowds armed with telescopes. Pronghorn antelope and coyotes prance in the grasses where mule deer and elk forage. Hawks, eagles, and ospreys circle the skies, occasionally diving into the Lamar River to talon out Yellowstone cutthroat trout.

Grizzlies roam here, too—plenty.

Owsley, 34, a fishing guide based in West Yellowstone, brought her father, Dichel Owsley, who lives in Ohio, to the Lamar Valley to catch cutthroats a few years back. She located the day's best catch with her ears. The Owsleys were walking along a grassy bank next to the stream when Alice heard "that unusual sucking-snap sound" of a cutthroat feeding. Like a military scout, Owsley held her right arm out at a 90-degree angle and whispered, "Stop! There's a cutthroat around here."

The sound kept coming, but Owsley scanned the river in vain for its source. Then she saw her clue. Rings rolled out from under the very stream-bank where she and her father stood. The trout was literally underneath them.

Bison gather to eat green, springtime grasses in the broad Lamar Valley. All the big, native North American mammals that explorers like Lewis and Clark saw still roam free here and are on full display in this one-of-a-kind place. PHOTO BY NATE SCHWEBER

Owsley and her father tiptoed away from the bank to avoid sending down vibrations that would spook the fish. She sent her father downstream where he could cast up toward the trout, and she positioned herself across the river to watch. She could see the big cutthroat holding in slack water below the overhanging, grassy bank. It would shoot into a current seam to gobble food and then dart back.

Owsley told her dad to cast into the bubbly seam, not into the slack water, or else the current would grab his line and rip his fly across the water. The elder Owsley did as he was told. His daughter held her breath and watched.

"I saw the fish come out from the bank and move to eat the fly," she said. "It was a moment of tension watching this happen thinking, 'Oh, please set the hook. You don't even have to land it; just feel the tension in your line and complete this process.'"

The cutthroat slurped the fly, and Dichel raised his rod. The formidable fish raced into the center of the river, looking for cover. Then it vaulted into the air. Exhausted, the 16-inch cutthroat with brilliant red gill plates came to his hand.

"It was great to share that with my dad on the river," Owsley said. "He was very excited."

Owsley starts fishing the Lamar River as soon as it clears from runoff. Because the valley is loaded with glacial silt that is fine and brown, the river often doesn't clear until July, and a good rain can quickly turn it back to the color of Yoo-hoo.

Despite the Lamar's reputation as a place where gaudy attractor patterns can fool nice fish, Owsley says to always pay attention for hatches, particularly stoneflies, Green Drakes, Pale Morning Duns, and occasionally caddisflies. In high summer, terrestrials like grasshoppers and crickets fish well, and smaller patterns, like Chernobyl Ants and foam beetles, fish great.

Because this is one of the last strongholds of the embattled Yellowstone cutthroat trout, as of this writing the park allows anglers to keep five nonnative rainbow trout per day. Rainbows threaten the cutthroat's survival by crossbreeding with them. Both cutthroats and cutthroat-rainbow hybrids (any fish with a red slash below its jaw) must be released immediately, unharmed.

Fish pack the entire length of the Lamar River and often fishermen do too, especially since illegally stocked lake trout in Yellowstone Lake collapsed the native cutthroat fishery in the nearby upper Yellowstone River. The Northeast Entrance Road parallels the Lamar River for all but its top reaches, which can make for lots of access but little solitude. Owsley recommends walking to get away from people. Every likely spot on this river holds fish, she

Surprise! A Lamar Valley grizzly bear, like this one, happened upon guide Alice Owsley one day as she led some clients from California to catch Yellowstone cutthroat trout in the Lamar River. PHOTO BY NATE SCHWEBER

said. It is a particularly good stream to hunt fish by locating and casting to one specific cutthroat at a time.

The Lamar Valley, named for former secretary of the interior Lucius Quintus Cincinnatus Lamar, who requested federal troops sent to Yellowstone in 1883 to protect its dwindling wildlife from poachers,[1] is also a good place to be hunted. One summer morning, Owsley and another guide took a Santa Barbara, California, man and his two sons, ages 16 and 12, fishing at a fairly remote spot in the valley. Owsley took the younger son a short distance downstream from the others and stood in ankle-deep water not far from a very large bush.

In midmorning the other guide came down to talk to Owsley. At just that moment, a grizzly bear stepped out from behind the bush.

"He was two fly-rod lengths away from us," Owsley said. "And I'm sure he was looking for food."

The guides whipped out their cans of bear spray, popped off the safeties, and waved their arms and yelled.

"My reaction was like, 'Ah! Bear!'" Owsley said. "The hair was standing up on the back of my neck, but I had to be a little more composed because I was guiding."

The griz took a few steps toward them and stopped, spooked by the commotion. Owsley said she knew not to run, and she talked to the bear in a commanding voice "to try and sound bigger than I am."

The griz shuffled away from the guides but headed up the river toward the oldest son and the father, who just so happened to be fighting a cutthroat at that moment. Owsley grabbed onto the 12-year-old for his safety and shouted upstream at the others. The father broke his fish off and sent the 16-year-old swimming in his waders to the far side of the river.

"It kind of sunk in to the boys later that it was really cool," Owsley said. "Like, dude, this is for real. We're not at the zoo; a hungry grizzly bear just walked past you, and I'm not sure it doesn't think 12-year-olds are tasty."

The griz eventually ambled away from the river and crossed Northeast Entrance Road, creating a flash mob of gaping tourists.

Owsley believes the bear was a young male, probably around 300 pounds. She has been back to that spot often but never saw that griz again.

"He got damn close," she said.

30 Yellowstone River at Lower Grand Canyon

Parker Heinlein

Telling secrets about fishing spots is tantamount to treason in some angling circles. Parker Heinlein, a longtime outdoors columnist for the *Bozeman Daily Chronicle*, reached a point where he feared that keeping his secret might do more harm than good.

Trout: Native Yellowstone cutthroats averaging 12 to 16 inches.

Bugs: Stoneflies, including Salmonflies, around the time the river opens on July 15. Pale Morning Duns, Blue-Winged Olives, and caddis.

Suggested fly box: Dave's Hoppers size 6 to 14; crickets size 8 to 14; Parachute and Chernobyl Ant patterns size 14 to 18; foam beetles size 14 to 16; size 14 attractor dry flies, including Royal Wulffs, Humpies, and Elk Hair Caddis; Parachute Adamses size 10 to 18; Pheasant Tail, Hare's Ear, and Prince nymphs size 14 to 18; black, tan, and olive Woolly Buggers size 4 to 8.

Key techniques: Search the water with high-floating dry flies, particularly near the bank, behind rocks, along current seams, and in eddies. Watch for rising trout and cast to them.

Best times: High summer and September.

Directions: Take the Specimen Ridge Trail from the Yellowstone River Trailhead just past the Yellowstone River bridge on Northeast Entrance Road, or from the Specimen Ridge Trailhead a couple miles farther east. When the trail forks, go left and take the Agate Creek Trail 4.1 miles down to the Yellowstone River. There is a backcountry campsite here.

Special rules: Catch-and-release for all cutthroat.

The breathtaking Yellowstone River in its seldom-visited lower Grand Canyon section. The water teems with cutthroats and the banks are filled with wild raspberries. PHOTO BY NATE SCHWEBER

Recently, Heinlein noticed that he hasn't seen as many anglers as he used to in the lower Grand Canyon of the Yellowstone River, his favorite fishing spot in the park. Folks he did see tended to be old-timers like him. Sure, he's known sportsmen who were threatened after they spilled about their secret spot, but for the sake of the future, Heinlein decided to share his.

"I like to think there's a lot of hard-core young guys who love to fly-fish, and it bugs me that there aren't more of them humping in there for the day," Heinlein said from his home in Malta, Montana. "Where are they?"

Heinlein has long made near-annual pilgrimages to the lower Grand Canyon, downstream from Seven Mile Hole and upstream from the Black Canyon. He's opening up about it now because he'd like the next generation of outdoors enthusiasts to know Yellowstone as thoroughly as he does.

It's not so hard to hike down to this rugged stretch of canyon where 12-, 14-, and 16-inch cutthroat trout rise from the Yellowstone River's teal and turgid depths like rosy-cheeked golden submarines. It's the hike out that hurts.

"It'll kick your ass if you're not in shape," Heinlein said. "Especially the climb out. That's never gotten any easier."

It's difficult, but worthwhile, to hike to parts of the Yellowstone River that are off the beaten path. To have a river like this to yourself is an incredible feeling. PHOTO BY NATE SCHWEBER

But the rewards are plenty in this remote region of the park. The canyon walls are majestic, and the Yellowstone River surges between them with awesome force.

"It's marvelous country," Heinlein said, "as grand as it can be."

The same is true about the fishing. Heinlein said this stretch is "full of cutthroat, and they're always eager to bite." In years past, he and his fishing buddies would try to go the whole day using a single Joe's Hopper pattern and "just wear that fly out," he said. Today he brings Stimulators, Woolly Buggers, and hopper patterns that he fishes upstream along the mighty river.

"It's always been pretty foolproof," he said. "You could drag a fly upstream that looked like a water skier and you could catch fish."

It is big water, though—not for wading. The banks are steep, the rocks are jagged, and the river runs deep, fast, and powerful. Heinlein advises not visiting until runoff has subsided.

Heinlein discovered the lower canyon in the early 1970s after he graduated high school and moved from his hometown of Evanston, Indiana, to Cooke City, Montana, and took a job working for an outfitter. An elderly couple from Ohio chartered a pack trip into the lower canyon. Heinlein said he "just went along to feed the horses."

"I thought, 'Wow, what an amazing place,'" he said.

He's seen bighorn sheep, elk, bison, and grizzly bears in the canyon, but the animal he remembers most was the first mountain lion he ever saw in the wild. Heinlein said that on a spring trip he climbed a ridge above his camp to a sagebrush-covered horn. He noticed movement on the hill up above him and saw the massive yellow tail of a big lion. It was feeding on an elk.

"It was just one of those things I'd always wanted to see and then, all of the sudden, it was right there in front of me," he said. "And it wasn't a part of any scripted wildlife viewing session."

Heinlein came back in the evening and saw the lioness with two cubs. He took photos of the feline family running with the Yellowstone River churning in the background.

Heinlein suspects the lower Grand Canyon doesn't get many human visitors because it is tough and remote. The route in is via the Specimen Ridge Trail and then down the Agate Creek Trail.

"You drop into a canyon, go around a corner, and there's no sign of civilization in sight," he said.

Heinlein laments the fact that most park visitors don't experience the backcountry, preferring instead to stay close to the road. According to 2010 statistics, of the more than 3.6 million people who visited Yellowstone, less than one percent spent a night in the backcountry.[1] There are lions, bears, silence, and hard hikes in Yellowstone's backcountry. There are also fantastic trout that are hefty and willing. Heinlein can't help wondering, Have people forgotten? Or have they just lost their nerve?

"I used to see more people back there," he said. "And I've fished this place for 40 years now."

31 Nez Perce Creek

Sallysue C. Hawkins, Otis Halfmoon

The junction where Cowan Creek pours into Nez Perce Creek is a peaceful backcountry pool in a meadow deep in grizzly country where little resident brook trout mingle with occasional big browns that run up from the geyser-fed Firehole River in high summer to escape the heat.

Sallysue C. Hawkins and Otis Halfmoon have both visited these cool waters to better know their family histories, which joined together in the hot summer of 1877 just like the streams. When they were both young they visited Nez Perce Creek with their fathers—not in search of fish, like so many visitors do, but rather to better comprehend perhaps the most amazing human drama in the history of Yellowstone National Park.

"It's an incredible story that has been passed down in my family through the generations," said Hawkins.

It's a story that Halfmoon knows the other side of.

"I thought of what the Nez Perce went through there in 1877, their suffering," he said. "And I thought of what the Cowans went through."

Cowan Creek is named in honor of Hawkins' great-grandparents Emma Cowan and her husband George who was shot three times, including once in the head, by members of the Nez Perce tribe, which included Halfmoon's great-great grandfather Red Owl, and his pregnant great-grandmother, whose traditional name does not translate to English. In this remarkable encounter, which George miraculously survived, Emma was taken captive by the Nez Perce, but was treated with a kindness that she marveled at for the rest of her life. She told stories of the Nez Perce's hospitality to her daughter Ethel May, who passed them down to her granddaughter, Hawkins.

It all happened along the banks of Nez Perce Creek, which was named in honor of the tribe.

For this chapter, Hawkins' cousin, Sharon Strand, another Cowan great-granddaughter, shared a never-published transcript that George Cowan dictated to his daughter Ethel in April 1920, which gives his firsthand account of the story.[1] Hawkins has the original manuscript, in Ethel's handwriting.

The Cowans, from Radersburg, Montana, were among the first tourists in the then-five-year-old national park. That same summer hundreds of Nez Perce—including revered leader and peacemaker Chief Joseph—fled their homeland in Oregon's Wallowa Valley and ran from the U.S. Cavalry on an incredible, bloody, 1,500-mile journey that took them through Yellowstone. Their flight ended in a tragic battle in the Bear Paw Mountains in North-central Montana, just shy of the Canadian border.

Hawkins said her grandmother told her that her father, George Cowan, planned the trip to Yellowstone because her mother, Emma, then 24-years-old, had just lost a child and he wanted to distract her from her grief. The trip fell on the Cowans' second wedding anniversary.

In her own published memoirs, Emma expressed delight at the fishing on the way to the geysers, particularly at the headwaters of the Madison River.

Trout: Browns, rainbows, and brookies averaging 6 to 12 inches.

Bugs: Mayflies, caddisflies, and terrestrials.

Suggested fly box: Parachute Adamses and Pale Morning Duns size 14 to 20; Royal Wulffs and Yellow Humpies size 14 to 16; tan Elk Hair Caddis size 14 to 16; Hare's Ear, Copper John, Pheasant Tail, and Prince nymphs size 14 to 20; Dave's Hoppers size 6 to 14; crickets size 8 to 14; Parachute and Chernobyl Ant patterns size 14 to 18; foam beetles size 14 to 16; black, tan, and olive Woolly Buggers size 4 to 8.

Key techniques: Fish upstream and tight to the banks, particularly with terrestrials. Also work areas behind structure, near undercut banks, and along current seams. In late summer, these fish can get very spooky.

Best times: High summer and fall.

Directions: Take the Mary Mountain Trail $6^1/_2$ miles south of Madison Junction or $9^1/_2$ miles north of Old Faithful. Hike in a mile or two to get above the hot springs.

Special rules: Catch-and-release for rainbow and brown trout. This stream doesn't open until mid-June because of bears. Watch for signs at the trailhead. Make sure all gear used in any other water has been cleaned and dried in order to protect against the spread of invasive species, such as whirling disease and New Zealand mudsnails. Barbless hooks only. Check the most current regulations.

A small brown trout from Nez Perce Creek in Yellowstone. This was the first stream in the park to be stocked with Von Behr brown trout, which originally hail from Germany. PHOTO BY NATE SCHWEBER

She wrote that while camped there on August 14, 1877, "we caught some delicious speckled trout."[2] They were westslope cutthroats.

While Emma's grief was diminishing, the Nez Perce's was growing. For years the tribe had endured as white settlers, wanting more grass for their cattle, encroached on lands in the Wallowa, Snake, and Clearwater Valleys that were promised to the Nez Perce in treaties. As tensions mounted after gold was discovered on Nez Perce land, some tribal members agreed to live on small reservations. In June 1877 several frustrated non-treaty Nez Perce attacked and killed a number of settlers, thus starting the Nez Perce War. Around 800 Nez Perce made a run for their freedom, hoping to join the Crow Nation in eastern Montana and live by hunting buffalo, or else escape to Canada to live with Chief Sitting Bull and his Sioux.[3] They were chased by hundreds of soldiers under the command of U.S. Gen. Oliver Howard, who was nicknamed "The Christian General" for his tendency to make policy decisions based on his fiercely held religious beliefs.[4]

Two weeks before the Nez Perce encountered the Cowans, the tribe suffered a brutal massacre in Montana's Big Hole Valley at the hands of around 200 soldiers led by U.S. Col. John Gibbon who—a year after helping identify the deceased at Custer's Last Stand—gave the order to take no prisoners. The cavalry was augmented with whiskey-fueled civilian volunteers. Exhausted from their trek, the Nez Perce set up camp, not knowing that General Howard had used a new invention, the telegraph, to inform Colonel Gibbon of their whereabouts. The cavalry struck at dawn, ambushing the Nez Perce in their wickiups. Author Dee Brown, in his seminal Native American history, *Bury My Heart at Wounded Knee*, wrote that 80 Nez Perce were killed, "more than two-thirds of them women and children, their bodies riddled with bullets, their heads smashed by bootheels and gunstocks."[5]

The Nez Perce who escaped fled with broken hearts and frayed nerves. The survivors followed the Madison River upstream toward its headwaters in Yellowstone at a junction with a river that, five years earlier, had been named in honor of Gibbon.[6]

One of the Nez Perce soldiers killed by Gibbon's men at the Battle of the Big Hole was Five Wounds, Halfmoon's paternal great-grandfather. Halfmoon's parents brought him to the Big Hole Battlefield as a boy and told him family stories. Five Wounds, they said, made a suicide charge at soldiers and was shot from behind. In the early 1990s Halfmoon worked as an interpreter at the Big Hole Battlefield and was there when archaeologists uncovered a 45-70 slug in the exact spot where Five Wounds fell. The bullet was mushroomed, indicating that it had impacted with flesh. Halfmoon believes it was the very shot that felled his forefather.[7]

Five Wounds had gone on the journey with his chiefs, having left behind on a reservation his 7-year-old son William, Halfmoon's paternal grandfather. Halfmoon's maternal great-great-grandfather, Red Owl, and his great-grandmother survived the Big Hole and were then part of a tiny group that escaped to Canada during the final battle. Later they moved back to America, onto reservation lands.

"By the time they got to Yellowstone, the Nez Perce people were very much hurting," Halfmoon said. "And a lot of that pain is still there."

On the afternoon of August 23, 1877, George Cowan met a scout in the Lower Geyser Basin from an army party that included Civil War icon Gen. William Tecumseh Sherman, who President Ulysses S. Grant had put in charge of Native American wars. The scout told the Cowans about the Big Hole battle, but promised them that the Nez Perce were not coming to Yellowstone because they were scared of geysers.[8] George was assured that he and his family were "as safe in the park as we would be in New York City," he recalled. That night Emma strummed her guitar and sang campfire songs in celebration of the last night of her vacation. She never knew that Nez Perce scouts were listening.[9]

Emma woke George up early the next morning, telling him that she could "hear Indians talking" outside their tent. George dressed quickly and went to meet them carrying his .45 caliber needle gun, then down to its last five cartridges. A young man named Red Scout, a skilled English speaker, told George that he and the men belonged to the Flathead tribe and were on their way to the buffalo hunting grounds of eastern Montana. George, an attorney, said that he "therefore subjected this talking Indian Charlie to what might be termed a rigid cross-examination and at length so cornered him in his statements that he was forced to aknowledge that they were Nez Perce Indians."

George was soon surrounded by around 200 of them. His temper flared when he saw a member of his party about to dole out flour and sugar to around two dozen Nez Perce hanging around the back of his baggage wagon.

"I immediately ran up using my gun as a sort of club weapon, made the Indians disperse or stand aside," George said. "If the Indians got any of our supplies, they would be taken by force."

Red Scout took note.

The Cowans tried to flee, but a line of mounted Nez Perce halted them at gunpoint. Red Scout informed George that he and his party were to be marched seven miles up the creek, then known as the East Fork of the Firehole River, to see Chief Looking Glass, the leader of his band who Red Scout added was "friendly with the whites." When the wagons could go no farther, they were ransacked, and the group continued on horseback.

In the meadow where Cowan Creek joins Nez Perce Creek, the Cowans met with Chief Looking Glass, Chief Joseph, Chief White Bird, and a sub-chief named Poker Joe, who earned his sobriquet in Montana's Bitterroot Valley from his love of gambling.[10] Poker Joe, acting as translator, told the Cowans that the chiefs wished to free them, but under one condition. Give the Nez Perce their fresh horses and saddles for fleeing, and their guns and ammunition for hunting buffalo, and they could take with them an equal number of worn-out Nez Perce steeds, which would get them back to the white settlements. Under the circumstances, what could the Cowans say?

Poker Joe also warned the Cowans of the limits of the chiefs' power over some of the distraught Nez Perce warriors.

"(He) said that the young warriors having lost many friends and relatives in the Big Hole fight were mad and angry and were hard to keep in control by their chiefs," George said.

Poker Joe told the Cowans to travel fast through the woods away from the main trail, lest they be spotted again. "Injuns heap mad," one account quotes him saying. "They kill maybe."[11]

The Cowans didn't heed his warning. After half a mile of struggling over downed timber and through bogs, they returned to the trail.[12] Almost at once around 75 Nez Perce between the ages of 18 and 25 ambushed them. One was Red Scout, who George noted was "conspicuous in the command of this party of young Indians." Red Scout told the Cowans that the tribe had changed its mind about letting them go. As the gang marched the Cowan party back upstream, two warriors rode ahead—George believed it was to make sure the chiefs were nowhere near—and then came charging back. Emma wrote that "shots followed and Indian yells and all was confusion."

Cowan Creek, on the left, was named for early tourists George and Emma Cowan while Nez Perce Creek, on the right, was named in honor of the Nez Perce Tribe. Here their fates ran together, like these streams, in the summer of 1877. PHOTO BY NATE SCHWEBER

George took a bullet blast through his left thigh. He saw another Nez Perce aiming a rifle at his head, so he leapt off his horse to avoid being hit. His wounded leg buckled, and he rolled down a knoll and came to rest lying down against a fallen tree. Red Scout and another Nez Perce man ran to him, but Emma reached her husband first. She threw her body over George to shield him. Red Scout pointed "a large dragoon revolver" at George's head, but Emma stayed in front of that "immense navy pistol"[13] and "begged the Indian to shoot her first." Red Scout "seemed disinclined to harm her," George said. Red Scout did catch Emma's right wrist as she tried to cover George, and he lifted her away as she clung to her husband's neck with her left arm. This pulled George into a partial sitting position and, thus exposed, the other Nez Perce warrior reached into his blanket, drew a revolver, and fired the kill shot. Point blank.

"The ball struck me on the left side of my forehead," George said. "I saw the smoke issuing from the pistol, and heard the shot, but was rendered unconscious."

Moments later Poker Joe, sent by Chief Looking Glass and Chief White Bird, rode up to the melee on horseback to halt the violence. Red Scout, who knew he had disobeyed his chiefs, protected Emma and her siblings after George was shot and helped Poker Joe quell the crowd, which included men throwing rocks at George's bleeding head. A year later Red Scout, who was one of just a few Nez Perce to escape into Canada, spoke to a journalist named Duncan McDonald, whose father was a Scottish fur trader and whose mother was a Nez Perce woman. Red Scout confessed that he had been "in the wrong" and explained why he safeguarded Emma and her 13-year-old sister Ida.[14]

"I had not the heart to see those women abused," Red Scout told McDonald, as quoted in an 1878 article in the *New North-West*, a newspaper in Deer Lodge, Montana. "I thought we had done them enough wrong in killing their relations against the wishes of the chiefs."[15]

The Nez Perce weren't finished with George Cowan. He awoke hours later on the opposite side of the downed tree covered in blood, his pockets turned inside out and emptied. He pulled mightily on a branch to stand upright. Then he turned and saw a lone Nez Perce waiting for him on horseback. The man dismounted, dropped to a knee, and fired a single shot that ripped through George's left hip and came out his abdomen.

"This felled me to the ground again, falling with my face downward," George said. "I turned my head so that its side rested on the ground and felt the warm blood running from my nose occasioned by its contact with the ground."

Finally, three bullets later, the Nez Perce left George Cowan for dead.

The Nez Perce took Emma and her sister captive along with their brother Frank, who the tribe hoped could guide them up the creek and across the park. In the Nez Perce camp that night near Mary Mountain, Emma wept on a blanket not far from Chief Joseph. She remembered him being "somber and silent, foreseeing in his gloomy meditations possibly the unhappy ending of his campaign."[16] The family story passed down to Hawkins was that the chief was angry with the young men who shot George.

"Chief Joseph wasn't happy with them for doing that," Hawkins remembers hearing her grandmother say. "He said, 'We're not here to do that, we're leaving to Canada.' He didn't want any more problems with the cavalry and settlers."

Hawkins said that Chief Joseph directed a woman in the tribe to give Emma a baby to hold, a gesture meant to cheer her spirit. When Emma took the child, she wrote that she saw "the glimmer of a smile," on Chief Joseph's face.[17] The infant's mother asked Emma's brother, "Why cry?" He said it was because Emma believed that her husband had just been killed. The Nez Perce woman replied, "She heartsick."[18]

George Cowan, the Rasputin of early Yellowstone, was not dead. A Civil War veteran who was raised on the Wisconsin frontier, he moved to Last

Chance Gulch in Helena in 1865 to prospect for gold. A lawyer by trade, he was tapped by Montana Territorial Governor Thomas Meagher in 1867 to lead soldiers to fight Native Americans.[19] By the banks of Nez Perce Creek, George crawled on his elbows into a willow thicket and then managed to cross the stream. It took him four days to crawl 10 miles back to his camp in the Lower Geyser Basin. There, two of General Howard's army scouts discovered him. Their first words were, "Who the hell are you?" When George answered, they replied, "Why, we expected to bury you."

In a diary of the Nez Perce War, Army scout William Connolly noted that on August 30, 1877, he "found a wounded man shot 3 times by the Nez Perce Indians."[20] The other scout was reportedly Col. J. W. Redington.[21] The army men attempted to comfort poor George by building him a campfire. That night the campfire spread into a small forest fire that nearly killed him again.

"I crawled through this fire for perhaps thirty yards until I got clear of it," George said. "Burning both my hands and knees in so doing."

Emma woke the morning after her capture to find a Nez Perce woman trying to keep her warm by rebuilding the campfire by her side. The woman "then came and spread a piece of canvas across my shoulders to keep off the dampness," Emma wrote.[22] Her sister Ida slept nearby on buffalo robes prepared by Nez Perce women, who also gave her bread and brewed her tea made from willow bark. The Nez Perce women slept surrounding their frightened charge in order to keep her safe.[23]

The tribe continued east, crossing the Yellowstone River at what is now Nez Perce Ford. On the far side, Nez Perce women offered Emma a lunch of Yellowstone cutthroat trout, giving a clue as to what the tribe ate on part of their journey. Emma declined. She wrote, "From a great string of fish the largest were selected, cut in two, dumped into an immense camp-kettle filled with water and boiled to a pulp. The formality of cleaning had not entered into the formula. While I admit that tastes differ, I prefer having them dressed."[24]

Poker Joe again released Emma and her siblings, and this time he rode with them back across the Yellowstone River and half a mile downstream until they were well along the trail. He had given Emma and her family their bedding, a waterproof tarp, bread, matches, two old horses, and a jacket for young Ida. The chief shook their hands and said, "Ride all night. All day. No sleep."[25]

This time, they took his advice.

George and Emma were reunited days later at the Bottler's Ranch, home of early settlers in the Paradise Valley south of Livingston, Montana. On the way home their story turned slapstick. Seven miles from Bozeman, George and Emma's two-seat wagon flipped over and tossed them out before careen-

Chief Joseph was one of a few Nez Perce chiefs who led their people on a run for their freedom up Nez Perce Creek in the summer of 1877. When he surrendered to the U.S. Cavalry that October just 40 miles south of the Canadian border, he was the only chief left.

ing down an embankment and coming to rest upside down in some pine trees above a river.[26] Then in Bozeman, as George rested in a hotel bed, his doctor sat down beside him and collapsed the bedframe. George went sprawling out on the floor and there suggested that someone use artillery on him, since nothing else could finish him off.[27]

Hawkins said that her grandmother was always proud of the fact that her father lived. He was too.

"He was lucky to survive and he knew it," Hawkins said. "He was also pretty tough."

Later in his life George confessed to his daughter Ethel that perhaps his well-known bluntness might have escalated the situation, particularly with regard to Red Scout.

"I think my great grandfather realized he could've handled it a little more diplomatically," Hawkins said. "It's one of those incidents where hotheadedness prevailed, both with the young Indians and my great grandfather."

George Cowan was headstrong. Literally. From 1877 on he carried around a watch fob made from the bullet that a field surgeon cut out of his skull. The slug was mushroomed from its impact with flesh. The fob is still a family heirloom.

"That's where we get our hardheadedness," Hawkins said.

George and Emma moved from Radersburg to Boulder, Montana, in 1885 and then to Spokane in 1910. He visited the park three more times in his life, always going back to revisit the spots where he was so tested. He passed away in 1927 and Emma followed in 1939. Theirs was, by all accounts, a happy ending.

The Nez Perce story, by contrast, ended in sorrow. By October, the beleaguered tribe made it within 40 miles of the Canadian border, so close that many thought they were safe. Unfortunately, as with the Battle of the Big Hole, the Nez Perce could not outrun the telegraph. A message went out, and U.S. Gen. Nelson A. Miles attacked the Nez Perce at the foothills of the Bear Paw Mountains.

The awful, final battle lasted for five days. Poker Joe was killed. Chief Looking Glass too. Only a few, including Chief White Bird, Red Scout, and Halfmoon's surviving relatives, snuck to Canada under cover of darkness. Chief Joseph surrendered to General Howard, who had finally caught up and promised that upon surrender the 500 remaining Nez Perce would be taken back to their reservation in Lapwai, Idaho. Under those conditions, Chief Joseph agreed. There the heartsick chief made his immortal speech saying, "From where the sun now stands, I will fight no more forever."

That winter, General Sherman broke General Howard's promise and ordered the Nez Perce penned and shipped on unheated rail cars to a prisoner of war camp in Kansas and then later to a reservation in Oklahoma where many died of disease. For years Chief Joseph pleaded with leaders in Washington, D.C., for his people to be returned to their homeland. Finally in 1885 some of the Nez Perce were allowed to return to the reservation in Idaho, but Chief Joseph was still considered too dangerous to join them. He was exiled to the Colville Reservation in north-central Washington where he died in 1904. His doctor said the cause of death was "a broken heart."[28]

In the few years after the Nez Perce's run through Yellowstone, in which two other unlucky tourists were killed and others wounded,[29] park superintendent P. W. Norris evicted the Sheepeaters, the only Native Americans to call the Yellowstone region their year-round home. Though the Sheepeaters played no role in the Nez Perce War, Norris feared their presence would detract tourists.[30]

When Halfmoon visited Nez Perce Creek, he had a revelation about his tribe's journey. The Nez Perce had made incredible time running from General Howard, even traveling uphill through thick timber over the rugged Bitterroot Mountains with women, children, their injured, wickiups, and hundreds of head of livestock. In Yellowstone, though, their pace slowed. Some historians said it was because they didn't know their way. Halfmoon thinks it was something else.

"I saw the trees and I felt the cool air in Yellowstone Park and it reminded me of the Wallowa Valley," he said. "I realized that it must've been at this point that these people became very homesick, realizing that they would never see the trees or feel the air of their home again, and they realized by then that if they were caught they would be slaughtered. These feelings slowed them down."

George and Emma Cowan returned to Yellowstone three more times in their lives, as shown in this photo from the early 1900s. They always revisited Nez Perce Creek.

Reflecting in her memoir on the treatment she received at the hands of the Nez Perce, Emma wrote, "Knowing something of the circumstances that led to the final outbreak and uprising of these Indians, I wonder that any of us were spared." In perhaps an unwitting nod to the Nez Perce's pursuer, "Christian" General Howard, Emma added, "Truly a quality of mercy was shown us during our captivity that a Christian might emulate."[31]

That message was passed down in family lore.

"My grandmother always told me that my great-grandmother and great-grandfather never harbored any animosity toward the Nez Perce," Hawkins said. "They understood later what the Nez Perce were going through, that they were being driven from their homes."

The story of the Cowan family and the Nez Perce goes on. Halfmoon is a national park ranger who worked for years at the Bear Paw Battlefield and is an expert on the Nez Perce War of 1877. He had searched for years for descendants of George and Emma Cowan. When contacted for this book, he called back within minutes.

"You found Cowans, eh?" he said.

Halfmoon explained that beginning in 1977, the centennial of the war, the Nez Perce began an annual powwow on their reservation in Lapwai. The tribe has made it a tradition at the Chief Joseph and the Warriors Powwow to honor descendants of the cavalry who chased the Nez Perce. It is to recognize their shared history, Halfmoon said.

He extended the same welcome to the Cowan descendants.

"We would like to honor them," he said.

Thus a June 2011 email that I sent from New York City addressed to Hawkins, her cousin Sharon Strand, and Halfmoon marked the first time there was contact between the Cowan family and the Nez Perce tribe since their ancestors met so fatefully in Yellowstone Park almost 134 years earlier. Halfmoon called Strand on the telephone and invited her and her family to the Chief Joseph and the Warriors Powwow. The timing didn't work out (when I finally tracked down Halfmoon, it was less than a week until the powwow), but the two had a friendly chat and as of this printing were making plans to one day meet each other.

The Nez Perce Creek that the Cowans and the tribe encountered on their historic Yellowstone visit had no fish, as it sat above an impassible falls on the Firehole River. In 1890 Nez Perce Creek became the first stream in Yellowstone to be stocked with Von Behr brown trout, a species of fish that originally hails from Germany.[32] These trout flushed up and down the watershed and, in the next few decades, were bolstered by additional stocks of brown, rainbow, and brook trout throughout the Firehole, Gibbon, and Madison River systems. The result was that by the time Emma Cowan died in 1939 these rivers were all great sportfisheries, but their native westslope cutthroat trout, which she delighted in catching and eating in the days before her capture, were either exterminated, hybridized, or pushed into just a few tiny, inhospitable headwater streams where no other trout lived.[33]

Thus Nez Perce Creek trout provide a metaphor for European settlement of North America, with regard to native people.

As this book is about fishing, I had to ask both Hawkins and Halfmoon if on their visits to Nez Perce Creek they ever wet a line. No, they said.

I asked the same question to Stan Hoggatt, a tribal historian.

"Out of all my Nez Perce acquaintances I don't know anyone who has ever fished there," he said. "That would be the furthest thing from their minds when they are visiting those sites."

32 Yellowstone River at Nez Perce Ford

Bob Jacklin

Bob Jacklin, who was inducted into the Fly Fishing Hall of Fame in 2004, knows exactly where he'd like to take his final fishing trip.

"I've said it publically: if the good lord gave me one last day to fish, I would fish the upper Yellowstone River in the old Buffalo Ford area," he says.

Today that spot is called Nez Perce Ford. It is a stretch of 150-foot-wide river that, due to a series of sandbars and islands, can be shallow enough to wade across when spring runoff subsides. It is named in honor of the Nez Perce tribe's crossing of that river in 1877 on their long run from the U.S. Cavalry.

Jacklin has had a long run of a different sort. He has sold flies and led guide trips from the West Yellowstone shop that bears his name for more than 35 years. He also coauthored a book called *Fly Fishing the Yellowstone in the Park* and has made several fishing DVDs.

In Jacklin's youth his favorite section of the Yellowstone River teemed with slabs of gold-and-crimson native Yellowstone cutthroat trout. "So many you wouldn't believe," he says. In the past decade, the trout bounty collapsed—victims to the triple blow of drought and whirling disease, but mostly the illegally stocked, nonnative lake trout in Yellowstone Lake. Many anglers who used to stand shoulder-to-shoulder in the Yellowstone River to catch native cutts have shifted to the northeast corner of the park, where they now crowd the Lamar River and Soda Butte Creek.

But monster survivors remain in the upper Yellowstone. What the native trout around Nez Perce Ford today lack in numbers, they make up for in size. Cutthroat of two feet and multiple pounds, while not common, are the fish most often caught here. Some guides refer to fishing this area as "big-game hunting."

The trick to catching these buffalo trout is to find one, Jacklin said. They most often reveal their lie by rising. Once spotted, Jacklin recommends drifting a Golden Stonefly, a size 12 Adams, or an Elk Hair Caddis over its nose.

"There's lots of insect hatches, caddis to Salmonflies," Jacklin says. "And the fish gorge themselves."

The Yellowstone River inside the park opens to fishing on July 15 to allow time for the cutthroat to spawn. Several small sections of the river near Nez Perce Ford stay closed year-round to protect cutthroat. Anglers should keep an eye out for the signs.

Jacklin, an expert, estimates on a good day today he could catch a couple to a few trout in the Nez Perce Ford section. Most of what he catches there are memories.

On August 8, 1967, Jacklin, then in his 20s, fished the then-Buffalo Ford with his father. There he saw the biggest trout he'd ever seen—rising. Jacklin dusted a size 12 Adams just upstream from the monster's maw. A splash and a rod-buckling battle later, that trout flopped in his father's net.

Trout: Native Yellowstone cutthroat trout averaging 18 to 24 inches.

Bugs: Stoneflies, including Salmonflies, around the time the river opens on July 15. Pale Morning Duns, Blue-Winged Olives, Green Drakes, and caddis.

Suggested fly box: Salmonflies size 2 to 6; Golden Stoneflies size 6 to 8; Adamses and Parachute Adamses size 8 to 18; Pale Morning Duns and Blue-Winged Olives size 16 to 20; tan Elk Hair Caddis size 14 to 18; Pheasant Tail, Hares Ear, and Prince nymphs size 14 to 18; Stimulators size 14 and 16; Joe's, Dave's, Parachute, and Rubber-Leg Hoppers size 6 to 14; crickets size 8 to 14; Parachute and Chernobyl Ant patterns size 14 to 18; foam beetles size 14 to 16; black, tan, and olive Woolly Buggers size 4 to 8.

Key techniques: Sight fish and cast to them. Watch for rises and, in clear water, watch for fish finning in the water.

Best times: Earlier in the season is better. By late summer, many of the big cutthroat that come into this section to spawn have returned to Yellowstone Lake.

Directions: Grand Loop Road parallels the Yellowstone in this section. Look for the picnic area pullout for Nez Perce Ford.

Special rules: Catch-and-release for all cutthroat; catch-and-kill for any lake trout; season opens July 15. Watch for signs indicating sections of the river that are closed for fishing to protect spawning trout.

A group of bison swimming across the Yellowstone River is an exciting thing to see in the park. Rules mandate catch-and-release for all bison hooked in the Yellowstone River. PHOTO BY NATE SCHWEBER

As these were the days before drought, whirling disease, lake trout, or the parkwide policy of catch-and-release for all cutthroat, that 24-inch, four-pound cutt now adorns the wall at Outpost Restaurant, next door to Jacklin's Fly Shop.

"Every August 8, I think about that day," Jacklin says. "That's a very, very special day."

Jacklin is a proponent of the park's lake trout netting program to keep the lakers in check.

"If more of that happens, we could turn that back into a good fishery again," Jacklin says. "I've got high hopes."

33 Clear Creek

Dave Sweet

Dave Sweet dreams of once again fishing Clear Creek, a little stream that pours into the east side of Yellowstone Lake. He remembers how once it was so full of cutthroat trout "you could walk from one side to the other on their backs."

That was before lake trout showed up in Yellowstone Lake.

Sweet discovered Clear Creek in the late 1980s when he and his wife ran a guest ranch just outside Yellowstone's east entrance. The ranch took so much work that Sweet had little time to fish as he catered to as many as 60 guests a night. Once he recommended Clear Creek to three brothers from Ohio who were followed all the way back to their car by a grizzly bear that they threw a candy bar to.

When he did get a chance to go fishing, Sweet wanted to get away—far away. Clear Creek was perfect.

"It was just choked with cutthroats," he said. "It was a really neat little stream."

Sweet said he would see some cutts paired up on spawning beds while others held in feeding lanes and splashed at bugs.

Sweet had tremendous success fishing nymphs such as Hare's Ear, Pheasant Tail, and Prince nymphs and what he calls "big, ugly nymphs," like Montana nymphs, Bitch Creek nymphs, and Yuck Bugs.

"If they were still on their spawning beds after the creek opens, you're trying to make 'em mad as much as get them to eat," he said.

Dry flies were also wildly productive, including Humpies, Elk Hair Caddis, and later in the summer, grasshopper patterns.

He said he would work the creek upstream from where it intersects with the Thorofare Trail, casting under the pine trees to Clear Creek's riffles, meandering pools, and gravel beds. He said he never went too far. He didn't have to.

"It was almost stupid easy," he said. "I'll be honest; it didn't seem to matter much what fly you used. It wasn't what you'd call highly technical fishing, but gosh it was fun."

Sweet said he was devastated by the collapse of the Yellowstone Lake cutthroat population. "This was supposed to be the mecca" for Yellowstone cutthroats, he said.

Sweet is trying to play an active role in the fish's recovery. He leads a committee called "Save the Yellowstone Cutthroat," which is part of the East Yellowstone Chapter of Trout Unlimited. He is also project manager for the Yellowstone Lake watershed for Trout Unlimited. Through his organizations, he has funneled tens of thousands of dollars to researchers pioneering ways to eradicate lake trout.

Sweet has also ventured out on the gill-netting boats that for the past several years have dredged up lake trout by the hundreds of thousands.

Trout: Native Yellowstone cutthroats, including lake spawners, averaging 16 to 22 inches.

Bugs: Stoneflies, including Salmonflies, around the time the river opens on July 15. Pale Morning Duns, Blue-Winged Olives, and caddis. Also terrestrials, including hoppers, ants, and beetles.

Suggested fly box: Yellow Humpies, Royal Wulffs, Royal Coachman Trudes, tan Elk Hair Caddis, and yellow Stimulators size 14; Parachute Adamses size 8 to 18; Pale Morning Duns and Blue-Winged Olives size 16 to 20; Pheasant Tail, Hare's Ear, and Prince nymphs size 14 to 18; Dave's Hoppers size 6 to 14; crickets size 8 to 14; Parachute and Chernobyl Ant patterns size 14 to 18; foam beetles size 14 to 16; black, olive, and tan Woolly Buggers size 4 to 8.

Key techniques: Sight fish and cast to them; search the surface with attractor drys or dredge the holes with Woolly Buggers or gaudy nymphs.

Best times: After August 11, when this stream opens, because of bear danger. By late summer, many of the big cutthroat that come into this section to spawn have returned to Yellowstone Lake.

Access: Park at the Nine Mile Trailhead on the East Entrance Road, about nine miles from Fishing Bridge and about 20 miles from the park's east entrance. It's about a $3^{1}/_{2}$-mile hike to Clear Creek.

Special rules: Catch-and-release for all cutthroat; catch-and-kill for any lake trout. Season opens August 11 because of bear activity. Handle spawning trout delicately.

Clear Creek was the site of a fish weir, built in 1945, that annually counted spawning cutthroats running up from Yellowstone Lake. In a generation, the cutthroat counts dropped from a high of more than 70,000 to just a few hundred because of predatory lake trout stocked illegally in Yellowstone Lake. PHOTO BY NATE SCHWEBER

"The scientists will say that if you capture enough lake trout you can start a collapse of that population," Sweet said. "Unfortunately, right now we don't even know how many lake trout are in the lake, so how will we know whether we're having a positive impact? There are strong indicators that this may be too little too late."

While intrepid anglers will still find a few fantastic cutthroats on Clear Creek, Sweet won't be one of them until Yellowstone Lake rebounds. Sweet says he hasn't fished Clear Creek, or any water in the upper Yellowstone, for nearly a decade, because, in his words, "The few number of spawners going back up there need to be totally left alone."

But in his dreams, he's an old man once again casting flies to a Clear Creek full of cutthroat.

"Hopefully 10 years from now we can look back and say, 'Wow, that population has recovered!'" he said. "I hope I get to fish it again."

34 Gallatin River

Dan Vermillion

The Gallatin River trickles out of icy, 10,000-foot-high Gallatin Lake and pours down beside Highway 191 in Yellowstone's northwest corner. The river has been guide Dan Vermillion's favorite spot to fish since he was a boy.

"If you want a place to have a great experience—and one of the things I look for in having a well-rounded experience is finding the best that Mother Nature has to offer—the Gallatin in Yellowstone is definitely that kind of place," said Vermillion, who runs the Sweetwater Fly Shop in Livingston.

A strong, healthy rainbow trout from the rushing Gallatin River. When hooked, this river's rainbows have a tendency to leap two feet high and five feet downstream.
PHOTO BY NATE SCHWEBER

The Gallatin has been called one of Yellowstone's most straightforward streams. Its trout—a collection of rainbows, browns, and cuttbows—all hide in all the likely spots. They camp behind boulders and rocks, along current seams, under overhanging banks, inside riffles, throughout eddies, and in the heads and tails of pools, Vermillion said.

"Anywhere the fish can kind of get out of the current," he said.

The flies to catch them are similarly straightforward. Vermillion recommends classic attractors such as Stimulators, Royal Trudes, Royal Wulffs, and terrestrials like hoppers and ants. Often, Vermillion said, he fishes a hopper/dropper combination, usually a Stimulator with a Copper John or Pheasant Tail nymph hung off the back.

Most of the fish average between 10 and 14 inches, he said, adding that "there are bigger ones in there that will surprise you."

I caught plenty of rainbow trout in the Gallatin, all chrome and red like an old-fashioned fire engine. They scarfed dry flies, and their first move when hooked was to vault two feet in the air and five feet downstream. One time

---

Trout: Rainbows from 8 to 18 inches and browns that occasionally get even bigger; outside shot at smaller cuttbows, brook trout, mountain whitefish, or even a westslope cutthroat.

Bugs: Golden Stoneflies, Pale Morning Duns, Blue-Winged Olives, drakes, *Baetis*, and caddis. Also terrestrials, including hoppers, ants, beetles, and spruce moths.

Suggested fly box: Yellow Stimulators size 6 to 14; Parachute Adamses size 10 to 16; Elk Hair Caddis size 10 to 16; Royal Wulffs, Royal Trudes, and Yellow Humpies size 12 to 18; Prince, Pheasant Tail, and Hare's Ear nymphs size 12 to 16; Dave's Hoppers size 6 to 14; crickets size 8 to 14; Parachute and Chernobyl Ant patterns size 14 to 18; foam beetles size 14 to 16; black, olive, and tan Woolly Buggers size 4 to 8.

Key techniques: Fish close to the bank along undercuts, also deep runs, current seams, and behind rocks. Hopper/dropper rigs, for example a size 10 Elk Hair Caddis, imitating a spruce moth, and a Beadhead Prince dropper, work great on this river.

Best times: After the river clears from spring runoff, usually early July, through to season's end.

Access: Highway 191 follows the Gallatin River for much of its length in the park.

Special rules: Catch-and-release for all cutthroat and whitefish.

Wildlife, like this cinnamon-colored brown bear, abounds on the banks of the
Gallatin River, making this a great place to have a well-rounded day of fishing.
PHOTO BY NATE SCHWEBER

using a nymph, I hooked . . . ye gods, was that an 18-inch rainbow that
snapped my line?

The Gallatin River is a high mountain freestone stream, and it is generally swollen with runoff opening day in May through mid-July. The
Shoshone tribe originally called this stream *Cut-tuh-o'-gwa*, meaning "swift
water," until Lewis and Clark renamed it in honor of Thomas Jefferson's secretary of the treasury, Albert Gallatin.[1] Vermillion said his favorite times to
fish the Gallatin are July, August, and September.

"It's neat water. It's fun. It's pretty. It's not hard fishing, and it doesn't
get a lot of pressure either," Vermillion said. "It's a good place to take kids
fishing because they'll get a lot of opportunities to find fish."

Access is easy for much of the Gallatin's length in the park, as Highway
191 follows the stream out toward Bozeman. "You can park your truck on
the highway, walk 50 feet, and catch a fish," Vermillion said.

The Gallatin's scenic meadows are alive with wildlife, including elk,
moose, wolves, and as photographer and fly fisher Jess McGlothlin found out
one October evening, grizzly bears too.

McGlothlin, 23, and her brother Jake McGlothlin were shooting video of
the Gallatin's flow about a quarter mile from the park's border for part of a
DVD series they were making called "Rivers in Motion." Jake was wading in
the river and Jess was standing on the bank when she said she heard rustling

Much of the lower Gallatin River in Yellowstone is easy to access as it is paralleled by Highway 191. Native Americans called this river *Cut-tuh-o'-gwa*, which means "swift water." Lewis and Clark renamed it in honor of Albert Gallatin, Thomas Jefferson's secretary of the treasury. PHOTO BY NATE SCHWEBER

and underbrush crackling behind her. She whirled around, and out of a bramble walked a young cinnamon-colored griz, old enough to have already grown its distinctive hump.

"I don't know who was more surprised, me or the griz," said McGlothlin. "It was about eight feet away, ridiculously close."

McGlothlin said she raised her arms and yelled at the bear. The little griz spooked and ran right back into the brush.

Vermillion's most memorable day on the Gallatin happened on the river's east fork near Bozeman. It was when he took a newbie named Barack Obama fly-fishing for the first time.

The trip was notable because in 2008 when Obama campaigned in Montana—a rare move for a Democratic presidential candidate in a traditionally red state with a paltry three electoral votes—he said that when the election was over he wanted to come back and learn to fly-fish. It was a campaign promise he kept.

Obama came to Belgrade, Montana, for a town hall meeting on August 14, 2009. Ten days earlier his aides gave him a fly rod for his 49th birthday.

Vermillion ended up loaning the president his waders and noted, "I'm a lot fatter than he is."

The worst rainstorm of the summer scuttled Vermillion's plans to take the president to a spring creek along the Madison River. So they went to a stretch of the East Gallatin River, a few miles from where it meets the branch that begins in Yellowstone. Over the next three hours the president hooked and lost about a half-dozen trout and joked about his "long-distance catch-and-release skills," Vermillion said.

When their time was nearly up, Vermillion suggested taking a shortcut across a field back to the caravan of waiting black SUVs. The First Family would spend the next day on an official visit to Yellowstone National Park.

Vermillion said President Obama asked his security detail how he was doing on time. They told the president that it was time to go but that he didn't need to rush.

"So the president said, 'Let's fish our way back,'" Vermillion said. "And we did."

Notellum Creek

Guy Muto

*H*ow many times has a trout blogger been stalked 2,000 miles? This thought ran through my mind as I slid the 20-year-old Chevy pickup I had just bought off Craigslist into park. It was dark, it was raining, and I was wired from the flight from New York City to Bozeman (where I got the truck) and then the drive to West Yellowstone. I didn't really know where I'd spend the night, so I was drawn to a late-night gas station where I thought I might find "Yellowstoner," the mysterious guy who writes my favorite trout blog, Fly Fishing in Yellowstone National Park.

Described by fans as "a better fishing report than this world deserves," Fly Fishing in Yellowstone National Park is the first thing I read every morning. Its tone is whimsical and teasing. It's loaded with news, tips, information on hot fly patterns, and the most up-to-date Yellowstone fishing reports. It's not trying to sell anything, which makes it a refreshing change from web sites run

---

Trout: Yellowstone, westslope, and Snake River finespotted cutthroats; rainbows; browns; brookies; grayling; and whitefish.

Bugs: Mayflies, caddisflies, and terrestrials.

Suggested fly box: Size 14 attractor dry flies, including Royal Wulffs, Humpies, and Elk Hair Caddis; Parachute Adamses size 10 to 18; Pheasant Tail, Hare's Ear, and Prince nymphs size 14 to 18; Dave's Hoppers size 6 to 14; crickets size 8 to 14; Parachute and Chernobyl Ant patterns size 14 to 18; foam beetles size 14 to 16; black, tan, and olive Woolly Buggers size 4 to 8.

Key techniques: Early baseball player Wee Willy Keeler's oft-quoted advice for batters was to "hit 'em where they ain't." That's good advice for fishing Notellum Creek.

Best times: All season long.

Directions: Study a map. Ask a sage. Walk.

Special rules: Let the natives go.

---

by fly shops. It also just hints at the best spots to fish but doesn't get too specific. Sometimes the hot spots are marked with just an arrow on a satellite map under the label "Notellum Creek."

"No tell 'em." Get it?

I figured I had to interview the writer for this book. But I couldn't find his contact information anywhere, just that nickname "Yellowstoner." It took a lot of long-distance calls before a nameless trout guide dropped the dime that "Yellowstoner" might just be the guy who works nights at the Phillips 66 station in town.

I thought I saw him standing outside the gas station's side door smoking a King Mountain cigarette. He had a bushy, white Santa Claus beard and belly to match. A trucker's cap covered his short, gray hair, and his T-shirt read "Firehole Fillup." I introduced myself and offered the best explanation I could for being there. His face blossomed into a jolly grin that showed off his teeth—all three of them.

I expected this character would be quite the guy, and in a literal sense it was true. He told me his name was Guy Muto. Thus began a summer-long conversation that was the best I had about trout in Yellowstone.

"My secret is that I catch fish," he chuckled, "where other people don't fish."

Bacon Rind Creek, Duck Creek, Specimen Creek, and upper Fan Creek; the Firehole River above Biscuit Basin; the Gallatin River above the Buckhorn Trailhead; and the Gibbon River above Virginia Cascades—these are some of Guy's favorite Notellum Creeks. Also, the upper Yellowstone and Snake Rivers. Plus Obsidian Creek and Arnica Creek. Oh yes, and Winter Creek. How many people, he asked, have even *heard* of Winter Creek?

"I'm old and cranky, have strong and perfectly formed opinions, despise corporate conformity in fly fishing, and am greatly bemused at the self-limiting attitude of conformist fishing," he wrote me in an e-mail.

He told me several times that what he sees too often are anglers who come to Yellowstone looking for "scalps."

"The fly fishers of today are just like the old French fur traders," he says. "They say, 'I did the Madison,' 'I did the Firehole.' Well, they drove past 14 calving buffalo, four rare thermophillic pools, and nine bristly aster clusters."

He went on: "What they've done is they've collected the scalp. Most of them are fishermen first, second, and last. They're not much concerned about Yellowstone."

Guy is concerned about Yellowstone—its botany, biology, geology, geomorphology, sedimentology, and on and on. Fishing, he says, "is a means to get deep inside the park, into the parts that fascinate me."

He told me that last bit between bites of lobster, jasmine rice, and asparagus at the Bar N Ranch, a fancy restaurant filled with taxidermy, on a sweet

A sparkling rainbow trout caught on a big grasshopper pattern in one of Yellowstone's many "Notellum" creeks.
PHOTO BY NATE SCHWEBER

spread along the South Fork of the Madison River about six miles from West Yellowstone. A bowl of mushroom soup arrived, and Guy told me to put a spoonful under my tongue. "What's the secret ingredient?" he asked as he nodded yes to a bottle of Pierrette et Marc Guillemot-Michel Quintaine. "It's cinnamon. Cinnamon and mushrooms is a classic that Americans have forgotten."

I thought to myself that I'd never seen anyone get so much delight from so few teeth. I also expected that the meal would be the most expensive date on which I ever took a 70-year-old man. But I'd made him a deal: grant me an interview, and I buy dinner—his choice of restaurant. At least the trout almondine (naturally) beat the hell out of the granola, gorp, and freeze-dried food I ate for every meal, weeks on end.

Guy said he moved to West Yellowstone in the summer of 1988 "to watch it burn," leaving his job as a college professor in Oklahoma. He worked for a stint as a park ranger in a booth but shakes his head and says the gig "wasn't for me." Born in an East L.A. slum and raised surfing and racing hot rods, Guy first visited the park in the late 1940s "when I was wee," he says. He returned for stints in the 1960s, first while he was earning a master's degree in anthropology from Idaho State University and then while earning his PhD at Washington State University. A pioneer in the study of lithic technology (Stone Age tools), Guy's work took him all over the six warmest continents. He returned to Yellowstone because he loves it here.

"It's a neat place," he smiled, nodding slowly. "It's just a neat place."

Guy started writing the blog Fly Fishing in Yellowstone National Park around 2005 after he couldn't keep up with e-mails from friends asking where they should go fish. Today it's one of the top-read trout blogs online. Interestingly, Guy's job at the gas station puts him in the unique position to get the best fishing news around. He gives a six-cent discount on gasoline to locals and offers the best cigarette and beer prices in town, plus free ice. So all the fishing guides and trout bums buy from him. They tell him their secrets.

Guy has two tips for catching the best and the most trout in Yellowstone. The first is as simple as time: Walk. Get away from other people. Find a ribbon of water and follow it upstream. Too many anglers miss out on fantastic fishing just because they don't hike away from the road, he says.

"If I had to sum it up like a law of the universe, it's that the farther upstream you go, the better the catching is," Guy says. "Also, I don't care what the fly shops say. I've never met a trout with a PhD or one that wouldn't take a Goofus Bug under the right conditions."

His second secret is to employ *seasonal transhuminance*. It's a term that anthropologists use. In fishing terms, it means go where the trout are biting.

"There are fishing spots that bloom and disappear," he says. "You have to know the park."

The payoff for walking to the right places at the right times is a catch of terrific trout in an uncrowded spot, trout that scarf classic patterns like Royal Coachmans, or a Prince nymph if you want to be fancy. These trout, Guy says, are "so pretty you could wear them as a ring." Experiences like these beat the ones sought by the "scalp collectors," he says.

"They seek the same satisfaction that I'm seeking, but they are doing it by somebody else's recipe," he said. "I know that there are places I can go to catch fish at certain times and no one even knows about it, let alone cares. That feels good. It feels special."

Even the trout themselves take on added significance in these places, he says.

"I don't know if it's mystical or cerebral, but I feel a connection to those critters," he says. "I have an admiration for trout."

Guy introduced me to a Montana dessert: rotating bites from a lump of vanilla ice cream, swigs of hot, black coffee, and sips of cold Disaronno amaretto liqueur. The bill came from a young lady voted West Yellowstone's homecoming queen two years running. Guy held his hand three feet off the floor and said he's known her family "since she was stealing candy." I whipped out my credit card, but Guy yanked the check folder away.

"Wait," I protested, "we had a deal!"

Guy smiled and tucked three hundred-dollar bills into the leather folder. He told the queen to keep the change.

On the night I met him, Guy gave me the password to access the Internet in the Laundromat attached to the gas station, so I always had a place to charge my cell phone and upload my photos. He poured me coffee, so I could stay up late typing my notes. And he let me in on a secret place to park where I could sleep in the bed of my pickup and not be hassled by cops. He volunteered his photos for this book. Then there were those countless conversations about Yellowstone trout.

I thanked him for the meal, his hospitality, and his stories, and I used every synonym I could think of. He was gracious about the former, and commented on the latter.

"The stories I have of Yellowstone," he says, "are the stories of fulfillment."

35 Cache Creek

Ronnie Wright

For Ronnie Wright, Cache Creek embodies the myth of the phoenix, that brilliant bird that would burn to ashes only to be reborn even more beautiful than it was before.

In the fiery summer of 1988, Wright, a longtime pack outfitter from Cooke City, Montana, saw Cache Creek, his favorite Yellowstone fishing spot, turn into an inferno.

"It was devastating to watch," he said. "There was great fishing in there."

Trout: Cutthroat trout, cuttbows, and rainbow trout averaging 8 to 16 inches.

Bugs: Terrestrials, mayflies, and caddisflies.

Suggested fly box: Dave's Hoppers size 6 to 14; crickets size 8 to 14; Parachute and Chernobyl Ant patterns size 14 to 18; foam beetles size 14 to 16; size 14 attractor dry flies, including Royal Wulffs, Humpies, Elk Hair Caddis, and Parachute Adamses; Pheasant Tail, Hare's Ear, and Prince nymphs size 14 to 18; black, tan, and olive Woolly Buggers size 4 to 8.

Key techniques: Stalk the bank, watching for rising trout in fish pools, undercut banks, current seams, runs, and pocketwater behind boulders.

Best times: August and September.

Directions: Park at the Soda Butte Trailhead along East Entrance Road and hike 1.4 miles to the Lamar River Trail, follow the Lamar River Trail 1.7 miles to the Cache Creek Trail. The first backcountry campsite is 5.5 miles from that junction.

Special rules: Catch-and-release for all cutthroats.

It's a healthy hike to get to Cache Creek above Waab Springs, but this makes for plenty of solitude on a stream teeming with native Yellowstone cutthroat trout.
PHOTO BY NATE SCHWEBER

Cache Creek got its name from early Lamar Valley explorers who hid caches of supplies at the stream's mouth. Wright first visited the stream when he guided clients there in the early 1980s. He came away enthralled by the freestone stream's friendly and healthy population of native Yellowstone cutthroat trout.

Then in 1988, as a full third of Yellowstone National Park burned, Wright took a TV news crew on horseback to the top of Republic Pass to watch the fire in Cache Creek below. In nearby Cooke City, residents were terrified that the flames chewing up the Cache Creek Valley would march down the adjoining Republic Creek Valley, which leads straight into town.

As Wright and the crew neared the top of Republic Pass, a massive gust of hot wind blew Wright's horse down to its knees. He stumbled and shouted for the other riders to dismount and hold on to their saddle horns to brace against the brutal updraft.

Wright fought his way to the ridge top. When he looked down at Cache Creek, he couldn't believe the thing roaring toward him.

"It looked like an atomic bomb went off," Wright said. "There was just a big mushroom cloud coming up out of there."

Wright's heart went out to the trout down below. Thousands upon thousands of gorgeous, native, little cutthroats were being suffocated in ash. Wright literally watched his favorite fishing spot go up in smoke.

The average size of the trout in upper Cache Creek has increased since the fires of 1988 cleared the timber and allowed more grasshoppers, beetles, ants, and other bugs to make their way into the water—and into the bellies of native Yellowstone cutthroats. PHOTO BY NATE SCHWEBER

"It's just amazing how Mother Nature does things in just such a big way," Wright said.

The updraft from the blowup was too intense for any of the film crew to shoot. "Everyone just had to hang on," Wright remembers. They hustled back to Cooke City where Wright spent an anxious night expecting the mountains around his home to glow orange.

But fires that big make their own rules. Instead of burning into Cooke City, the flames leapt the top of Pilot Ridge and raced down Pilot Creek to scorch the Sunlight Basin. Cooke City had been saved, but Cache Creek was lost.

For years the creek's waters ran black with ash each time it rained. The forests that lined the banks were denuded to black poles leaning crooked or down as if drunk or dead. Whenever Wright came to Cache Creek, looking for the golden glimmer of life, cutthroats once again filling the valley, he found nothing but water washed gray with silt.

In time, though, the cutthroats returned. To his astonishment, Wright watched the fishery go from good to great.

"Actually the fish are probably even a little bit bigger than they were before the fire," Wright said. "It stands to reason because so much of that creek was up in the trees with not much grass; now there's more grass and more insects because the fires opened it up."

Cache Creek cutthroats average between 10 and 14 inches with healthy numbers stretching a foot or more. On occasion, Wright said he's caught a few that went 16 inches.

The fish are usually easy to take on attractor patterns, Wright said. He recommends Royal Wulffs, PMDs, and hoppers.

"There are no big secrets as far as fly patterns," Wright said. "There are good numbers of cutthroats, and they're usually pretty willing."

The trout hang in what Wright describes as "riffles and really nice pools and bends."

Hot, toxic water from Waab Springs runs into Cache Creek not far above where it joins the Lamar River. Few if any fish live around the mouth of the spring, Wright said. Anglers need to either fish the lower part of the stream or make the arduous, but worthwhile, trek to the creek above Waab Springs.

The trail to get to Cache Creek includes a ford of Soda Butte Creek and goes through the Lamar Valley floor where hikers will likely see antelope and bison. I saw my first badger in the wild up the Cache Creek Trail. The hike to the upper reaches of the creek has many ups and downs, as the trail cuts across several small streams that feed into the creek. There are several back-country campsites as well as stock campsites on the upper parts of the trail.

Today, Wright said, he loves visiting Cache Creek for what it represents as a place to see firsthand the power of nature's rejuvenation.

"It's come back," he said. "Good and healthy."

A native backcountry Yellowstone cutthroat trout from Cache Creek. These fish have rebounded after many were killed from ash and erosion in the aftermath of the 1988 fires. PHOTO BY NATE SCHWEBER

36 Lava Creek

Dale Sexton

Many park visitors know Lava Creek as a picnic area. Waterfall lovers know it as a stream that slides over pretty Undine Falls before rushing through a canyon on its way to the Gardner River. A few fishermen know Lava Creek as a fun stream packed with friendly brook and rainbow trout, and even a few small brown trout too.

Dale Sexton knows Lava Creek as the place where in the span of just a few minutes he managed to surprise a mother black bear with cubs and then piss off a grizzly.

Trout: Brook trout averaging 6 to 10 inches; slightly bigger browns, rainbows, cutthroat, and whitefish near the Lava Creek's junction with the Gardner River.

Bugs: Stoneflies, mayflies, caddisflies, and terrestrials.

Suggested fly box: Size 14 attractor dry flies, including Royal Wulffs, Humpies, Elk Hair Caddis, and Parachute Adamses; Pheasant Tail, Hare's Ear, and Prince nymphs size 14 to 18; Dave's Hoppers size 6 to 14; crickets size 8 to 14; Parachute and Chernobyl Ant patterns size 14 to 18; foam beetles size 14 to 16.

Key techniques: Dapping and short casts with dry flies are fine ways to work this small stream.

Best times: Anytime after spring runoff.

Directions: Park at the Undine Falls pullout about 4 miles east of Mammoth Hot Springs, or drive to the picnic area a half mile farther east, right where the creek flows under Grand Loop Road.

"Every time I see Lava Creek, I'm always thinking about that crazy experience," said Sexton, 46, who runs Timber Trails, an outdoors store in Livingston.

Sexton became enamored with little Lava Creek because it was an easy place to stop and pick up brook trout. He calls it "an idyllic little trout stream." In his old career as a fishing guide, he would take an elderly client who couldn't walk far to the Lava Creek picnic area. There the man would easily swipe a few trout from Lava Creek right by the bridge. I tried this, too, and I caught vivid, orange-bellied brook trout on nearly every cast with a bushy dry fly.

Sexton fished Lava Creek around the picnic area, which lies above Undine Falls. A half mile upstream from the picnic area, Lava Creek becomes unmanageably cluttered with deadfall and downfall. Throughout this section, Sexton caught shiny brook trout about six to nine inches long. He also fished the creek near its confluence with the Gardner River. There he caught rainbows, brookies, and small browns.

Lava Creek runs maybe 15 feet wide and is a "typical mountain freestone," Sexton said. It was named for the basalt and rhyolite lavas that it runs through.[1] It has riffles, runs, and pools where its trout congregate. Good patterns are big, bushy, attractor dry flies like Royal Wulffs, Royal Trudes, and Stimulators in size 12 to 14.

Lava Creek gushes with runoff until around the first week in July. From then until the snows choke it with cold, Lava Creek fishes great, Sexton said.

One part of Lava Creek that Sexton hadn't fished until a few years ago was the canyon beneath Undine Falls. One September day in 2007, he brought his wife, Hannah Sexton, and their friend Rick Hypes to the Lava Creek canyon via the trail that runs alongside. On his back, Sexton carried his and Hannah's then 18-month-old daughter Meryl. Hannah was also six months pregnant with the couple's second daughter, Palen.

The trio of adults took turns trading around one rod. One of them would stand in the middle of Lava Creek and catch a brook trout or a rainbow. Then the rod got passed along.

"We had enough entertainment to keep us involved for an hour or so," Sexton said.

Then the group started marching the mile and a half back to their car, which was parked at the picnic area. They were single file, and Sexton was in the lead.

Coming up over a hump in the trail, he saw a mother black bear with two young cubs just 10 yards away.

Alarmed, Sexton backed off and warned the others, "We've got a bear right here." He made sure his spray was at the ready. Fortunately, the mother

Colorful and relatively easy to catch, pretty brook trout are the main fish species in the upper parts of Lava Creek. PHOTO BY NATE SCHWEBER

black bear stayed calm as she hustled her babies down the slope and up into a tall, old-growth Douglas fir tree.

"It was pretty cool to watch those guys scamper up that tree as quickly as they did," Sexton said. "And with the mother, it didn't seem like she was alarmed or afraid or upset that we were there."

The group detoured off the trail and swung around wide to the left to give the black bear family plenty of room. They rejoined the trail uphill from that Douglas fir where the bear cubs clung to the branches. Invigorated by the encounter, Sexton announced he had a great idea. He would bushwhack to a vantage point off-trail to take pictures of the bear cubs in the tree, with his daughter on his back.

"I wanted my little one to get another look at them," he said. "Not that she could understand or comprehend, but just for her to be in that kind of proximity."

Hannah Sexton protested, but her husband was already gone, with their daughter and the bear spray.

Sexton got some great shots of those black bear cubs. He estimates he was gone 5, maybe 10 minutes tops. When he returned, his wife was steamed. She scolded him for tromping off to look at bears with their daughter, leaving her and Rick alone, unguarded. What if another bear came along?

Sexton sweet-talked that he'd kept a safe distance from the little bears and their mama. And he wasn't really gone that long.

"Besides," he said, "the prospect of another bear coming along is so remote."

No sooner had the words left his mouth than a grizzly bear appeared on the edge of Lava Creek just 75 yards away. It was mad.

The griz had its front legs atop a big, downed log on the bank of the creek. It shuffled back and forth, the way an angry bear does. It stared at the hikers from two cobalt eyes inside a blocky face hunkered below its big, griz hump.

"I was like, 'Oh my God, there's a griz,'" Sexton said. "And that bear, unlike the black bear, was in a very aggressive posture."

The stare-down went on about ten seconds. Sexton and the griz locked eyes, and then the bear "wheeled around and burst away in the blink of an eye," he said.

"I've seen a lot of grizzlies in the backcountry, and with each one I never really thought that I ruined his day except this one," he said. "The contrast between the grizzly bear and the black bear was just remarkable."

But the bear stories made the fishing in Lava Creek that much better.

"So often it's not as much about the fishing," Sexton said, "as it is about what Yellowstone has to offer as a wildlife haven."

37 Soda Butte Creek

Fanny Krieger

It must've been a funny scene, the elderly lady catching cutthroat trout with the big buffalo standing next to her on the banks of Soda Butte Creek.

"It was really a fantastic experience," said Fanny Krieger, 81.

Krieger had wanted for years to fish Soda Butte Creek, which glides through the northeast corner of Yellowstone. Soda Butte empties into the Lamar River near a large, mound-like extinct geyser from which the creek gets its name. Northeast Entrance Road traces Soda Butte Creek almost from the park's eastern border to its confluence with the Lamar River in the Lamar Valley.

Trout: Cutthroat trout, cuttbows, and rainbow trout averaging 12 to 20 inches.

Bugs: Terrestrials, mayflies, and caddisflies.

Suggested fly box: Dave's Hoppers size 6 to 14; crickets size 8 to 14; Parachute and Chernobyl Ant patterns size 14 to 18; foam beetles size 14 to 16; size 14 attractor dry flies, including Royal Wulffs, Humpies, Elk Hair Caddis, and Parachute Adamses; Pheasant Tail, Hare's Ear, and Prince nymphs size 14 to 18; black, tan, and olive Woolly Buggers size 4 to 8.

Key techniques: Stalk the bank, watching for rising trout, and fish to them.

Best times: August and September.

Directions: Northeast Entrance Road follows Soda Butte Creek for most of its length in the park.

Special rules: Catch-and-release for all cutthroats. Consider harvesting any brook trout as park biologists electrofish this stream every summer to remove brook trout that wash down from outside the park.

Stunning mountain vistas, abundant wildlife, and a healthy population of native cutthroat trout make Soda Butte Creek one of the most rewarding spots to fish in Yellowstone. PHOTO BY NATE SCHWEBER

A few years back, Krieger took a trip to Yellowstone with friends, and together they hired a guide. When she learned they would fish Soda Butte Creek, Krieger was pleased. It had long captured her imagination.

"When he said we were going to fish there, I said, 'Oh, great,'" she said. "I was excited."

Krieger had twisted her right foot on a hike before her Soda Butte trip and suffered a slight hobble. Her guide took her to a spot on the creek's bank a short distance from the road. Krieger said she fished a "gentle spot" with "not too much current," and she said she saw the cutthroats "were all lined up against the far bank." The fish seemed to almost float in air. "I had never seen water so clear," she said.

Krieger could easily send her fly over to the other side and she said, "Almost every cast, a fish took it."

"It was almost as if they were waiting for me," she said. "It was just beyond belief."

She described the joy she felt fishing Soda Butte Creek.

"When you put the right fly in the right place and the fish comes from down below and slowly comes up and grabs it, it's just thrilling," she said.

Soda Butte, similar to the Lamar River, fishes with nice hatches of Green Drakes, Pale Morning Duns, and a few caddis. Terrestrials, including

Wild bison often stand side-by-side with cutthroat anglers on Soda Butte Creek in the park's wildlife-rich Lamar Valley. PHOTO BY JESSICA LOWRY-VIZZUTTI

hoppers, ants, beetles, and crickets, are a favorite on this stream. This is a creek that is loved for its population of Yellowstone cutthroat trout, which are now in some trouble because brook trout that were stocked high up the creek outside the park and had been kept out of park waters by toxic tailings from the McLaren Mine near Cooke City are now leaking down because the creek's channel was altered.[1] Park fisheries managers electroshock Soda Butte Creek every late summer to harvest as many brookies as they can, said top Yellowstone fisheries biologist Todd Koel. Rainbow trout have also recently migrated up from where they were stocked decades ago in the Lamar River, he said.

On that day Krieger first fished Soda Butte Creek, she noticed that just downstream her friend Barbara Klutinis, who went on to film a DVD about women who fly-fish, wasn't having any luck. So Krieger offered to share her spot.

"I said, 'Barbara come here,'" Krieger said. "And she got to catch a fish."

Klutinis said she was touched by her friend's gesture.

"I thought it very kind and considerate of Fanny," Klutinis said. "But that is also how she is."

Klutinis moved on, but Krieger was not alone.

"Suddenly, I had this weird feeling like something was watching me," Krieger said. "I turned around, and there was this huge buffalo, just huge, looking at me."

Krieger was in midcast when she noticed the bison about 15 feet away. It had walked up to her right side from downstream. Krieger thinks she didn't notice because she had been concentrating so intently on her fly. She said she quickly reeled in while "the buffalo kept me company." Krieger backed away from her spot and watched the bison cross the mountain stream, "just going on its merry way."

Krieger hustled back to her friends and told them breathlessly, "You'll never believe this; I was just fishing with a buffalo."

"My heart was pounding, but it turned out to be very benign, kind of fun," she said. "Another experience while fly-fishing."

Krieger's late husband Mel Krieger taught fly casting for decades until his death in 2008. Fanny Krieger didn't take up fly fishing until the middle of her life, after her two children were grown. Recently, she taught her four grandchildren to fly-fish.

Krieger said that her fishing trip to Soda Butte Creek encapsulated everything she loves about fly fishing for trout, a sport she describes as "gentle" and "graceful."

Fanny Krieger, shown here holding a trophy New Zealand rainbow trout, was thrilled to fish Soda Butte Creek for the first time. She came away with stories about cutthroat trout and a big bull bison. PHOTO COURTESY OF FANNY KRIEGER

A 12-inch cutthroat trout from Soda Butte Creek. The trout tend to grow smaller farther upstream, particularly above Icebox Canyon. Near the confluence of the Lamar River, the cutthroats are larger. PHOTO BY NATE SCHWEBER

"It always gets you to beautiful spots out of the city where you get into a rhythm and watch the trees, the flowers, the skies, the mountains, the snow, and the friendly animals that come to visit you," she said.

Speaking from her home in San Francisco, Krieger said she wanted to visit Soda Butte Creek again, for the one-of-a-kind experience it gave her.

"I can't imagine fishing where buffalo run wild anywhere else," she said. "We have buffalo here in Golden Gate Park, but they're in a pen. There's no fishing there."

38 Pebble Creek

Tom Travis

om Travis concedes that as Pebble Creek flows through the campground that bears its name, the little trickle can seem underwhelming. It is precisely the kind of dribble that sends scores of anglers flocking to nearby Soda Butte Creek.

"It sure doesn't look like much," said Travis, 60, a longtime outfitter who works out of Livingston.

Couple that with the fact that the forested area north of the Pebble Creek Campground is serious griz country. It's the reason why Travis calls

---

Trout: Native Yellowstone cutthroats averaging 8 to 13 inches.

Bugs: Terrestrials, caddis, and mayflies.

Suggested fly box: Size 14 attractor dry flies, including Royal Wulffs, Humpies, and Elk Hair Caddis; Parachute Adamses size 10 to 18; Pheasant Tail, Hare's Ear, and Prince nymphs size 14 to 18; Dave's Hoppers size 6 to 14; crickets size 8 to 14; Parachute and Chernobyl Ant patterns size 14 to 18; foam beetles size 14 to 16.

Key techniques: Cast bushy dry flies upstream into pocketwater; also behind rocks, along current seams, around deadfall, and over pools and runs.

Best times: July through September.

Access: Park at the Pebble Creek Campground or the Pebble Creek Trailhead along Northeast Entrance Road. Either fish the canyon section near the campground, or hike 3^1/$_2$ miles up into the valley and follow the trail for backcountry campsite 3P1 down to the creek.

Special rules: Catch-and-release for cutthroats.

Just upstream from the Pebble Creek Campground lies a fascinating little canyon that the creek cuts through. PHOTO BY NATE SCHWEBER

Some say Pebble Creek's cutthroats may be the most beautiful in all of Yellowstone. The ones in a meadow section about a four-mile hike above the campground are a little bigger. PHOTO BY NATE SCHWEBER

this northeast Yellowstone stream "another little secret place in the Lamar Valley."

"You get about four miles back up in there, and it opens up into a meadow. And the size of the trout always surprises everybody," Travis said. "You've got fish going from 7, 8, 9 inches to 10, 12, 14 inches."

Pebble Creek cuts through a narrow canyon above the campground before it opens up into its meadow section. Access to the river via the Pebble Creek Trail can be tricky in this section, as the path takes the ridge high above the water. Travis gets there by wading up the creek itself, fishing all its little pools.

"You'd be amazed how many fish you can catch in those holes; they're just alive with fish," he said. "They all hold four or five fish."

In the meadow section, Travis likes to get out of the water and move slowly along the banks, working each pool thoroughly, enjoying the bigger cutthroats. "I'd rather fish than hike," he said. Fishing that meadow can make for a "delightful day of fishing," Travis said.

It can also make for some drama. On one summer afternoon, Travis cast a grasshopper pattern into one of Pebble Creek's meadow pools with a big rock jutting up from the middle. He gaped as a 17-inch cutthroat appeared and nudged the hopper with its nose. "This wasn't a very big pool, but it was a very big fish," Travis said. "I remember it distinctly." He cast again, and the big trout reappeared, eyeballing the fly and following it as it floated downstream. Travis switched to a Rubber-Legged Hopper pattern. Again the big cutthroat gave it a bump, followed it, and watched it drift by.

Pretty little waterfalls abound on Pebble Creek in the canyon section between the campground and the upstream meadows. Despite the fact that some of the falls seem impassible for fish, cutthroats abound throughout Pebble Creek and biologists say there was never a record of them having been stocked. PHOTO BY NATE SCHWEBER

Finally, Travis tied on a black cricket pattern. He expected the same result. "First cast he hit that thing like a tramp after a sandwich," Travis said. "I was shocked."

Instead of rolling near the surface the way many cutthroats do, this one dove right to the bottom and wrapped Travis's line around that big rock centerpiece.

"He got it snugged up enough that I had to pass my rod around this stupid rock with one hand," Travis remembers. "But that was quite a fish, especially for in there."

Terrestrial fishing can be "like dynamite" on Pebble Creek during late summer and early fall afternoons, Travis said. In addition to hoppers and crickets, Travis likes to throw unusual ants. Instead of tiny size 18 to 20 ants, he likes them size 14. Sometimes he'll even throw in an ant that is hot-pink-colored, a pattern he designed as a gag for a friend but which ended up to be a savagely effective fly.

"Pebble Creek can be really fun because it's not heavy-duty match-the-hatch stuff," he said.

During spring runoff, Pebble Creek "really rips," Travis said. It doesn't usually clear until the first week of July when Parachute Adamses and Elk Hair Caddis make for good patterns. Good subsurface bets include Prince nymphs, Hare's Ear nymphs, and earth-tone San Juan Worms, Travis said.

"Pebble Creek goes through a lot of woodland, and when it rains, you wind up with a lot of angleworms in the creek," he said.

The worm doesn't always go to the early bird on Pebble Creek, Travis said. Often the stream doesn't begin fishing well until midmorning. "It needs time to warm up," he said. Fishermen can find trout action on Pebble Creek until dark, but Travis doesn't recommend it because of bears.

"Don't stay until it's too late and then have to walk out in the dark," Travis said. "You have to use some common sense. Have a whistle and bear spray; there's no sense being foolish about this."

Animal encounters happen unexpectedly up at Pebble Creek. One day Travis was sitting cross-legged by a pool in the forest section above the meadow when he heard rustling behind him. He turned to see a bull moose walking toward him. Afraid that any sudden movement might anger the animal, Travis sat there while the moose walked "four steps away from me, stuck his muzzle down in the creek, and got a drink."

"I was close enough to hear him swallow, and I'm looking at him thinking, 'God, I hope you're in a good mood,'" Travis said.

The moose returned Travis's stare when his thirst was quenched.

"He looked at me and then walked back into the woods as if to say, 'Okay, you can fish again,'" Travis said.

39 Cougar Creek

Patrick Byorth

Patrick Byorth pulled the snorkel mask over his eyes and dug his toes into the pebbles at the bottom of Cougar Creek so that when he lay down in the bracing, cut-glass-clear water he could look 10,000 years back in time without getting washed away.

Cougar Creek's westslope cutthroat trout seemed only too happy to check out their reflections in Byorth's mask.

Trout: Westslope cutthroat trout and cuttbows averaging 6 to 10 inches.

Bugs: Terrestrials, caddis, and mayflies.

Suggested fly box: Size 14 attractor dry flies, including Royal Wulffs, Humpies, and Elk Hair Caddis; Parachute Adamses size 10 to 18; Pheasant Tail, Hare's Ear, and Prince nymphs size 14 to 18; Dave's Hoppers size 6 to 14; crickets size 8 to 14; Parachute and Chernobyl Ant patterns size 14 to 18; foam beetles size 14 to 16; black, tan, and olive Woolly Buggers size 4 to 8.

Key techniques: Dap bushy dry flies or make short casts upstream behind rocks, over pools, along current seams, and near undercut banks. Prompt territorial strikes from these little fish by teasing Woolly Buggers through their holes.

Best times: July through September.

Directions: Park at the Seven Mile Bridge Trailhead along West Entrance Road just east of the bridge over the Madison River. Take the Gneiss Creek Trail 1.4 miles to its fork in a large meadow, go right, and follow the Cougar Cabin Trail 2.3 miles to the stream.

Special rules: Catch-and-release for cutthroats.

In early summer the trail to upper Cougar Creek crosses a meadow colored yellow and lavender from massive blooms of arnica and lupine wildflowers.
PHOTO BY NATE SCHWEBER

"I saw these beautiful, highly golden and speckled fish with big, bright slashes on their chins, and I thought, 'These things have been here forever,'" said Byorth, 47, a staff attorney for Trout Unlimited's Montana Water Project.

Cougar Creek cuts through a cozy trench of granite and volcanic rock. Much of the 15-foot-wide creek's flow comes from cold springs. The temperature and scarcity of food keep fish sizes down to a foot or less. It also makes for a thin distribution of them. Underwater, Byorth said, he would see just a westslope cutthroat or two in each of Cougar Creek's pretty little pools. None of them seemed scared of a man in a snorkel.

"I have this image in my head of this fish just alive with colors," he said. "Just vivid."

Cougar Creek is unique in that it's bisected into two sections by a vast marsh. Byorth calls the marshy area "just a wall of willow and alder, literally a swamp" with "no discernible channel" and "plenty of peat bogs." Before this was a marsh, it might have been a giant complex of beaver dams 5,000 to 10,000 years ago, Byorth said.

Cougar Creek's water seeps through this marsh before it collects into a recognizable stream again, crosses the park boundary, and then pours into Hebgen Lake. Byorth believes the marsh kept the westslope cutthroats in the

Bison skull along the bank of Upper Cougar Creek, where herds of this animal may have roamed for millennia. Occasionally the herd that roams the Madison Valley migrates close to this small, fascinating stream.
PHOTO BY NATE SCHWEBER

headwaters of Cougar Creek mostly safe from introduced species like brown trout, which eat small fish, and rainbows, which crossbreed with cutthroats. Unfortunately, according to park fisheries biologists, upper Cougar Creek was stocked with rainbows and Yellowstone cutthroat trout. Genetic tests in the 1990s, which were not as accurate as they are today, showed that about half the cutthroats in upper Cougar Creek were hybridized, top Yellowstone fisheries biologist Todd Koel said.

Still, upper Cougar Creek trout bear a strong resemblance to the original westslope cutthroats, especially through a snorkel mask.

"As much as I love to fish, there's a whole different world that we don't get to see by casting a fly," he said. "You put your face down into a stream and the whole world opens up."

For example, on the creek bottom, Byorth said, he found "big, bruiser" Cougar Creek caddisfly cases that were "spangled with mica."

"They were really bright and shiny," he said. "It was fascinating to be snorkeling along and see these glistening, giant caddisfly cases more than an inch long."

In 1995 a West Virginia jeweler named Kathy Stout had the idea to put caddis larvae in aquariums filled with tiny, colored gemstones. She sealed the cases with epoxy and lacquer and made necklaces and earrings. Today she has aquariums filled with 2,000 to 4,000 caddisflies building cases out of tiny chunks of gold, sapphire, ruby, turquoise, and other gemstones, which she then sells at craft shows.[1]

"When I first saw caddis cases, I said, 'Wow, this is nature making art,'" she said.

It's been happening on upper Cougar Creek for millennia.

Byorth always packed his fly rod into upper Cougar Creek along with his snorkel, but he said it was easier to peer at these trout than to catch them. In the spring, he used Beadhead Hare's Ear and Pheasant Tail nymphs. In the summer, he used Royal Coachmans and Parachute Adamses. The tricky part of catching Cougar Creek's westslopes was not spooking them through the translucent water.

"If they see a shadow or a person standing up on the bank, they're ducking for cover," he said. "The trick is not to make long casts but to crawl on your hands and knees or drift just off the edge of the bank where they can't look up and see you."

For Byorth the jewels of visiting Cougar Creek were the beauty of the three-mile hike in, the solitude, and the animals he saw along the way. At the start of one hike, he had to walk through a herd of bison in a meadow. "I was thinking how it had been that way for 15,000 years," he said. Later Byorth saw a black bear, "as fat and black as can be," standing in tall grass that was "blowing in the wind in synchronicity with the thick hair on its back."

"It was a great image," he said. "As much as the fish were the job, the whole experience kind of outdid the fishing itself."

When I visited Cougar Creek in July, there were no bison, but the vast meadow to the north of the Madison River was thick like a shag carpet with arnica and lupine flowers. The trail faded away. Weeks later I would return to find a pair of rangers leading a dozen Youth Conservation Corps members to repair it, and I had to bushwhack through downfall scattered like a box of toothpicks dropped on the floor, with nine-foot pine saplings growing through it as thick together as blades of grass. The stream was a fascinating place. At one spot, I found remains of a bull elk; its antlers planted in the ground, and its skull hanging upside down. Just a little farther up, I found a porcelain-perfect bison skull that looked exactly like the Charles M. Russell art on the tails side of the Montana state quarter. I caught a handful of little cutthroats, or probably cuttbows, colorful like fruit candy. Some I caught on dry attractors, but most I caught on the biggest, gaudiest streamers in my box after I noticed that these ferocious little trout were guarding their territories. I lost an 11-inch giant that I swear looked like a pure-blooded westslope. I was crestfallen.

Byorth visited Cougar Creek in the mid-1990s when he worked as an arctic grayling restoration biologist. Although arctic grayling might have historically been kept out of upper Cougar Creek by the big marsh, grayling and westslope cutthroats used to fill the entire Madison River drainage. The grayling started to go extinct around the turn of the twentieth century right after the newly built Madison River Dam at Ennis cut off scores of the fish from their upstream spawning grounds.[2] The final nail in the Madison grayling's coffin was the Hebgen Dam, which flooded Horsethief Springs, the fish's most important spawning habitat around Yellowstone, Byorth said.

Biologists harvested eggs from Big Hole River grayling, which are today the last contiguous stream-dwelling population in the lower 48. They created a stock of the fish in Axolotl Lake in Big Timber, Montana.[3] Byorth brought eggs from Axolotl Lake to upper Cougar Creek and distributed them around springs to try and reestablish a population of stream-dwelling grayling in Yellowstone, of which there hadn't been any for decades. He returned regularly to check on the eggs. Most of them hatched, he said. But then it appeared that all of them died.

Fortunately, Byorth's successor built on the lessons learned from Cougar Creek and perfected the use of streamside incubators. Using the incubators, biologist James McGee brought grayling back to the upper Ruby River in 1997. As of this writing, a self-sustaining population was surviving in that river,[4] and biologists are considering other streams in Yellowstone where grayling could live.

Meanwhile, it's likely that there are still a few pureblood westslope cutthroats in Cougar Creek that are doing just fine—same as they have for 10,000 years.

"You don't go to Cougar Creek to catch a big trout," Byorth said. "You go for the pleasure of catching a rare trout."

40 Hellroaring Creek

Phil Adams

For a modern-day mountain man like Phil Adams, Hellroaring Creek near the Yellowstone National Park boundary has the allure of being a place where the only signs of man are 5,000 to 10,000 years old.

Adams, 52, used to spend months at a time in the primitive Absaroka-Beartooth Mountains north of Yellowstone, and he would crisscross the

---

Trout: Yellowstone cutthroat trout and rainbow trout averaging 8 to 14 inches.

Bugs: Terrestrials, caddis, and mayflies.

Key patterns: Size 14 attractor dry flies, including Royal Wulffs, Humpies, and Elk Hair Caddis; Parachute Adamses size 10 to 18; Pheasant Tail, Hare's Ear, and Prince nymphs size 14 to 18; Dave's Hoppers size 6 to 14; crickets size 8 to 14; Parachute and Chernobyl Ant patterns size 14 to 18; foam beetles size 14 to 16; black, tan, and olive Woolly Buggers size 4 to 8.

Key techniques: Cast bushy dry flies upstream into pocketwater; also behind rocks, along current seams, around deadfall, and over pools and runs.

Best times: July through September.

Directions: Park at the Hellroaring Trailhead 15 miles east of Mammoth Hot Springs or about four miles east of Tower Junction and hike about two miles, across the suspension bridge above the Yellowstone River, to Hellroaring Creek.

Special rules: Catch-and-release for cutthroats.

Although Hellroaring Creek got its name from a nineteenth-century explorer who called it "a hell-roarer," the stream is easy to wade and ford in high summer. PHOTO BY NATE SCHWEBER

park's backcountry border in the Hellroaring drainage to look for Native American artifacts—and trout.

"Hellroaring Creek is chock-full of fish," he said.

Hellroaring Creek flows south into the park, down from the Hellroaring Plateau, a vast, jagged wilderness area from which streams like Slough Creek and Buffalo Fork originate before pouring into Yellowstone. In fact it was one of Adams's forebearers, a hunter and explorer named A. H. Hubble, who gave the stream its name in 1867 when he reported to his companions after a hunting trip that the creek was "a hell-roarer."[1]

For ages the sky-high plateau was where Native Americans from the Shoshone Indian band known as Sheepeaters journeyed to make arrowheads from the region's abundance of obsidian and petrified wood. In places, Adams said, he's found pieces he believes were left by Sheepeaters "everywhere you look."

"That whole area is almost aglitter with chips and shavings," Adams said.

The Sheepeaters were the only group of Native Americans to live year-round in the high, frigid Yellowstone region. For thousands of years, stronger, more technologically advanced tribes lived in the lush, bison-rich prairies and valleys of the American West, gaining tools and technology from Europeans like horses and guns. But the Sheepeaters, who never acquired horses and instead used dogs to haul around their goods, remained isolated and reliant solely on their limited means of hunting and gathering. As their name suggests, they trapped bighorn sheep in the rugged, steep country. They also ate Yellowstone cutthroat trout. Because the Sheepeaters lived in one of the last places in the region to be explored by Europeans, they were able to sustain their ancient lifestyle longer than other tribes that were more quickly displaced by white settlers.[2]

Adams said he and fellow backcountry explorers carbon-dated human bones they found in the Hellroaring region and found that some of them were around 10,000 years old.

"That's a long time ago, considering that us white guys have only been here 120 years," he said.

Adams said that in the vertiginous backcountry he would locate fish just like the Sheepeaters: by following a creek from the trickle of its high-country headwaters down to where it became big enough to support fish. It was by doing this that he crossed into Hellroaring Creek in Yellowstone Park via a route alarmingly called "The Suicide Trail."

"It's aptly named because it's a narrow ridge with a precipice on the side and goat hair caught on the grubby rocks," he said.

The terrain around Hellroaring Creek is steep, jagged, and rugged. Hellroaring Creek was so named because it is a torrent during springtime runoff. The rest of the year, it gushes over stones and surges through rocky canyons.

Hellroaring Creek offers fine fishing for native Yellowstone cutthroat trout all the way up to the park border and beyond. Humans have caught cutthroats in this stream for millennia. PHOTO BY NATE SCHWEBER

Cameron Mayo, owner and operator of Absaroka Beartooth Outfitters, which guides throughout the Hellroaring region, calls Hellroaring Creek an "unbelievable fishery."

"We've caught fish in Hellroaring from 8 to 18 inches," said Mayo, 28. "We've caught 20-inch fish out of there right on the park boundary, and they're all native Yellowstone fish."

August is the best time to fish Hellroaring, he said, when the runoff is down and the fish are at the back end of the growing season. Mayo recommends Parachute Adamses, Royal Wulffs, and Dave's Hoppers during the summer months. Copper John and Prince nymphs take cutthroats from Hellroaring's deeper holes, he said. All of the trout glisten like arrowheads.

Just outside the border of the park, Adams said, he often used very different tactics to catch trout. Many times he dug through rotten logs for a grub and then baited a hook attached to six feet of fishing line tied to the end of a willow switch. He would crawl to the bank of Hellroaring Creek on his belly, inching along as not to cast a shadow over, or sound waves down to, his quarry.

Sometimes he would plunge his arm into the creek up to his shoulder, his nose and mouth just barely above water. He calls this "hand fishing."

"You reach down under a cut bank or a root, and you feel a little bit of them," he explains. "You tickle them up their bellies, then under their pectoral fins; they actually sort of settle in your hands and then, once your fingers are under their gills, thunk! Up and over your shoulder."

Adams adds, "I've caught many fish like that."

(It's worth noting here that hand fishing and killing cutthroat trout are illegal within the boundary of Yellowstone National Park, as is fishing with bait on all but a few park waters set aside specifically for children.)

Adams, a Montana native who speaks in a voice that can echo across mountaintops, used to travel into the high country as soon as the snow cleared with two mules, a stockpile of bacon, and Bisquick. He also brought field books for identifying trees, wildflowers, and constellations, plus volumes of Robert Louis Stevenson poetry. In the high country, he said, he learned to rely on himself, build shelter and fire, and stitch and be stitched with fishing line. He said he even cut a spiritual deal with the grizzly: in exchange for safe passage, he would never hunt nor guide anyone to hunt any bear. "Call it karma, call it ridiculousness, call it hippieish; it worked," Adams said. "And there are a lot of grizzly bears in that area."

Adams said living in the backcountry gave him "a feeling of peace and well-being as well as being on edge."

He and a few friends traversed game trails, scoured Prairie Dog towns where the soil-tilling varmints helped unearth arrowheads, and found scores of what they believe to be artifacts, such as sandals in caves up Hellroaring

Creek and wooden fish-drying racks strung between pines near Slough Creek. The latter burned in the 1988 fires.

"We were all amateur archaeologists," he said.

Over the years, Adams said he has learned to leave artifacts alone. "Taking them destroys the archaeological integrity of the sites," he said.

Of all modern Americans, Adams is one of the few who has come the closest to living like the Sheepeaters, summering in the Yellowstone region high country, foraging on wild foods. Despite his bare-handed bravado, Adams said, there is one modern invention that he wouldn't want to ever live without—something he always keeps in his wallet.

"In the backcountry, you realize that one of the best things man ever made was the metal fish hook," he said. "It's such a nice thing."

41 Black Canyon of the Yellowstone

Michael Leach

The top and west corner of Yellowstone National Park is unlike anywhere else in the region. It is a high desert, filled with prickly pear cactus, juniper trees, and even rattlesnakes.

The Yellowstone River spaded a mighty canyon through here, every inch of it some of the roughest and most rugged terrain in the park. Through the rock walls swim native Yellowstone cutthroat trout that anglers say pulse with the richest color around.

Perhaps to emphasize how unknown this area is, and how shadowy its legends are, it is called the Black Canyon. The Black Canyon lies downriver from the great Grand Canyon of the Yellowstone and is yin to that famous attraction's yang. It is Michael Leach's favorite spot.

"It's the biggest, wildest canyon in the lower 48," he said. "It almost has this gravitational pull on people who like to explore."

Leach, who founded Yellowstone Country Guardians, an organization that advocates for the park's wildlife, first ventured into the Black Canyon in 2002. He wanted to "experience one of the classic backpacking trips in the Northern Rockies," he said. Three years later, when he bought a home in Gardiner, Montana, the Black Canyon became his place of refuge, the spot he would go to rejuvenate after a hard season of work. Leach knows a place in the canyon that he won't disclose, a several-mile hike from his home in Gardiner, that he nicknamed "The Sacred Hole." It is home to countless cut-throats and a slinky family of otters. Leach took his baby daughter Kamiah to this spot when she was six months old, "just so she could stand in that water, because the water is so full of life it's pulsing."

The 19-mile course through the Black Canyon, from the Hellroaring Trailhead down into the town of Gardiner, drops 1,000 feet of elevation; but it's all over rough terrain. The river cuts through big, dark cliffs that form a tight canyon with basalt and rhyolite all around. There are a few magnificent backcountry campsites, one even on a sandy beach by the Yellowstone River. Still, Leach calls it "as rugged a place as I've ever fished."

In the early 1870s, Lt. Gustavus Doane, who named this place, described the Black Canyon as "grand, gloomy, and terrible; a solitude peopled with fantastic ideas, an empire of shadows and of turmoil."[1]

The native Yellowstone cutthroat that swim the Black Canyon are the most extraordinary Leach has ever seen. It's as if, he said, all the darkness of the canyon, its austerity, and its lacking of the lush green that blankets the rest of Yellowstone Park are compensated for by the colors of its cutthroat.

"Something about living in those deep, vibrant, green waters of the Black Canyon, with the walls so black and steep, just pours out in the vibrancy of those fish," he said.

Black Canyon cutthroat start feasting on stoneflies, golden stones, or even the giant Salmonfly, right around the time the Yellowstone River crests back from the 20,000 cubic feet of water per second that rage through the

---

Trout: Yellowstone cutthroat trout, cuttbows, rainbow trout, and brown trout averaging 10 to 20 inches; brook trout to 18 inches; and mountain whitefish.

Bugs: Stoneflies, including Salmonflies, around the time the river opens on July 15. Pale Morning Duns, Blue-Winged Olives, and tan caddis. Terrestrials, including hoppers, ants, beetles, crickets, and spruce moths.

Suggested fly box: Salmonflies size 2 to 6; Golden Stoneflies size 6 to 8; Parachute Adamses size 8 to 18; Pale Morning Duns and Blue-Winged Olives size 16 to 20; tan Elk Hair Caddis size 14 to 16; Pheasant Tail, Hare's Ear, and Prince nymphs size 14 to 18; Stimulators size 8 to 14; Rubber-Leg Hoppers size 6 to 14; crickets size 8 to 14; Parachute and Chernobyl Ant patterns size 14 to 18; foam beetles size 14 to 16; black, tan, and olive Woolly Buggers size 2 to 8; white Muddler Minnows size 2 to 4.

Key techniques: Search the water with high-floating dry flies or hopper/dropper rigs. Work water near the bank, behind rocks, along current seams, and in eddies. Strip Woolly Buggers through deep holes. Watch for rising trout and cast to them.

Best times: July, August, and September.

Directions: Park at the Hellroaring Trailhead or the Blacktail Deer Creek Trailhead and hike in the riverbank, or climb down to the riverbank from the High Bridge in Gardiner, Montana, and bushwhack to the park border and then uphill to the Yellowstone River Trail.

Special rules: Catch-and-release for all cutthroat and whitefish.

canyon like burned tea during spring runoff. The water usually begins to clear in early or mid-July and giant Salmonfly nymphs crawl to the banks and molt. Leach matches Salmonflies with a Sunken Stone imitation. On the heels of the Salmonflies comes a hatch of big Golden Stoneflies, which Leach matches with Gould's Golden Stone patterns.

Around the middle of August, terrestrial fishing kicks into high gear. Leach remembers incredible days fishing tan and cinnamon-colored Chubby Chernobyl's sizes 12 and 14. Also small yellow hopper patterns and black cicadas and crickets with foam bodies.

Particularly early in the year, Leach said he'll trail a Minch's bead-head and copper nymph or a size 14 Prince nymph 24 to 30 inches off the back of his dry fly. His tippets range from 3X early in the year to 5X late in the year, and he prefers to fish the Black Canyon with a 6-weight rod in order to better throw big bugs around in the canyon's sometimes blasting wind.

On rare occasions Leach will fish streamers in the Black Canyon, like size 2 and 4 black and olive Woolly Buggers and white Muddler Minnows. But he notes, "You don't go into the Black Canyon to nymph or streamer fish, you come to catch trout on dry flies."

Because parts of the canyon are so barren, Leach said, he feels a rush each time he sees a glowing cutthroat rise from the river's depths.

"To watch the Yellowstone cutthroat—its take is so slow and so deliberate—it's almost like foreplay," he said. "There's something almost sensual about it. Most fish pound a hopper, but a cutthroat will come up and sip it or slurp it. In some of the quieter pockets you can actually hear them."

Leach described Black Canyon cutthroat as "chunky, fat, and wild," usually stretching around 16 inches but occasionally popping more than 20. Once hooked, they use the Yellowstone's hydropower to "give you a great ride in that fast water," he said.

The water can also give incautious waders a ride. Once, Leach said, he fell in and was swept a football field downstream before he could crawl out. Other anglers haven't been as lucky and have drowned. A sturdy pair of hiking boots is a must, particularly because getting from the trail down to the riverbank makes for some of the hardest parts of the trip. I even slipped in over my head trying to refill my water bottle off a giant boulder the size of a 5-story building.

Dehydration is another killer in the Black Canyon. Temperatures can top 100 degrees and feel "like a furnace" on summer days, Leach said.

The Black Canyon doesn't have the best animal habitat in the park, but bison, elk, bighorn sheep, and the omnipresent grizzly bear all maraud through here. The canyon has a bigger population of some of Yellowstone's rarer, but still dangerous, animals, including the park's highest concentration of mountain lions and rattlesnakes, Leach said.

Michael Leach, shown here with his daughter Kamiah, says the Black Canyon of the Yellowstone has a "gravitational pull on people who like to explore." PHOTO COURTESY OF MICHAEL LEACH

Leach saw his first rattler on one of his early Black Canyon explorations. He heard the telltale shake while marching the sage- and grass-covered trail. Then he watched the six-foot serpent sidewind across his path.

"The first time you see a rattlesnake it sends chills up your spine," he said. "It added to the mystique and wildness of the Black Canyon."

Going down to the river in the dark canyon lifts Leach's spirit and soul "in a way that other waters just can't," he said.

"People say Yellowstone is the Yankee Stadium of fly fishing. I say Yellowstone is a church to those whose temples are the rivers and the mountains," he said. "The Black Canyon is the Vatican of fishing in Yellowstone."

Based on Leach's description, plus books and magazine articles I researched that called the Black Canyon one of the best hikes in the Rocky Mountains, I was excited to take this trip along with my stepfather Bill. But when I contacted park rangers to make backcountry campsite reservations, I got troubling news: instead of making the full, nearly 20-mile Black Canyon hike from the Hellroaring Trailhead down to Gardiner, Montana, we were told we would have to hike out halfway through the Blacktail Deer Creek Trail, thereby missing about 8 miles—practically half—of the Black Canyon of the Yellowstone.

Knowles Falls makes an impressive spectacle in the middle of the Black Canyon of the Yellowstone, a place that nineteenth-century explorer Lt. Gustavus Doane described as "grand, gloomy and terrible ... an empire of shadows and turmoil." PHOTO BY NATE SCHWEBER

I investigated and learned that about the last half mile of the Yellowstone River Trail runs through five private properties in the town of Gardiner, Montana. In 2009 one landowner named Ken Ballagh, once the principal at the town's school, closed the section of trail that runs through his property, which stretches from a bluff on a hill overlooking the Yellowstone River down to the high-water mark. Almost simultaneously Ballagh filed papers with the county to run a guest house out of a red barn built on his land so he could make money renting beds to Yellowstone tourists. According to public records in Livingston, only about 220 feet of the 20-mile Yellowstone River Trail runs through Ballagh's property, but it is crucial to access the Black Canyon of the Yellowstone.

Ballagh's move upset a lot of people. "I think everybody in the community is in agreement that it's not right," said Lynn Chan, a member of the Park County Parks Board who publically petitioned Ballagh to change his mind. Neither Park County, Montana, nor the National Park Service, being strapped for cash and leery of getting into a dispute involving private property rights, challenged Ballagh. The Bear Creek Council, a park watchdog group based in Gardiner, hired an attorney to see if there might be any way to use litigation to re-open the trail, which historians say has likely been used by Native Americans for millennia. Ever since Yellowstone was created, even after the land that Ballagh now owns was first developed in 1974, hikers, anglers, horseback riders, and outfitters used that trail under a gentleman's agreement. However no easement was ever put down in writing. Ballagh used that technicality to close the trail. "To my way of thinking, that trail is such an important access to the park," said Julia Page, president of the Bear Creek Council. "Can't we come to some sort of equitable way to make this work?"

Ballagh said he made his decision after partiers used the trail to reach the Yellowstone River below his house and left beer cans, condoms, and debris from bonfires. "It just got out of hand," Ballagh told me in September 2011. Nothing came of suggestions to boost law enforcement patrols and have local volunteers regularly clean up the riverbank. Some residents suspected Ballagh simply didn't want Yellowstone visitors crossing his property unless they paid him his $250 a night fee. He denies this. Still, as evidenced by a guest raving online that Ballagh taught her to fish on his "private beach at the Yellowstone River," it's clear that the disputed section of Yellowstone River Trail is still accessible, for a price.

Under Montana law streambanks below the high-water mark are public property and can be accessed from places like bridges and public lands. My stepfather Bill Innes and I, not wanting to miss the full Black Canyon, decided to follow the Yellowstone River Trail to the park border and then drop down to the riverbank and hike out the last half a mile to the High Bridge in Gardiner. We were glad we did. The final 10 miles of the Black Canyon wove through some of the most incredible country we had ever seen; orange, chiseled cliffs cutting away into that great river; jagged mountains, churning Knowles Falls. I caught a surprising 16-inch brook trout, a dancing 18-inch rainbow, and a streetfighting 22-inch cutthroat right at the mouth of Bear Creek, just a few miles from Gardiner. Bill and I would have missed all of it had we stopped at the new sign bolted to a tree halfway through that read, "DEAD END TRAIL—NO ACCESS TO GARDINER, MONTANA."

In 2009 a Gardiner, Montana, guest-house owner named Ken Ballagh closed a 220-foot stretch of the Yellowstone River Trail that runs through his private property, prompting park officials to route hikers out halfway through the Black Canyon via the Blacktail Deer Creek Trail. This dead end sign, nailed to a tree in the middle of the Black Canyon, warns hikers that following the historic trail down to the town of Gardiner is now considered trespassing. PHOTO BY NATE SCHWEBER

The hike out below the high-water mark was tough; we had to scramble around boulders, through willows, and over deadfall—and then make the steep hike up to the road by the bridge. We picked up as much trash from the riverbank as we could carry, but Bill, 63, took a nasty fall and suffered a bloody gash on his arm.

In the future the Forest Service may build a connector trail from public land along the Jardine Road on the mountain above Ballagh's property down to the Yellowstone River Trail. It's better than nothing, but no longer would Gardiner residents have an in-town trailhead they could walk to. Yellowstone backpackers would also then be faced with a mighty uphill climb for the last leg of their 20-mile hike; plus they would no longer have the unique experience of being able to hike out into a town after days in the wilderness and belly right up for a beer at the Two-Bit Saloon, order a bison burger at The Corral Drive In, or buy an ice cream cone at Yellowstone Gifts.

Still, thanks to Montana's excellent stream access law, you can still hike in and out of the Yellowstone River Trail from the High Bridge in Gardiner. You could even pause beneath the Ballagh property to enjoy the fishing on your own private beach.

Chasing Rare Cutthroats on High Lake, Sedge Creek, and Goose Lake

Jeff Reed

Not all the native cutthroat news from the Yellowstone region is bad; in fact, some of it is very encouraging and some of it is just, well, unexpected.

Much of this story centers around a trek I took with Jeff Reed, a sinewy and fast hiker with a passion for rare, native cutthroat trout in Yellowstone. We went to Sedge Creek to look for a special type of cutthroat, one that isn't genetically programmed to run to Yellowstone Lake. On our way in via the Pelican Valley Trail, a pair of Australian tourists stopped us and warned us that they'd just seen a testy mama griz with two cubs huff off behind a grassy hill. Our path to Sedge Creek would take us right by them.

To make bear noise, Reed and I talked about High Lake, way up in the Gallatin Mountains in the northwest corner of the park. It was a place I'd recently visited, as had he, to look for another rare fish in Yellowstone, the westslope cutthroat trout.

"I read about the project," Reed said, "and I wanted to just see one of those westslopes in Yellowstone."

In 2007 biologists stocked High Lake with westslopes[1] and created an important reservoir for this native fish in the nearly 8,800-foot elevation lake, the highest stillwater in the park that supports trout.

Until the turn of the twentieth century, westslope cutthroats flourished on the west side of the Rocky Mountains in Yellowstone and beyond. They filled the Madison and Gallatin Rivers and thrived down through the great Missouri River. By the 1930s, introduced brown, brook, and especially rainbow trout, with which the native westslope cutthroats interbreed, almost wiped them out.[2] Biologists and native trout lovers rejoiced in the late 1990s when a population of what was believed to be pure westslope cutthroats were

High Lake is the highest elevation stillwater in Yellowstone that supports fish. It's a 20-mile round-trip hike, but views of westslope cutthroat riseforms on a back-country lake that mirrors skyscraping Electric Peak are worth the effort. PHOTO BY NATE SCHWEBER

confirmed in the North Fork of Fan Creek inside Yellowstone. However in 2003, additional, intense lab tests showed that two-tenths of one percent of those trout's genes came from rainbow trout; they were not genetically pure.[3]

Quick on the heels of that disappointment came another eureka discovery. In 2005 Yellowstone officials heard that a U.S. Forest Service ranger found a few hundred westslopes in a small, unnamed tributary of Grayling Creek just inside the park's western border.[4] Around 1910 workers on the old Highway 191 built a roadbed across this tiny, spring-fed stream. The roadfill isolated a population of around 700 genetically pure westslope cutthroats upstream, and it kept out nonnative rainbows, which were stocked downstream in Grayling Creek starting in 1923.[5] Less than two miles of stream inside Yellowstone National Park held the last of its native, genetically pure westslopes.

Biologists took to calling this little stream, "Last Chance Creek," as in the last chance for westslope cutthroats in Yellowstone.

Around the same time, a biologist working with a grant made another fascinating discovery in Oxbow and Geode Creeks, small tributaries to the Yellowstone River in the Black Canyon section of the park. These streams

Jeff Reed, owner of the Rivers Bend Lodge on the banks of the Yellowstone River in Emigrant, Montana, scouts Sedge Creek for a rare type of native Yellowstone cutthroat. PHOTO BY NATE SCHWEBER

were considered so insignificant that only Oxbow ever warranted mention in a previous Yellowstone angling guide, and it was described as "fishless."[6] Lo and behold, it turned out that both Oxbow and Geode Creeks each held robust populations of more than 10,000 genetically pure westslope cutthroat trout, said Todd Koel, the park's top fisheries biologist. Records from the 1920s show that these streams were stocked with "blackspotted trout" from an unspecified location, he said. Modern genetic tests showed that these trout are actually pure westslopes, which were kept isolated from downstream Yellowstone cutthroats and rainbows by waterfalls, Koel said.

"We assume that the original westslope cutthroats planted in Geode and Oxbow Creeks came from somewhere around here," he said.

Biologists took the westslopes from "Last Chance," Oxbow, and Geode Creeks to the private Sun Ranch, which lies outside the park in the Madison Valley, Koel said. The giant ranch has its own trout hatchery with a population of genetically pure westslope cutthroats culled from one of the last, tiny remaining populations of that fish in the Madison drainage.

From those four sources, park biologists bred a population of pure westslopes, with genetic diversity from several strains, and used a helicopter to stock them in High Lake.

Biologists built a fish barrier on the East Fork of Specimen Creek downstream from High Lake to keep out nonnative fish. Pure westslope cutthroats were reintroduced to this stream in 2010. PHOTO BY NATE SCHWEBER

In 2006 fisheries biologists poisoned High Lake, which was historically fishless until it was stocked with Yellowstone cutthroats in 1937.[7] They also built a fish barrier out of logs on the East Fork of Specimen Creek just upstream from its junction with the main stem to create a westslope sanctuary all the way up to the lake.

In 2010 biologists learned that the westslopes planted in High Lake were successfully spawning, Koel said. That year they also brought five-gallon buckets filled with thousands of westslope eggs on horseback to the East Fork of Specimen Creek above the fish barrier. The idea was that trout hatched in the stream would be more likely to hold in the stream and less apt to flush down to the Gallatin River below. Nearly all the eggs hatched as planned, and biologists expect that within a few years the East Fork of Specimen Creek will have its own fishable population of westslopes.

As its name suggests, it's a long, uphill climb to get to High Lake, but it's a beautiful one. The fish barrier lies a short bushwhack down to the East Fork of Specimen Creek about a mile up from where it pours into the main stem. It's a heartening thing to see for people rooting for native cutthroats to make a comeback.

Majestic Electric Peak towers to the east above High Lake, and the hulking mountain's reflection paints the top of this lake. On summer evenings, saucer rings from rising westslope cutthroats pock this seven-acre jewel.

The westslopes have sides that are more silvery than their golden Yellowstone cutthroat cousins. Their backs range from olive to emerald, and their bellies often turn salmon-colored. A soft, almost metallic pink covers their gill plates, and true to their name, the undersides of their jaws flash fire-engine red. The 8- to 12-inch ones I met at High Lake eagerly scarfed Parachute Adams drys and put up spirited fights.

Sedge Creek, by contrast, was a puzzle. Reed and I reached the small, twisting mountain stream by its mouth at chalky Turbid Lake. Aeons ago, Yellowstone Lake was much bigger, and what is now Turbid Lake was part of the lake bottom. When Yellowstone Lake shrank around 8,000 years ago, it isolated Turbid Lake, which has acidic, poisonous water because of thermal springs on its floor. Consequently, the Yellowstone cutthroat trout that live upstream in Sedge Creek evolved with the unique characteristic that they do not run downstream toward Yellowstone Lake.[8]

In the early 1980s, biologists planted Sedge Creek cutthroats in a section of the South Fork of the Yellowstone River and in Scenicio Creek, a tributary to Atlantic Creek, both high in the Bridger-Teton National Forest, south of the Yellowstone Park border. Historically, those sections of stream were fishless because they are above waterfalls that blocked trout migration. Populations of

A pure westslope cutthroat trout from High Lake. In 2007 park officials stocked High Lake with westslopes, creating a reservoir for this fish, which had been all but extirpated from Yellowstone Park. PHOTO BY NATE SCHWEBER

Sedge Creek cutthroats, with their quirk of not migrating downstream, are now established in those remote places, said Jason Burkhardt, a biologist with the Wyoming Game and Fish Department.

Reed and I fished Sedge Creek a couple miles upstream and didn't see a single trout—no rises, no splashes, no flashes, and no shadows. Ominously, we didn't even see baby trout darting around the shallows.

Nearby Pelican Creek was the first water in Yellowstone to be confirmed infected with whirling disease.[9] Biologist Koel would tell me later that volunteer anglers caught cutthroats in Sedge Creek as recently as the couple years prior to my visit. An angler I spoke to named Joe DiSilvestro, of Phoenix, said he hiked to Sedge Creek in the late 1990s in search of the special cutthroats, saw only a couple, and caught none. "I just don't think their population is very large," DiSilvestro said. Glen McFaul, who accompanied DiSilvestro on this cutthroat quest said, "In all the years we've fished for native cutthroats, we never came across a fish population that spooky." Still, Reed and I couldn't help but wonder why we couldn't find any Sedge Creek cutts.

"Wouldn't it be a shame if something happened to these special cutthroats?" Reed said, peering down into the creek for some sign of trout life.

Reed is a Billings native who spent his summers helping his parents at a bed-and-breakfast that they ran in the Paradise Valley, just outside Yellowstone. Later he earned a PhD in Sheffield, England, and then founded a successful computer company in Seattle. Wanting to spend more time in the Montana wilderness he loves, in 2004 Reed bought 120 acres of Yellowstone riverfront property in the Paradise Valley, with a spectacular view of towering Emigrant Peak, and built the Rivers Bend Lodge not far from his parents bed-and-breakfast. The lodge is luxurious, rustic, sustainable, and decorated with Reed's collection of old Montana maps and Yellowstone photographs. His library is filled with volumes on his favorite topics—Yellowstone Park and Paradise Valley history. On the short drive from Yellowstone to the lodge, Reed pointed out vital cutthroat trout spawning streams as well as crucial big-game habitat, plus new developments—such as a golf course—that are changing the nature of the Paradise Valley.

"I've always loved this land and its native wildlife," Reed said.

At least for westslope cutthroats in Yellowstone Park, the future is getting brighter. In the fall of 2011, biologists poisoned Goose Lake, a short walk from Fountain Flats Drive near the Firehole River, to remove nonnative rainbow trout. Soon they will stock the water with pure westslope cutthroats. This will give park officials access to a brood stock of pure westslopes somewhere other than the private Sun Ranch, and a place easier to access than High Lake.

It will do the same for the angling public.

"I'm real excited about getting a native westslope spot that is so accessible for people," Koel said.

42 Solfatara Creek

Christopher Oertle

Remember the pure joy of fishing? The elation of that first trout hooked on a fly?

For Christopher Oertle, he only has to think back to the fall of 2010 when Yellowstone's Solfatara Creek gave him a little brown trout for a sweet-sixteenth present that he'll never forget.

"I just got this explosive bite, and as I started to pull it in, I got really excited about what was going on," said Christopher, who turned 16 in September 2010, "realizing I'd just caught my first fish fly-fishing on my own."

Trout: Browns, rainbows, and brookies averaging 5 to 12 inches.

Bugs: Mayflies, caddisflies, and terrestrials.

Suggested fly box: Parachute Adamses and Pale Morning Duns size 14 to 20; Royal Wulffs and Yellow Humpies size 14 to 16; tan Elk Hair Caddis size 14 to 16; Hare's Ear, Copper John, Pheasant Tail, and Prince nymphs size 14 to 20; Dave's Hoppers size 6 to 14; crickets size 8 to 14; Parachute and Chernobyl Ant patterns size 14 to 18; foam beetles size 14 to 16; black, tan, and olive Woolly Buggers size 4 to 8.

Key techniques: Fish upstream and tight to the banks, particularly with terrestrials. Also work areas behind structure, near undercut banks, and along current seams. In late summer, these fish can get very spooky.

Best times: High summer and fall.

Directions: Park at the Norris Campground, 21 miles south of Mammoth Hot Springs and about a mile north of Norris Junction, and follow Solfatara Creek upstream.

Special rules: Catch-and-release for rainbow and brown trout.

Solfatara Creek is a gentle little stream that winds through a meadow near the Norris Campground on its way to the Gibbon River. Wide spots stretch 10 feet from bank to bank. Skinny spots are long-jumpable. Deep pools reach a man's neck; shallow parts barely wet ankles. This rocky-bottomed stream holds rainbow, brown, and a lot of brook trout. Most of them are fairly small, but they tend to get larger near where the creek joins the Gibbon River.

Christopher's family made a tradition of staying at the Norris Campground during a decade of annual summertime visits to Yellowstone. Beginning when he was 12, Christopher said that he fished Solfatara Creek with his spinning pole every evening before a campfire dinner with his family. He never caught anything, he said, and he lost a lot of expensive Panther Martin spinners in the bushes. But he enjoyed being out in the meadow with "the bison, the bull elk, and sometimes a wolf or two."

In August of 2010, Christopher enrolled in the River Guardian Fly Fishing School in Gardiner, taught by Michael Leach. He learned the basics of casting, selecting fly patterns, and watching streams for signs of bugs and trout. With Leach by his side, Christopher even caught a few trout in the Yellowstone River, but not on his own.

About a month later, Christopher and his family made their annual stay at Norris Campground. Christopher and his sister Kiersten, a year his junior, went out to fish. She had also taken the River Guardian class.

About 30 minutes in, Christopher took a spot on Solfatara Creek just across from the A-22 campsite. "I was a little bit rusty," he said, "but I got back into my rhythm." He cast an Elk Hair Caddis upstream to a current seam running along an undercut bank. He mended his line a couple times and watched his drift.

A brown trout came up underneath his fly and burst completely out of the water. It hung suspended, glistening in the air for a split second.

"It was lucky for me because I had just enough time when he was out of the water to get my fly hooked into its mouth," Christopher said.

The trout "gave quite a fight," Christopher said. He said he played the fish by pulling it in two feet and then letting it out for six inches, "so he wouldn't pop my line."

"In the middle of the river, he did a hop, skip, and a jump across the water," he said, "which really helped me out because when he was out of the water, I could spin as fast as I can."

Christopher said he felt "disbelief" as he reeled in his catch, "like electricity was going through my body." Unlike the fish he had caught in class, this Solfatara Creek trout was all his own.

"It was important for me to catch that by myself," he said. "Just to realize it's not impossible to catch a fish."

With the little fish at his feet, Christopher leaned down and quickly unhooked it with his hemostats. He felt a paramount duty to release that fish as quickly as possible because "him being out of the water would be like us being in the water," he said.

"I was trying to be very gentle and keep him as calm as possible," he said.

Though his camera was in his pocket, Christopher never used it. He did show his catch to one person—his sister. She had already caught a trout that day and was leading by one in their sibling rivalry.

"We ended up tying that day," Christopher said. "And that satisfied me."

Only after the little trout swam away did Christopher let his feelings wash over him.

"The excitement came more after I released the fish because I got to hold it," he said. "I was proud."

Later, around the campfire, his parents Chris and Gina Oertle were thrilled too. They told Chris they wished he'd taken a picture of his trout, and he conceded that he did, too. "But I just knew the importance of getting it back in the river," he said.

I fished Solfatara Creek over several days, trying to catch a brown trout just like Oertle's. I caught a dozen brook trout instead. One of them went 13 inches, a surprise in this small stream.

The Oertle family was so moved by their annual visits to Yellowstone that they pulled up roots from their home in Redmond, Oregon, and, after stops in Butte, Montana, and Virginia, settled in Gardiner, Montana, in 2010.

Though he's near the beginning of what will surely be a lifelong love of fly fishing, the story of Christopher's first Solfatara Creek trout holds a lesson for all anglers: keep a sense of curiosity and wonder.

"You might be an expert fisherman," Christopher said seven months after his first fly cast, "but wherever you go, there's always going to be room for learning."

43 Slough Creek at Lamar Confluence to Slough Creek Campground

Dean Reiner

Sensitive readers please excuse the following description from Dean Reiner about what it feels like to land a 30-inch trout (thirty, he swears!) from the lower meadows of Slough Creek.

"Ooh," he squeals. "It's better than sex."

Lower Slough Creek's grassy, sagebrush flats, stomped flat by herds of buffalo, packs of wolves, and ambling grizzlies, harbor those mythical 30-inch trout, all brassy cutthroats and flashy cutthroat-rainbow hybrids. Reiner knows the trout actually grow that long because after catching a few that boggled his sense of size, he took out his tape measure—three-zero. A photo of that fish hangs on the wall at Hatch Finders Fly Shop in Livingston, which Reiner, a Philadelphia native, has run for 12 years.

"I didn't believe it until I actually caught one and put a tape to it," he said.

The prospect of a 2½-foot trout draws anglers the world over to the Madison River in the fall for a shot at the big browns running up from Hebgen Lake. Other anglers risk bears and hypothermia chasing a fish that goes three-oh in places like the Lewis River Channel or—sssh!—the Bechler Meadows. In truth, there are few places and fewer times in Yellowstone where anglers have a shot at catching a battleship like that in a stream. But the huge cutthroats and cuttbows in lower Slough Creek hide in plain sight all season long.

"You can see them from the bluff overlooking the creek," Reiner said. "On a sunny day you look down, and you think they're rocks. Then you realize, by God, they're fish!"

He adds, "But just because you can see them doesn't mean you can catch them."

"PhD Pool" is the name Reiner gave to the first of the three pools he fishes between the Slough Creek Campground and the canyon where the creek empties into the Lamar River. He said he dubbed it "PhD Pool" because "you need a doctorate degree to fish it." The pool is almost parallel from the third pullout along the dirt road that leads to the Slough Creek Campground and backcountry trailhead.

Another pool lies about an eight-minute walk downstream from PhD Pool, this one nearly parallel from the second left-side pullout on the campground road. The third pool is about a quarter mile below that one, just above the canyon that Slough Creek pours through before emptying into the Lamar River.

The key to catching lower Slough's giant fish is being there at the right time, fishing the right fly, and targeting the right fish, Reiner said. Early in the summer and again in September are Reiner's favorite times to fish lower Slough Creek. Key hatches include medium-sized caddis, yellow sallies, and crane flies, plus tiny *Baetis* and midges in the size 20 range. One of Reiner's favorite patterns for PhD Pool is a *Baetis* Thorax Dun.

Trout: Cutthroat trout and cuttbows that average 12 to 22 inches with a few eye-poppingly bigger ones mixed in; also small rainbow trout.

Bugs: Mayflies, including Green Drakes, Pale Morning Duns, and *Baetis*; caddis; stoneflies, including Golden Stoneflies, little yellow stoneflies, and Salmonflies; and terrestrials, including hoppers, ants, beetles, and crickets.

Suggested fly box: Green Drakes size 8 to 12; Elk Hair and X-Caddis size 14 to 18; yellow Stimulator size 8 to 12; Salmonflies size 6; Parachute Adamses size 14 to 18; crane flies size 12 to 16; *Baetis* Sparkle and *Baetis* Thorax Duns size 20 to 22; Pheasant Tail, Prince, and Hare's Ear nymphs size 14 to 20; Dave's Hoppers size 6 to 14; crickets size 8 to 14; Parachute and Chernobyl Ant patterns size 14 to 18; foam beetles size 14 to 16; black, tan, and olive Woolly Buggers size 4 to 8; midges.

Key techniques: Sight and stalk specific fish; cast to rising trout; search water with a hopper/dropper rig; strip Woolly Buggers.

Best times: July through October.

Directions: Find the Slough Creek road on the Northeast Road about 6 miles east from Tower Junction or about 27 miles west from the northeast entrance.

Special rules: Catch-and-release for all cutthroats; consider harvesting any rainbow trout.

A trail winds down to lower Slough Creek, above its confluence with the Lamar River. This water is home to big, wary, and hard-to-catch cutthroats and cuttbows.
PHOTO BY NATE SCHWEBER

Terrestrials are good bets in high summer, particularly grasshoppers, beetles, and ants. Reiner cautions that standard patterns won't do.

"Your flies have to be tied sparse—not the way you want them tied, the way the fish want them tied," he said. "If you overdress a fly, they know it's not real. They're very educated."

Reiner cautions that anglers should be ready to cycle through every pattern in their fly boxes. They should also be ready for agonizingly long looks, and then refusals, from big trout.

"These fish will take their sweet time coming up, and they'll put a magnifying glass on your fly," he said. "You have to have nerves of steel, and remember, if you have any drag on your fly, you're done."

Reiner remembers a 30-inch cutthroat that he tempted for close to three hours, tying on every pattern in his box, watching one refusal after another. Finally, the huge fish committed on an itty-bitty *Baetis*, mauling and charging in the water until "he decided to roll over" and come to the net.

September is Reiner's favorite time to fish lower Slough Creek because of its big Green Drake hatch. The drakes, which like muddy bottoms, crawl out of their nymph shucks near shore and float downstream as their wings dry out. Reiner says he finds the hatch with his ears.

"They make an audible 'pop!' You can actually hear them hatch," he said. "When I hear that, I say somebody's calling my name."

Locating feeding trout is another key, Reiner said. If trout are hugging the bottom, they are "just laughing at you; you're wasting your time," he said. His technique is to take a seat by the streambank and just watch. When he sees a rise, he'll key in on that area until the trout rises again. The big trout often move from their lies in the pools into feeding lanes in runs and riffles during a hatch, he said. During a good hatch, Reiner sees trout "whacking" flies. Only then will he start casting.

"They have to be rising before you'll actually get something to come up," he said.

Hooking up can be just as tricky. Anglers must time their hook set to the dive after the trout's rise. Set the hook too quick with a cutthroat, as is necessary with other trout species, and the fly will come flying out of that fish's mouth.

Also, because 6X tippet is often needed on Slough Creek's slow, polished-glass surface, anglers must take care not to break their line. "You just raise the rod tip up," Reiner said.

Then there's the fight. Many of the fish in Slough's lower reaches are cuttbows, crosses between the rainbows that swim up from the Lamar River and the cutthroats native to the drainage. A big cuttbow packs the bulldog shake of a cutthroat with the turbo-thrust of a rainbow.

Bison often graze the meadows through which lower Slough Creek flows near its confluence with the Lamar River, pictured in the background here. PHOTO BY NATE SCHWEBER

Bison, wolves, elk, coyotes, grizzlies, antelope, and other animals roam the grassy banks of Slough Creek in its lowermost meadow. PHOTO BY NATE SCHWEBER

"The cuttbows are big and fast, and they're mean," Reiner said. "They're not going to sit there and say, 'Oh, gee, I'm hooked again.' You hook one of those guys, they come out of the water. They're rather feisty."

Besides the gobsmacking 30-inch trout, the lower part of Slough Creek has a lovely, easy atmosphere, Reiner said.

"If it's a nice day, I'll get there early and sit on a spot," he said. "The sun comes up; it warms you; you hear the sound of the creek and the wind blowing through the willows and the sagebrush, maybe a coyote yip, a wolf howl or a buffalo snort. There's birds cruising around and chipmunks that are fun to watch."

Reiner said sometimes he'll even lie back and take a nap. Because it's close to a road, this part of Slough Creek can get busy on summer days with amateur anglers whom Reiner calls "dudes." Still, it's often less crowded than the stream's upper reaches, which fill with anglers who consider a back-packing trip to the top of Slough Creek almost a Yellowstone fly-fishing rite of passage.

Reiner, who said he discovered the great fishing on lower Slough "just by being lazy," said he's happy to leave the stream's hard-to-reach places to more ambitious anglers.

"The word is out to all these guys: 'You've got to go up to the second or third meadow,'" he said. "I've always said, 'Yep, fine, go ahead. I'll just stay down here and catch all the big fish I want.'"

44 Firehole River at Ojo Caliente

Delores Marsh

Delores Marsh still isn't sure if she actually walked on water to get away from the big bull buffalo that ended her 100-fish day in the Ojo Caliente section of the Firehole River a few years back.

But she's positive that she left the river walking high above the ground.

"I will never have another day like that," Marsh said. "And I will never forget it."

Trout: Rainbows and browns averaging 10 to 14 inches, with a few bigger ones too; brookies in the upper reaches; whitefish below Firehole Falls.

Bugs: Mayfly hatches, including Pale Morning Duns and *Baetis*; caddisflies, including *Nectopsyche* and White Millers; also Salmonflies, midges, and terrestrials.

Suggested fly box: Parachute Adamses size 14 to 20; Pale Morning Duns, Blue-Winged Olives, and Sparkle Duns size 16 to 18, Iris Caddis emergers, and Elk Hair Caddis size 14 to 20. Hare's Ear, Copper John, Pheasant Tail, and Prince nymphs size 14 to 20; soft-hackle wet flies size 14 to 20; black and olive Woolly Buggers size 6 to 10.

Key techniques: Match the hatch; fish nymphs when no fish are rising. Swinging soft-hackle wet flies can also be very effective here.

Best times: May through June; also September through November.

Access: Park at the picnic area near Fountain Flats Drive along the Firehole River.

Special rules: Fly-fishing only; catch-and-release for browns, rainbows, and whitefish.

The Firehole River at Ojo Caliente can sometimes appear to be boiling with rises from rainbow and brown trout. Matching the hatch and fooling these fish can be tricky. PHOTO BY NATE SCHWEBER

Ojo Caliente is an emblematic stretch of this one-of-a-kind river, with its geyser basins and herds of buffalo wandering the banks. The river's surface is smooth and glassy, perfect for spot fishing hot-rod rainbow and brown trout. Many a bald eagle competes with the fly anglers who work this stretch.

"It's probably one of the most lovely places in the park," Marsh said.

Marsh, 64, a nurse who lives in Bend, Oregon, makes annual treks to Yellowstone in the late summer with her friends Harry Harbin and his wife Judy Harbin. Marsh and Harry Harbin, the anglers in the group, make a point to fish a different spot each time they visit. In 2009 they followed a tip from a clerk at Blue Ribbon Flies in West Yellowstone and arrived at Ojo Caliente. It was around 11 o'clock in the morning on a sunny, early September day, and small Blue-Winged Olives were hatching.

"The trout were just sipping them in the riffles," she said.

Marsh found a size 20 imitation, bathed it in floatant, and tied it to her 6X tippet at the end of a 9-foot leader. She cast with her 4-weight rod and brought so many trout to hand that she lost count.

"Between the two of us, we easily caught more than 100 trout," she said.

The fish were thick, solid rainbows and browns, mostly between 10 inches and a foot with a few that stretched to 15 inches. "And these fish were fighters," Marsh said. They danced until they were inside her brand-new "ghost net," made of clear rubber mesh, an accessory she had bought specifically for this trip.

"Every fish had its own story," Marsh remembers. "Each way the fly floated was different, the way it drifted down a seam, the way the trout put its nose out of the water and took it."

Hours trickled by and a few cottonball clouds crawled across the warm, sapphire sky. The fish gorged themselves on the tiny mayfly duns as well as on Marsh's fly, which she said she watched glide down the riffles "until it just disappeared" into another trout's mouth. She had too much fun to even eat her own lunch.

"When you're experiencing fishing like that, you don't want to stop for anything," she said. "There's nothing better than standing with the current rushing all around you, with a buffalo standing behind you, holding a wild trout in your hand and not being able to wait to revive it and release it so you can catch it again. That's the experience of Yellowstone."

Marsh noticed a lone, bull bison upstream from where Harbin stood. In the late afternoon "that big ol' buffalo," as Marsh called it, started to chug down the far bank, "at a pretty good clip." The buffalo motored so intently that dust devils sprouted each time one of its hooves left the ground. Harbin was unconcerned, but Marsh was unnerved.

An iconic American animal, bison are showstoppers—and sometimes traffic stoppers—in Yellowstone. PHOTO BY NATE SCHWEBER

"I said, 'If that thing crosses the river, I'm out of here,'" she said. "There was no way I was going to let that bull buffalo give me a little love nudge."

Sure enough, the bison plunged into the river about 15 feet upstream from Harbin and cut a wake to Marsh's side. That buffalo came freight-training down Marsh's bank, and, she swears, she could literally see her reflection in that bull's big, black, eightball-sized eye.

She still isn't sure what happened next. Neither is Harbin.

"I turned around, and she was magically transported across the deep water up onto the other bank," Harbin said. "I accused her of walking on water."

Marsh, who stands roughly five feet high, doesn't deny it.

"In all reality, I can't tell you how I got to the other side, but I was motivated," she said. "I do know I had a terrible time crossing back over."

The bison incident was the only thing that entire day that put the fish down. Whether she passed over them or through them, the pod of rising trout that Marsh casted to had scattered, not to return.

Marsh left Ojo Caliente feeling like she was levitating.

"Not in all my years of fishing have I ever had a day like that before," she said. "It wasn't until we were walking back, realizing that we caught and released more than 100 trout, that I realized I was walking 10 feet off the ground."

45 Lewis Lake

Tom Bie

The Yellowstone landscape was chalked in a lunar glow, and the banks of deep, cold Lewis Lake were lined with a dozen or more crazed fishermen who, like werewolves, only came out underneath the full moon.

For years, Tom Bie, a former Grand Teton National Park fishing guide, counted down the days with his fellow guides until the September full moon. Then, in blackness, they lit out for Lewis Lake to catch hefty lake trout from shore as that big, pale orb rose in the sky.

Trout: Lake trout averaging 18 to 22 inches and brown trout averaging 14 to 20 inches with many a whole lot bigger; brook trout averaging 16 to 18 inches.

Bugs: Leeches, damselfly nymphs, scuds; periodic hatches of caddis and red ants.

Suggested fly box: Black, tan, and olive Woolly Buggers size 4 to 8; Clouser Minnows, JJ Specials, and Tequeelys size 2 to 6; Parachute Adamses size 12 to 18; Elk Hair Caddis size 14 to 16; Prince and Hare's Ear nymphs size 14 to 18; tan scuds size 14; Elk Hair Caddis size 14; red ants size 16.

Key techniques: Strip streamers and leech patterns; watch for hatches and rising trout.

Best times: May through June; also September through November.

Directions: South Entrance Road goes past the east side of Lewis Lake and has several pullouts. The Lewis Lake Campground has parking spaces.

Special rules: Limit five combined trout, including lake trout, brook trout, and no more than two brown trout; only one more than 20 inches.

"It was just a real different, unique experience," said Bie, today the editor and publisher of *Drake* magazine based in Fort Collins, Colorado.

On those few early fall nights when the full moon "makes the night like daylight," as Bie said, big Lewis Lake mackinaw cruise close enough that fly anglers can catch them on glow-in-the-dark streamers thrown from shore on sink-tip lines. To a handful of fishing guides, delirious after a summer of hard work and with just a short time to go before the end of the season, the opportunity to catch strange, big trout was too much to resist, even if it meant getting home at 4 o'clock in the morning and then waking two hours later for a full day rowing on the Snake River.

"We were looking for any sort of opportunity to go fishing after work or at night and not have to pass up a day of guiding," Bie said. "Hard-core fly-fishing guys are going to figure out every angle to catch a fish."

These troutheads were particularly eager to catch lake trout, a species of giant char far different than the cutthroats, browns, and rainbows they chased in rivers. Most of the year, Lewis Lake mackinaws stay down deep and are nearly inaccessible with a fly rod. But in September, under a full moon, they come near shore. Adding to the allure is the fact that a moonlight fishing session on Lewis Lake could yield as many as 30 fish weighing from three to five pounds each, "substantially larger than what we were getting out of the river," Bie said. Plus there was always the possibility of hooking up with a serious monster.

"Lake trout were kind of an exotic, fascinating species to us because we so rarely got a chance to catch them. We didn't really see why they were this horrendous, ecological disaster," he said. "And you could go out and fish for these lake trout and no one cared, because the park officials didn't even want them there."

Lewis Lake, named in honor of Meriwether Lewis—who never came within 50 miles of Yellowstone—was historically fishless until it was stocked with lake trout and brown trout in 1890. Those two species have both flourished in the lake, which is the third biggest body of water in Yellowstone.

Bie said fishing for lake trout at night in Lewis Lake was "fishing by feel." He would cast into the darkness, wait for his line to sink, and then slowly retrieve his streamer.

Sometimes the take of a lake trout would be very subtle, "and sometimes they would just hammer it," Bie said. He could tell when one of the fishermen in a float tube hooked onto a good one because they would start yelling, getting towed around by the big fish. "They probably had beer in their float tube, too," Bie said. When the shore anglers lined up next to him landed a laker, they turned their headlamps on to see and unhook the fish. "There would be this constant flashing of headlamps on and off," Bie said. "And you wouldn't hear anything but splashing."

A giant brown trout pulled from the dark depths of Lewis Lake underneath a full moon as a bull elk sounded its piercing shriek in the distance. Not a bad consolation prize after not catching any lake trout. PHOTO BY NATE SCHWEBER

Sometimes the lake trout would strike practically at Bie's ankles. He said he was continuously amazed at how far into shore the lake trout would follow his streamer.

"Right up to the point where you were about to raise up and make another cast," he said, "you'd get a strike."

Each time he caught a lake trout, which he described as "a beautiful fish with some very sharp teeth on them," he would "release it and then go for the next one."

Standing chest-high in cold, deep lake water catching big char from the Great Lakes under a Yellowstone full moon was "trippy," Bie said, particularly when he would gaze at the moonlit shadows of dead trees that burned in the fires of 1988.

"It makes the silhouettes of the landscape that much more eerie," he said. "But that's part of the attraction of Yellowstone; it's a freaky place."

On the drive back to Jackson as the first wisps of dawn cleansed the sky, Bie said he would enjoy the scenery.

"It was either full moonlight or almost dawn," he said. "One of the most gorgeous drives ever."

Greeting other guides on the river later that morning made for giggles stifled by yawns, Bie said. None of the clients knew what their boat captain had been doing all night long.

"That's the thing about Yellowstone," Bie said. "You could always do weird stuff."

Wanting to write with authority about this spooky experience, I went to Lewis Lake in the dark and tried to catch a lake trout in moonlight. I failed. But I caught something else instead: a six-pound brown trout, almost as big around as an NFL football.

Quagmire

There is still no definite answer to the million-dollar question, *how did lake trout get into Yellowstone Lake?*

Genetic tests showed that the lake trout that got loose in Yellowstone Lake came from Lewis Lake. The official consensus is that a rogue fisherman, a "bucket biologist," or maybe a small group, caught lake trout in Lewis Lake and drove them over to Yellowstone Lake. Scientific evidence suggests there may have been multiple illegal stockings between the mid-1980s and the mid-1990s.[1] The Park Service offered a $10,000 reward for information, posters for which still hang in the Bridge Bay Marina. Law enforcement investigated. Today the culprit is still unknown along with the question, *does he realize what he has done?*

A few speculated that maybe birds like eagles or osprey yanked mackinaw out of Lewis Lake and dropped them into Yellowstone Lake. Scientists are skeptical because it is rare that a raptor ever catches a deepwater dwelling lake trout, and it's even more doubtful that a breeding pair could survive the trauma of being clawed, suffocated, and dumped. Some have also hypothesized that perhaps the lakers were transported by helicopters that dipped water buckets into Lewis Lake to fight the great fires of 1988. Again, scientists are dubious that the buckets would have reached deep enough to scoop up lake trout, to say nothing of them surviving the ordeal. There is even an obscure reference to 10,000 "yearling lake trout" being stocked in "the Yellowstone River above the falls" in 1890 in a book by historian Hiram Martin Chittenden.[2] Modern historians are suspicious of this because the stocking doesn't appear in other records; plus if it were true, then why were lake trout not confirmed, nor their fast and terrible damage felt, for a century?

As is the case with quagmires, the question *how* is less important than the question, *what now?* In February 1995, the Park Service and U.S. Fish and Wildlife Service officials called an emergency meeting in Gardiner, Montana. Fearing that the lake trout population in Yellowstone Lake was about to blow up, they decided to fight back with the resources they had, which weren't much compared to the challenge, biologist Robert Gresswell said.

A netting boat pulls up to the Bridge Bay Marina after a day hauling destructive lake trout out of Yellowstone Lake. These boats could be the cutthroat's best hope for survival in the lake. PHOTO BY NATE SCHWEBER

First of all, Yellowstone Lake, at 89,000 acres and nearly four trillion gallons of water, is gargantuan.[3] It is frozen over half the year and has only a few marinas from which to launch fishing boats. Secondly, the Park Service was, and is, stretched thin for money and manpower. In the beginning, the Park Service could only scrounge up an old boat, man it with a skeleton crew, and use nets designed for fish sampling, not lake trout eradicating, Gresswell said. Around 2000, the Park Service got a second boat and a few more workers, and lake trout catches began to rise dramatically, but not in proportion to their exploding numbers.

It was obvious that the Park Service still needed more help. In 2008, after another emergency meeting, the Park Service hired Hickey Brothers Fisheries, a Wisconsin-based fishing crew that was one of many responsible for the overharvest and eventual collapse of the lake trout fishery in Lake Michigan, the ancestral home of the lake trout that invaded Yellowstone Lake.

Todd Stuth, captain and co-owner of Hickey Brothers, said that his crews net unwanted lake trout out of several Western lakes, but no longer fish for them at home. Through trying to preserve this fish's stocks in the Great Lakes, the Hickey Brothers have learned an enormous amount about lake trout habits, like where they congregate, when they spawn, and the best depths at which to find them. In Lake Michigan, the company uses this

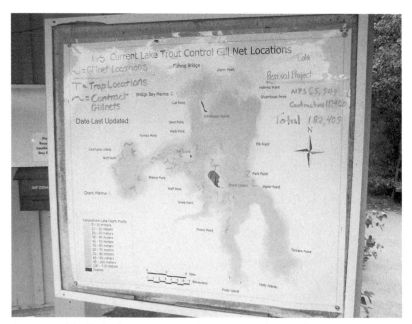

A map outside the Bridge Bay Marina charts spots on huge Yellowstone Lake where netting boats target voracious, nonnative lake trout. PHOTO BY NATE SCHWEBER

information to avoid lake trout; in Yellowstone Lake, they use it to kill them. They're getting better, he said.

"Every year we're able to learn more and drive those stocks down," he said.

The Hickey Brothers fish differently than the park crew. They use live entrapment nets that can help them harvest lake trout while releasing cutthroats alive. The company also lays gill nets in water thickest with cutthroats, unlike the park crews. The Hickey Brothers then check these gill nets hourly to minimize cutthroat kill but maximize the takeout of the really big lake trout that feed on adult cutts.

Biologists discovered some spawning areas after they tagged and tracked a few lake trout that they dubbed "Judas fish." One tiny factor that could play to the Park Service's advantage is that even in massive bodies of water like the Great Lakes, lake trout tend to spawn in just a few areas. Unlike other trout, which pair up, lake trout spawn in clusters. Females lay their eggs on rocky, underwater outcrops, and males swarm above them depositing their milt.

By following the Judas fish to the spawning beds where the lake trout congregate, workers have been able to harvest boatloads of them, many of them females just on the verge of laying tens of thousands of eggs.

A park employee hoists two large lake trout hauled out of Yellowstone Lake. In addition to the netting program, scientists are trying to develop alternative methods to help control lake trout in Yellowstone Lake in the hopes that its once-abundant cutthroat trout population might one day come back.

In the summer of 2011, scientists tagged 140 more lake trout in Yellowstone Lake and placed 28 acoustic receivers throughout the lake in order to monitor where these fish swim.[4] Biologists like Todd Koel and Gresswell hope that this will turn up even more spawning sites.

The netting program costs around a million dollars a year, park officials say. Workers puncture the air bladders of the dead lake trout and throw their bodies back into the lake so their nutrients will be reabsorbed into the ecosystem. Park officials explored the option of either selling the lake trout or donating them to food banks, but found that the costs of processing, freezing, and shipping the meat would take away from the amount of money that could be spent on the main objective: to eradicate this harmful, nonnative species.

Dr. Jackson A. Gross, a fisheries biologist who has worked to keep nonnative Asian carp out of the Great Lakes and battled introduced northern pike that are destroying salmon fisheries in Alaska, has partnered with Gresswell and used money donated from the East Yellowstone Trout Unlimited chapter to develop new ways to kill lake trout. Some of Gross's most promising ideas include using a giant water vacuum to suck up the lake trout eggs, shattering the egg membranes with sound waves, electrocuting the eggs, and suffocating them in silt.

These techniques could be used in tandem with the gill-netting program, he said.

"We keep thinking there's a silver bullet for everything," he said. "I'm talking about using multiple strategies in concert with each other."

A byproduct of Yellowstone Lake's sickened ecosystem is that many of the only cutthroat trout remaining are old and large, big enough not to be eaten by lake trout. Specimens like this one, spawning in one of the lake's eastside tributaries, are now a rare sight. PHOTO BY NATE SCHWEBER

Gresswell even dreams about a final strategy. Scientists have been able to genetically engineer fruit flies, pink bollworms, and some species of fish like carp and tilapia so that they produce only male offspring.[5] What if, Gresswell asks, the bulk of the lake trout in Yellowstone Lake were gill-netted, then most of the survivors' eggs were killed on the spawning beds using Gross's techniques, and then a few genetically engineered lake trout were planted so that the only baby lake trout born in Yellowstone Lake were all males?

"It's a pipe dream," Gresswell said. "But you could envision a possibility to get the very last one."

That dream is still many years away. As of this writing, thousands of man-hours and millions of dollars have been spent, and the greatest Yellowstone cutthroat trout fishery on earth is still gone. We'll never get the first two back. Time will tell if there's still hope for the last one.

46 Shoshone Lake

Bruce Staples

Because giant Shoshone Lake is the largest backcountry lake in the continental United States—no roads, no buildings, no telephone poles, nothing—Bruce Staples has visited this high, cold place since the early 1970s.

Shoshone's abundance of very big fish, lunker lakers, brawny browns, and even the occasional trophy brook trout made it his favorite spot.

Trout: Lake trout averaging 18 to 22 inches and brown trout averaging 14 to 20 inches with many a whole lot bigger; brook trout averaging 16 to 18 inches.

Bugs: Leeches, damselfly nymphs, scuds; periodic hatches of caddis and, in high summer, red ants.

Suggested fly box: Black, brown, and olive Woolly Buggers size 2 to 8; Clouser Minnows, JJ Specials, Tequeelys, Marabou Mudlers, Light Spruce, and Zonkers size 2 to 8; damselfly nymphs size 8 to 10; tan scuds size 14; Elk Hair Caddis size 14; Parachute Adamses size 12 to 18; Prince and Hare's Ear nymphs size 14 to 18; red ants size 16.

Key techniques: Strip streamers and leech patterns; watch for hatches and rising trout.

Best times: May through June; also September through November.

Directions: Park at the DeLacy Creek Trailhead, about nine miles south of Old Faithful and nine miles north of West Thumb, and hike about three miles to Shoshone Lake. Or park at the Dogshead Trailhead and hike about five miles in to Shoshone Lake.

Special rules: Limit of five combined trout, including lake trout, brook trout, and no more than two brown trout, only one more than 20 inches.

Shoshone Lake at the headwaters of the Lewis River Channel is an excellent place to fish in the fall for big, spawning brown trout and the lake trout that follow them. PHOTO BY NATE SCHWEBER

"It's like stepping back into the nineteenth century," said Staples, 70, a New England native who had worked for decades as a chemist at the Idaho National Lab.

Shoshone Lake, named in honor of the Shoshone tribe, was fishless until 1890 when it was stocked with lake trout and brown trout, both of which flourished in the big water. By the early twentieth century, Shoshone Lake had such a bounty that commercial fishermen worked the lake to supply Yellowstone Park hotels and restaurants with fresh dinners. Ultimately, decades of overuse, abuse, pollution, and trash led park supervisors to shut down the commercial enterprise and allow the dirt road that led to the lake to go to seed. The land returned to its primitive state.[1]

Early and late in the season, Staples packs a float tube in to Shoshone Lake and fishes scud, leech, and streamer patterns on full-sinking lines near weed beds, where trout congregate. Good days will yield as many as 30 lake trout between 17 inches and 21 inches with the occasional 5-pounder or a 2-foot-long brawling brown trout to keep things interesting. On very rare occasions, Staples said he has reeled in jewel-like, 18-inch brook trout that washed down from one of Shoshone Lake's feeder streams and grew giant in the depths.

Shoshone Lake doesn't offer easy fishing. Shore casting isn't a very viable option, save for late in autumn near the outlet to the Lewis River Channel where hormone-hopped brown trout congregate and big lakers follow—both mash streamers, Staples said.

Otherwise the vast water is best fished with a float tube, which must be packed in via the three-mile DeLacy Creek Trail or the five-mile Dogshead Trail beginning near Lewis Lake.

Another way to reach Shoshone Lake is to canoe in via the meandering Lewis River Channel. Staples said this was how he first began exploring, and fishing, Shoshone Lake. During some of his early visits, he said, he would only fish the deep parts of the lake, catching perhaps two fish in three days, lake trout in the neighborhood of 12 pounds.

Boat travel can be risky on Shoshone Lake. The lake is vast, and the water is frigid. Unpredictable storms frequently whip the surface into four-foot swells. Some boaters have drowned in Shoshone Lake; others have succumbed to hypothermia.

"The lake gets real rough," Staples said. "Just like Yellowstone Lake, it can be downright dangerous. When a snow squall or a thundershower comes up, you need to go to shore, hole up, and wait the storm out. By evening you can get back to your campsite."

As Shoshone Lake fishes best in June and again in late September and October, rugged weather is part of the package. Staples said he's been snowed on at Shoshone Lake around the Fourth of July. He remembers a foot of

Lake trout, like this one, are a common catch in both Lewis and Shoshone Lakes, as well as the Lewis River Channel, which runs between them. Big lake trout follow spawning brown trout into the channel in the fall.

snow piling up on the banks while he fished Shoshone Lake on a September day, before the mercury dropped to ten below zero in his campsite that night.

The bears can be pesky, too. Staples said he's never had a problem with a grizzly around Shoshone Lake, but black bears have raided his camp.

Once Staples said that he and six friends planned a "big ol' fish fry" on the lakeshore at the end of a multiday backcountry trip to Shoshone Lake. The anglers hauled in around two-dozen lake trout, perfect for fillets. "You batter them up, and they're superb eating," Staples said.

The fishermen put their trout on stringers, chains that hook through the fish's gills so they can be kept alive in the lake but anchored to shore, guaranteeing the freshest meal possible.

Around five o'clock in the afternoon, the men came to clean their catch and found nothing but fish heads bobbing on the ends of the stringers. Black bear prints covered the bank.

"It was pretty obvious a black bear had come by and ate all the fish," Staples said. "We had to go back out and catch more. As I recall, we had a midnight dinner that night."

Still, the weather and the bears, the big waves and the cold nights are all elements of what people like Staples seek when they come to Shoshone Lake—not a trace of man, nothing but nature in abundance.

"I love the ambiance of the place; you don't hear any man-made noises," Staples said. "And I know I can catch fish that average 19 or 20 inches."

47 Madison River at Barns Hole

Rich Jehle

It's not the fish Rich Jehle caught in the Barns Hole section of the Madison River that keep him coming back, even though those fish are the biggest ones he's ever landed in his life.

Jehle keeps coming back because of the one that got away.

Trout: Resident rainbow and brown trout averaging 8 to 14 inches as well as spawners from Hebgen Lake that average 16 to 20 inches with a large number of even bigger fish. Also plenty of whitefish and a very remote chance of catching a grayling washed down from Grebe Lake.

Bugs: Mayflies, including *Baetis*, Pale Morning Duns, Gray Drakes, and Tricos; caddisflies; stoneflies, including Salmonflies and little yellow stones; and terrestrials, including hoppers, ants, and beetles.

Suggested fly box: Black, brown, and olive Woolly Buggers size 2 to 8; Clouser Minnows, JJ Specials, Tequeelys, Marabou Muddlers, Light Spruce, and Zonkers size 2 to 8; Montana and Bitch Creek nymphs size 4 to 8.

Key techniques: Dredge nymphs deep; swing and strip streamers.

Best times: May and June; also September and October.

Directions: Follow the dirt road on the left-hand side of West Entrance Road about a half mile from the entrance gates to the park.

Special rules: Catch-and-release for rainbow trout, brown trout, grayling, and whitefish. Make sure all gear used in any other water has been cleaned and dried in order to protect against the spread of invasive species and disease, such as the New Zealand mudsnail. Check the current regulations.

In the fall, Barns Hole is packed with brown trout running up from Hebgen Lake—and the anglers who pursue them. PHOTO BY NATE SCHWEBER

"I tell you what," said Jehle, a park ranger in West Yellowstone. "Some of those fish in Barns Hole will clean your clock."

Jehle got his clock cleaned on his last cast on the last day of the 2006 season. He had waded across the Madison upstream from the second Barns Hole in order to fish the far bank, away from the crowds near the road.

It was almost dark, and Jehle had caught a few rainbows about a foot to 14 inches long plus some big whitefish. He said he fished a brown nymph that he tied with a sparkly tail, and he worked hard to keep the fly as close to the river bottom as possible.

Jehle cast and watched as his strike indicator "went down hard," in the middle of a strong, deep run. Jehle yanked back on his rod, setting the hook.

"This thing took off straight across the river, zipped my line out," Jehle said.

His rod buckled over and the reel screamed. The line was stripped to the backing in seconds. He said he could "tell that whatever I hooked was significantly bigger than anything I'd ever hooked in the Barns Hole before."

Suddenly, the line went slack. Jehle staggered, and his heart pounded. He never even caught a glimpse of the creature that mashed his fly; but when he reeled in his line, he got another clue about its size. The beast didn't snap his line. It broke his hook.

Jehle has seen anglers wrestle 8-pound browns from Barns Hole, and a friend of his caught one that went 9 pounds. He has a photo of a man hefting a 30-inch brown, which surely must've weighed 10 pounds, from that very river.

Could the one that got away have been one of those?

Barns Hole is world famous for its fall spawning run of massive brown trout up from Hebgen Lake, a trout warehouse just beyond the western border of the park. Big rainbows follow the browns. Anglers travel far and wide to take turns dredging the depths of Barns Hole. For West Yellowstone residents, fishing "The Hole" is practically religion.

"It's what everybody's doing; it's what everybody's talking about," Jehle said. "It's in the friggin' paper."

Barns Hole isn't a single spot, nor is it technically a hole in the traditional, pool-like sense of the word. Rather, Barns Hole is a series of broad, fast-moving, rock-bottomed runs. The area used to be the site of holding stations for horse-drawn carriages that brought tourists into Yellowstone in the park's early years.[1] The barns are nothing but rubble now. A dirt road about a half mile in from the west entrance leads about a mile down to the Madison River and forks right to the first Barns Hole. A left-hand fork leads to the second hole.

Barns Hole might be the single most crowded fishing spot in Yellowstone on a late September or October day. Jehle likens the first Barns Hole, where dozens of cars pack the parking lot on weekends, to an English chalk stream where anglers wait their turn.

"You fish it through and then go back to the end of the line," he said. "It's like riding on a merry-go-round."

One veteran Barns Hole visitor tells a story of how she and her friends made cards marked 0 through 10 and rated each angler fishing the hole like judges at the Olympics.

Jehle, a park ranger since 1987, said he never fished Barns Hole until 2003 because the crowds intimidated him. He only gave it a shot because he lives just five minutes away and heard stories about the big ones. He caught a story of his own fast.

"Within 10 minutes, I had this gigantic fish on there that took me 20 minutes to land," Jehle said of the first 22-inch, 4-pound rainbow he took from the hole. A year later in the same spot, he caught a brown trout about the same size, a fish that he notes is "fairly common" in Barns Hole.

"It took me a while to get the guts to go give it a try," Jehle said. "But once you get a taste of one of those big hogs yanking your rod in half, you'll put up with the crowds a little bit."

The bruisers start to muscle their way into Barns Hole in late September, and Jehle said the fishing only gets better the closer it gets to Yellowstone's season closer, the first Sunday in November. Because the fall-run fish are always on the move, anglers need to be constantly at the ready. Jehle

There are actually three spots considered "Barns Hole," and all of them are swift, fast runs. Barns Hole got its name from the barns that used to stand on the banks of the Madison River that held the horses that drew carriages bringing early tourists into Yellowstone. PHOTO BY NATE SCHWEBER

describes the process as "hours and hours of complete boredom interspersed by moments of sheer terror."

"The fish are always moving that time of year, so the 5-pounder that wasn't in that spot a minute ago is there now," Jehle said. "You really have to have some luck being in the right place at the right time with the right presentation."

Jehle recommends stripping big streamers to try and "aggravate the fish into striking," or dead-drifting big, gaudy stonefly nymphs "to get the big trout's attention." He said nymphers need to be vigilant to use plenty of weight and be ready for the river's might.

"One of the challenges of Barns Hole is it's not slow water," Jehle said "It's deep, fast runs, and while you get a long drift, you've got about five seconds because it's moving quick."

As with any place on the Madison River, or in Yellowstone Park for that matter, Jehle implores anglers not to get so focused on fishing that they miss out on their surroundings. Jehle has watched bald eagles swoop in to the trees over Barns Hole and has seen otters splash in front of him. Elsewhere on the Madison, he's had to take cover as a herd of bison swam across the river, straight at him.

"The Madison is just an exciting river because you never know what's going to happen," Jehle said. "You just know there are hogs in there."

48 Lewis River Channel

Greg Thomas

Since he learned to fish, Greg Thomas, author of fly-fishing guidebooks to Wyoming, Idaho, and Washington and editor of *Fly Rod & Reel* magazine, has been obsessed with *Salmo trutta*, the brown trout.

"I was just fascinated with brown trout to begin with," he said from his home near the banks of the famous brown trout waters of the Madison River in Ennis, Montana.

Trout: Lake trout averaging 18 to 22 inches and brown trout averaging 14 to 20 inches with many a whole lot bigger.

Bugs: Stonefly, caddis, and mayfly nymphs.

Suggested fly box: Black, brown, and olive Woolly Buggers size 2 to 8; Egg-Sucking Leeches size 4 to 8; Clouser Minnows, JJ Specials, Tequeelys, Marabou Mudlers, Light Spruce, and Zonkers size 2 to 8; Montana and Bitch Creek nymphs size 4 to 8; Copper Johns size 16 to 18; egg patterns.

Key techniques: Strip streamers and leech patterns; dead-drift nymphs and egg patterns.

Best times: May through June; also September through November.

Directions: Park at the Shoshone/Dogshead Trailhead near the northern tip of Lewis Lake and follow the trail 4.6 miles to the outlet of the Lewis River Channel on Shoshone Lake. The Lewis Channel Trail follows the stream.

Special rules: Limit of five combined trout, including lake, brook, and no more than two brown trout; only one bigger than 20 inches. Make sure all gear used in any other water has been cleaned and dried in order to protect against the spread of invasive species and disease, such as the New Zealand mudsnail.

The Lewis River Channel, shown here at its mouth with Lewis Lake, is an excellent place to catch lake trout as well as big browns. PHOTO BY NATE SCHWEBER

In Yellowstone, Thomas's quest for big browns led him miles through thick bear country to the Lewis River Channel, a four-mile stretch of stream that meanders between Lewis Lake and Shoshone Lake, the largest backcountry lake in the continental United States.

Thomas first visited the channel years ago when he lived in Jackson Hole, Wyoming, and asked the guides at local fly shops where the secret money holes were where the giant brown trout lived. That fall he found 3-, 5-, and 8-pound brown trout glistening in the Lewis River Channel like goldbricks at Fort Knox.

"You can see them stack up in these holes," Thomas said.

Astonishingly, the big browns are followed into the channel each fall by even bigger lake trout. The lakers possibly come to feed on brown trout eggs, or more likely, the brown trout themselves. Giants of 10, 12, and even 15 pounds are not uncommon.

"If you spend time there, you're going to run into one of those fish," Thomas said. "And hopefully you can hold on and land 'em."

Beginning around mid-September, when Yellowstone's crisp autumn air sharpens to a blade, the browns start pouring into the channel, which also has a sprinkling of brook trout.

"You see these gigantic golden sides and dark brown backs coming out of the water, rolling and jumping," Thomas said. "As an angler, if that doesn't get your blood boiling, you've got to check for a pulse."

The Lewis River Channel runs approximately four miles between Shoshone Lake and Lewis Lake, pictured here. A trail follows most of this distance. PHOTO BY NATE SCHWEBER

The party lasts until Yellowstone's fishing season closes the first Sunday of November, but anglers must beware. The brown trout aren't the only creatures in the Yellowstone autumn acting on ancient impulses. Bears abound, and as winter approaches, the bruins enter a state called hyperphagia. It's a feeding frenzy in which bears' tempers flare as they desperately stuff themselves to pack on fat for their long hibernation. Some of North America's most gruesome griz attacks came from hyperphagic bears.

"You can't go to the Lewis River Channel in the fall to fish for brown trout without giving equal thought to whether you're going to get out alive," Thomas said. "On the hike in, you'll see fresh bear sign. As you should be, you're on high alert, on edge, and it makes you feel alive."

It's at least a five-mile trek through lodgepole forest on relatively level terrain to reach the Lewis River Channel from the Dogshead Trailhead. In the fall, the air is filled with the whinnying sound of bull elk bugling.

The channel itself is a meadow stream, smoothing below undercut banks, through deep runs and pools, and occasionally bouncing over shallow riffles. The brown trout pack into pools and runs, and beneath the undercuts. Thomas said that in any given hole, the aggressive browns mash streamers stripped past their hooked jaws. After that, Thomas said, anglers may need to tie on an egg pattern or a size 18 or 20 Flashback Pheasant Tail to "nymph out" the cagey ones.

The upper part of the Lewis River Channel is a freestone stream. Here in the middle its character changes to flatter, broader, deeper water where lake trout congregate by the thousands. PHOTO BY NATE SCHWEBER

One of Thomas's favorite patterns for the channel is one he ties himself. It is a variation of the traditional Egg-Sucking Leech. Thomas said he ties the fly "much sparser" than ones sold in stores. He uses black marabou for the tail, two to three strands of peacock herl for the body, webby black hackle, and a wrap or two of hot pink chenille for the head. No weight.

Thomas said he dead-drifts that pattern through deep runs and pools. He also strips it like a streamer in Shoshone Lake, near the channel's mouth.

"One of the things all anglers have in common is we want to catch the biggest fish of any given species that we can," Thomas said. "This is one of the places in Yellowstone where you can catch a really large fish."

49 Madison River at Baker's Hole

Doug Peacock

Few people have seen as much of the interior of Yellowstone National Park as has Doug Peacock, a self-described "militant conservationist," Vietnam veteran, author, and fly fisherman.

His favorite fishing spot in Yellowstone is Baker's Hole on the Madison River. That section of the river actually S-curves in and out of Yellowstone Park along the border it shares with the state of Montana. Upstream from Baker's Hole, the river jags southeast through backcountry, eventually meeting up with West Entrance Road, which it runs beside to its headwaters at the

---

Trout: Resident rainbow and brown trout averaging 8 to 14 inches as well as spawners from Hebgen Lake that average 16 to 20 inches with a large number of even bigger fish. Also plenty of whitefish and a very remote chance of catching a grayling washed down from Grebe Lake.

Bugs: Mayflies, including *Baetis*, Pale Morning Duns, Gray Drakes, and Tricos; caddisflies; stoneflies, including Salmonflies and little yellow stones; and terrestrials, including hoppers, ants, and beetles.

Suggested fly box: Black, brown, and olive Woolly Buggers size 2 to 8; Clouser Minnows, JJ Specials, Tequeelys, Marabou Mudlers, Light Spruce, and Zonkers size 2 to 8; Montana and Bitch Creek nymphs size 4 to 8.

Key techniques: Dredge nymphs deep; swing and strip streamers.

Best times: May and June; also September and October.

Directions: Turn into the Baker's Hole Campground on Highway 191 just north of West Yellowstone, Montana.

Special rules: Catch-and-release for all species of whitefish, grayling, and trout, except brook trout.

---

junction of the Gibbon and Firehole Rivers. Peacock said he prefers visiting that dogleg section, which he calls "the wildest part of the Madison River."

"You have to bushwhack and wade through some beaver dams to get back there, but my favorite holes are the most remote," he said from his home in Emigrant, Montana. "That's the best fishing I've ever had."

For around a decade starting in the mid-1970s, Peacock said, come October he would park his small house trailer in the Forest Service campground at Baker's Hole and stay all month. He said he caught legions of brown trout, 2- to 4-pound runners from Hebgen Lake, plus one memorable monster that busted 7 pounds. "That's a bigger fish than I care to catch, really," he said.

Peacock became a fixture in the Yellowstone backcountry in the late 1960s after he returned from Vietnam, where he served as a Green Beret combat medic. As he chronicled in his riveting book, *Grizzly Years: In Search of the American Wilderness*, he was so seared and disillusioned from war that he sought out the remote, wild country of the Northern Rockies. Through his encounters with the awesome grizzly bear, he said, he regained his sense of humanity.

He also spent a lot of time fishing, but not for sport. "This is going to make the catch-and-release fishermen puke," Peacock said, "but we were really poor, and we lived off fish. We made trout chowder, trout noodle casseroles, trout meat sandwiches; we ate trout until they were coming out of our ears." Creel limits were different then. Today, it's catch-and-release for all brown and rainbow trout on the Madison River inside the park.

Back in the 1960s and 1970s, Peacock ventured into Yellowstone in April, when the snows began to melt, to track grizzlies. Come June, he would head farther north and west, to work as a ranger in the northern Cascade Mountains in northeast Washington and as a fire lookout in Glacier National Park. In September he would return to Yellowstone to photograph griz. Come October, his work would be done, and he would have weeks to fish the Madison River before ice drove him back to his wintering grounds in the Southwest near the Mexican border.

Peacock said he fell in love with the Madison at Baker's Hole because the trout were abundant and big. "Every day you could catch a dozen fish between 14 and 22 inches if you wanted," he said. Peacock began each day by fishing, then ventured into the park to watch wildlife, and returned an hour before sunset to fish some more, his beloved collie dog Larry lying patiently on the bank behind him.

At night Peacock and friends would play cards, drink whiskey, and tie flies. They kept their eyes peeled on hikes for materials like duck hackle or, best of all, blue heron feathers. They wound patterns that Peacock described thusly: "You don't know what the hell it is in the water, but the fish like it." His one suggestion for fly tiers embodies this spirit.

"You should have some fun inventing big nymph and streamer patterns because everything works there," he said.

It is ironic that Peacock spent so much time deep in the Yellowstone backcountry in spring and early fall looking for grizzly bears, because, come October, they would be all around him on the Madison River. Peacock said that when snow fell, he would be astonished at the number of grizzly tracks he found, some of them in his campground, some of them simply enormous. "You realize how many grizzlies are in a place like Baker's Hole," he said.

One of Peacock's most treasured memories is fishing Baker's Hole with his late father, Marion E. Peacock. A grizzly stood on the opposite bank. A moose foraged in the willows behind them. Peacock said that during moments like that, "you realize you're so lucky to be alive and so privileged to have all those components living in your life."

He added, "I was like a pig in shit."

Peacock fished Baker's Hole with many friends, including renowned fly tier Jack Gartside. One buddy whom Peacock brought to Baker's Hole, but couldn't get to wet a line, was author and activist Edward Abbey. Both men dedicated their lives to protecting wild places and wildlife. Abbey wrote about the character George Washington Hayduke, an environmental hero, in his rollicking masterwork, *The Monkey Wrench Gang*. Peacock was Abbey's inspiration for Hayduke.

Peacock helped bury Abbey, who died in 1989, "in a little illegal grave in the Arizona desert," he said. Peacock wrote about the burial in his book, *Walking It Off: A Veteran's Chronicle of War and Wilderness*. Of the character Abbey modeled after him, Peacock said, "I am whatever earthly is left of Hayduke; I buried the rest of him when I buried Ed."

Baker's Hole holds Peacock's memories of Abbey, of his dad, of Jack Gartside, and even of Larry, the faithful collie.

"I go there to visit my ghosts," Peacock said. "My father, my friends, my dog, Abbey—they're all gone. They all died early on me. But they're all there on the Madison in Yellowstone. I go back and talk to them."

Hotter and Drier

As complicated as it is dealing with lake trout in Yellowstone Lake, it could seem like tic-tac-toe compared to a problem that a chorus of scientists say jeopardizes trout survival in the coming centuries: climate change.

Matt Skoglund, an attorney with the Natural Resources Defense Council in Bozeman, calls climate change "the most dire threat that Yellowstone trout face down the road."

Years of drought that walloped Yellowstone in the first decade of the 2000s may have been a substantial third factor in the wipeout of Yellowstone Lake cutthroats because spawning streams dried up, biologists say. Three different seasons during that decade, park officials were forced to put extra fishing restrictions on more than 200 miles of streams, including the Madison, Firehole, Yellowstone, Lamar, Gardner, Gibbon, Snake, and Bechler Rivers as well as Slough and Soda Butte Creeks, to protect trout stressed by the heat and low water. During these spells, brown and rainbow trout overheated and died and could be seen floating down the Firehole and Madison Rivers.

Yellowstone's climate could spike by 10 degrees F and become like that of Los Angeles, California, by the century's end, according to a 2011 report by the Rocky Mountain Climate Organization and Greater Yellowstone Coalition.[1] The years 2001 to 2010 were the hottest ever recorded in the greater Yellowstone region, and they featured six of the seven worst fire seasons in park history. Summer temperatures rose a full degree more than the worldwide average, and tree rings showed there was less winter snowpack in the region than during any timespan since the thirteenth century.[2] Worldwide statistics showed that the years 2000 to 2010 were 10 of the hottest 11 years recorded since atmospheric measurements began in 1850.[3]

Steve Running, a University of Montana professor who was part of a team that won the Nobel Prize in 2007 for their research on climate change, said trout are at their most vulnerable in late summer, when water is lowest and temperatures are highest. Warmer temperatures and less snow means less water that trout need to survive those crucial times, he said.

"You don't want to paint a picture that a bad year would wipe all the trout out at once," he said. "But what you have to think of is the potential for a gradual, step-by-step decrease in trout starting at the smallest streams and working its way up."

As seems so often to be the case, Yellowstone's cutthroats could be hardest hit. According to that 2011 report, nearly half the cutthroat in the Yellowstone River basin could be wiped out by the century's end.[4] According to another 2011 report, authored by 11 researchers from Trout Unlimited, the U.S. Forest Service, the U.S. Geological Survey, Colorado State University, and the University of Washington, by 2080, native cutthroat trout across the West could lose almost 60 percent of the habitat they have left because of climate change, altered rivers, and competition from nonnative species.[5]

Jack Williams, senior scientist for Trout Unlimited, said there may be a "synergistic effect" between a warming climate and invasive species, such as more habitat for tubifex worms, which carry the exotic parasite responsible for whirling disease. Trout can be hurt in less direct ways, too, he said. For example, warmer temperatures have led to an explosion throughout the Yellowstone region in pine tree–killing beetles, and dead, rust-tinted trees are becoming an increasingly common sight in Yellowstone. More dead trees means less shade in the high country to slow summertime snowmelt. It also means more fuel for potentially devastating fires, which can choke out trout streams with ash and erosion.

Williams points out that despite the vitriolic politics involved with addressing global warming, an overwhelming 97 percent of climate scientists believe that toxic amounts of heat-trapping carbon in the atmosphere, from human-burned fossil fuels like coal, oil, and gasoline, is the cause.[6]

"I think there's an obligation that anglers have to make sure to understand issues like climate change," he said. "And realize that there is more we can do to protect trout."

50 Firehole River at Muleshoe Bend

Joshua Bergen

In the middle of the great park snakes a river like no other, a stream that has a diversity of life that is matchless, from the bison on its banks to the trout in its water.

It is the Firehole River on the last day of fishing season in Yellowstone. Just as the season blossoms here, it fades here, too.

Joshua Bergen, an outdoor writer from Belgrade, Montana, has a tradition to fish the Muleshoe Bend section of the Firehole River the first Sunday each November. He calls it his "closing day ceremony."

Trout: Rainbows and browns averaging 10 to 14 inches, with a few bigger ones too; brookies in the upper reaches; whitefish below Firehole Falls.

Bugs: Mayfly hatches, including Pale Morning Duns and *Baetis*; also midges.

Suggested fly box: Parachute Adamses size 14 to 20; Pale Morning Duns, Blue-Winged Olives, and Sparkle Duns size 16 to 18, Iris Caddis emergers and Elk Hair Caddis size 14 to 20; Hare's Ear, Copper John, Pheasant Tail, and Prince nymphs size 14 to 20; soft-hackle wet flies size 14 to 20; black and olive Woolly Buggers size 6 to 10.

Key techniques: Match the hatch; fish nymphs when no fish are rising. Swinging soft-hackle wet flies can also be very effective here also.

Best times: May through June; also September through November.

Directions: Park at the Midway Geyser Basin and walk upstream through Muleshoe Bend.

Special rules: Fly-fishing only; catch-and-release for browns, rainbows, and whitefish.

Joshua Bergen plays a brown trout at Muleshoe Bend on the Firehole River on the final day of the Yellowstone fishing season. This photo ran with a story he wrote about his experience for the *Bozeman Daily Chronicle*. "It's almost as if right when you needed it, the trout were there to give it to you," he said. PHOTO BY BEN PIERCE

Steam from the Midway Geyser Basin wafts thick on cold days above 7,000 feet. The fog reduces bison on the far bank to just dreamlike, primal shadows. Snowflakes parachute and ice crystals clog fly-rod guides. But the tourists are gone. The shoulder-to-shoulder anglers of high summer are a memory. Even Grand Loop Road is quiet. For Bergen, this spot on this river is just a place to be with friends and fish.

"It's pretty, placid, glassy water; and because the Midway Geyser Basin is right there, the steam floats past you, through you," Bergen said. "It's a one-of-a-kind experience, something you can't do anywhere else in the world."

The Firehole trout keep their springtime zip, even when their cousins in other streams are sleepy with cold. The Firehole is infused with enough hot runoff from geysers to keep it warm enough in the wintertime for bugs to hatch, warm enough for trout to still poke their noses into the air to swallow them.

Bundled in layers of warm clothes inside of thick waders, Bergen casts tiny Sparkle Duns to match the hatches of Blue-Winged Olives. Or he fishes subsurface with a Greg's Emerger to match *Baetis*. Or he swings a size 18, soft-hackle wet fly—a technique he calls "the way to catch fish on the Firehole."

Mostly, he thinks about the fishing season about to pass.

Because it is infused with thermal runoff from geysers, the water in the Firehole River stays warm enough late in the Yellowstone fishing season for trout like this brown to still attack flies with their early season gusto.

"It's so quiet, and there's no other people, so it gives you a chance to look back on your year," Bergen said. "And reflect on where you fished."

The first time Bergen visited the Firehole on closing day, he wrote a story about it for the *Bozeman Daily Chronicle*, where he worked as a reporter. The hour got late, and though he had caught many trout, his companion, the story's photographer, hadn't got a photo for the article yet. Soon the light would be gone.

As if on cue, Bergen drifted a delicate mayfly pattern over a steaming swath of river. A trout rose. Bergen got his fish, a spirited 13-inch brown trout. The paper got a picture.

"It was almost as if right then, right when you needed it," Bergen said, "the trout were there to give it to you."

Epilogue:
Pelican Creek

Pelican Creek could be the only stream in Yellowstone National Park where six inches is bigger than 20 inches.

I learned this a moment after I saw a cutthroat splash near the far side of the creek, sending ripples through water that just moments before had mirrored a big bull bison, now up the bank rolling in a wallow.

In that split second I had in my vision two species of animals for which the Pelican Valley could have been a waterloo, but was instead a watershed. Truly, if Yellowstone had a wildlife crucible, it would be this 50-square-mile wild, rolling valley of sage bluffs and grassy coulees ringed by pine forest.

I had the pleasure of visiting the Pelican Valley in late July 2011 with Bill and Joann Voigt and Rich and Sue Hamstra, coordinators of the park's volunteer fly-fishing program. The Voigts come to Yellowstone each summer from Pennsylvania, where Bill works in the athletics department at a university. Rich Hamstra is a pastor at a church in Michigan, and he told me on the trail that he decided to volunteer for the summer after he landed a grant that came with a single rule: "do something that makes your heart sing."

Park biologists started the volunteer fishing program in 2002. They were then, as they are now, so overwhelmed fighting the lake trout outbreak in Yellowstone Lake that they no longer had enough time or resources to devote to other park waters. The volunteer program solicits private anglers' help to collect data from streams and lakes, plus harvest nonnative trout from certain vulnerable fisheries.

The fact that I was hiking in to fish Pelican Creek was a big deal unto itself. The creek had been closed for the previous seven years because whirling disease was discovered there in 1998.[1] Whirling disease is a parasite, imported from fish hatcheries in Europe, that infects baby trout and eats away at their skeletons. Nerve damage often makes the trout fry swim in uncontrollable circles until they die. This is why the disease is called "whirling." Humans and birds can spread the bug.

By 2011 Todd Koel, Yellowstone's top fisheries biologist, decided that it didn't make sense to keep Pelican Creek closed to anglers out of fear that they might spread the disease. A bird might do it just as easily. Koel figured that he

After decades of poaching, park officials scoured Yellowstone in 1902 for a wildlife census and could find only 23 bison left, all of them in the remote Pelican Valley. A descendant of one of those survivors crosses Pelican Creek in the summer of 2011. PHOTO BY NATE SCHWEBER

could fight whirling disease as effectively by educating anglers to clean, inspect, and dry their waders. Plus if he reopened Pelican Creek, volunteer anglers might just be able to bring him news about what is going on with that fishery, which suffered disaster in the early 2000s.

Whirling disease in Pelican Creek, a vital Yellowstone cutthroat spawning stream, made for a double whammy because, at the time it was discovered, the park's robust Yellowstone cutthroat population was already fast on the decline due to predation from those illegally planted lake trout in Yellowstone Lake, into which Pelican Creek flows.

John D. Varley worked as a fisheries biologist in Yellowstone in the 1970s and remembers that for years when he counted trout in Pelican Creek, "the cutthroat fry were so thick there were parts of the stream that looked black."

Varley was working as the director of the Yellowstone Center for Resources in the early 2000s when Koel, who had inherited his responsibilities, reported the grim number of trout fry that he and his researchers had found in Pelican Creek that season. Zero.

"It was just inconceivable to me that they could run these survey lines on Pelican Creek and come up with a big goose egg," Varley said. "It was a very empty feeling."

In other streams infected with whirling disease, trout populations have rebounded via natural selection. The small percentage of trout that are genetically resistant to the disease, or those trout that happen to spawn at times or in places where they manage to avoid the parasite, live to thrive and reproduce, eventually refilling the water with healthy trout.[2]

The problem in Pelican Creek is twofold, Koel said. First, the concentration of the disease is extremely high because the stream's silty, muddy bottom makes perfect habitat for the tubifex worm, which hosts the whirling disease parasite during the first stage of its life. Koel and his team took healthy baby cutthroats inside fish cages and planted them in several sections along the length of Pelican Creek. When they came back and measured how severely the fish were infected, on a scale of one to five with five being the worst, all the little trout were fives.

The second problem is that even if a trout born in Pelican Creek managed to avoid whirling disease, it would probably migrate down to Yellowstone Lake and be gobbled by a lake trout.

Thus by the early 2000s the cutthroat trout population in Pelican Creek, where fish weirs used to count an average of 30,000 spawners each spring, collapsed.[3] Ominously, the few cutthroats that remained were almost uniformly old and large. Entire populations of young, small cutthroats were missing: a very bad sign for the future.

As we wound up the dusty trail toward the Pelican Valley, Voigt said that he had visited Pelican Creek two weeks earlier with some other volunteer anglers. They caught a couple 20-inch cutthroats.

"It was great to see those big, beautiful cutthroats back in Pelican," he said. "But it would be really encouraging to see some trout of different age ranges; little guys as well as big guys."

We stopped farther up to admire a stately bull bison silhouetted next to the blue creek water. Then we walked down a bluff to a green-grass stretch of bank. The water underneath smoothed into a dark pool. Voigt's college-age granddaughter Dana Megginson rolled up the cuffs of her jeans and caught minnows and what might have been baby trout in the shallows with a goldfish net. Voigt would examine these later for signs of disease. I saw the cutthroat rise along the far bank. Beyond it the wallowing bison sent up plumes of dust.

Bison and cutthroat; Yellowstone surf & turf.

In his remarkable book *Last Stand: George Bird Grinnell, the Battle to Save the Buffalo and the Birth of the New West*, author Michael Punke brings the story of North America's mass bison slaughter to an incredible climax in the Pelican Valley. It was here, just before the turn of the twentieth century, that most of the final few wild buffalo alive hid, after all the others across America had been annihilated. Hordes of poachers descended on early Yellowstone, because it became the West's last, best wildlife oasis, and the only place left to shoot a wild buffalo—whose scarcity caused prices for their stuffed heads to skyrocket. These outlaws pushed the frontline for the continent's largest land mammal all the way back to the hidden Pelican Valley, and here they came less than two-dozen bullets from doing to the park's last known buffalo herd what American hide hunters did to all the rest.

The most notorious poacher was named Edgar Howell. He was a Cooke City man so tough he would ski to the Pelican Valley over 8,500-foot Specimen Ridge through 10 feet of snow towing a 180-pound toboggan behind him wearing nothing on his feet but wool socks. A U.S. Army scout named Felix Burgess, aided by a civilian scout, captured Howell in March 1894 in a snowstorm so brutal that it cost Burgess a big toe to frostbite. The scouts tracked Howell down in the Pelican Valley after they heard six blasts from his rifle. Burgess used snowshoes to sneak up on the poacher as he hacked away at the head of one of five buffalo lying dead in the snow at his feet. The publicity surrounding Howell's arrest prompted congress to pass the Lacey Act, also known as the National Park Protective Act, which created a way for the burgeoning park administration to whack poachers with penalties harsh enough to deter them.[4]

The toll that Howell took on America's few remaining wild bison cannot be overstated. By the time of his capture, he had slaughtered an estimated 80 Yellowstone bison out of maybe just 200 left, combining with other poachers to pitch the animal on a nosedive toward extirpation. Just eight years after the Howell bust, officials scoured the park for a wildlife census and counted just 23 *(twenty-three!)* buffalo, all of them in the Pelican Valley.[5] These weren't just the last wild bison in Yellowstone, they were the last wild bison in the country, a country that a generation before was home to a millionfold more. Park officials took drastic action in 1902 to save bison by starting a buffalo ranch near Mammoth Hot Springs founded with a few pureblood animals taken from private owners in North Dakota and Texas. Descendants of bison from that now-closed ranch repopulated the park's Lamar, Hayden, and Madison Valleys.[6]

But the Pelican Valley herd sustained on its own.[7]

Watching that commanding buffalo across the creek I was struck by the gravity of the Pelican Valley; this remote place in this postage stamp park in this giant, vast nation. This is the only place in the country where bison have always roamed free; never fenced, never exterminated. Here. Only here.

Then the cutthroat rose again, shaking me from my reverie.

I waved my size 14 Elk Hair Caddis in the air and set it down gently on Pelican Creek. Voigt watched intently. A white mouth atop a crimson slash poked out of the beryl water; colors as modern as the American flag and as timeless as blood and bone. My fly vanished in halos of water rings. I tugged and something silver danced a jig in the deep. Voigt's eyebrows went up, his

Bill Voigt, coordinator of Yellowstone's volunteer fly-fishing program, examines a goldfish net full of minnows and maybe baby trout for signs of whirling disease, which was discovered in Pelican Creek in the late 1990s. The volunteer fly-fishing program helps park fisheries biologists learn more about trout populations throughout Yellowstone. PHOTO BY NATE SCHWEBER

eyes popped, and his lips spread into a grin. What do you know? A little cut-throat trout.

"Hey now," Voigt beamed. "That's great to see."

You've never seen two grown men so excited about such a small fish.

We put the squirming trout and a scoop of water into a yellow rubber bag. Voigt put his tape measure to it; six inches exactly. I snapped a photo. We poured the bag and its precious cargo back into Pelican Creek.

We hiked out of the Pelican Valley hours later with singing hearts. I had caught another 6-incher. Co-coordinator Hamstra caught one too, plus an 8-incher. Best of all, we had seen dozens of little guys rising. In November 2011 I was sent to Pennsylvania on an unrelated assignment for the *New York Times* and I met again with Voigt, on a break, to cast to wild brown trout on the Little Juniata River, a stream he has led efforts to clean of pollution. There Voigt told me that the last team of Yellowstone volunteer anglers to visit Pelican Creek that summer had caught around 60 little cutthroats. "It was wonderful," he said.

We all paused again in the Pelican Valley to marvel at that big, bull buffalo, still in the same spot he was that morning. As I continued on down the trail, I pondered the parallels between those two extraordinary and beautiful animals: bison and Yellowstone cutthroat trout, neighbors in the Pelican Valley since before Columbus. In my best Yellowstone memories I see them both, one in hand and one on the far bank.

Mercy, how they've suffered. Yellowstone cutthroat once swam thousands of miles of streams in Montana, Wyoming, Idaho, Utah, and Nevada. Dams, pollution, and alien fish cut them down to just a fraction of their historic range,[8] and now their biggest sanctuary, Yellowstone Lake, has been spoiled by lake trout. The poor buffalo once owned the North American plain, and then in a blink of history's eye they were just millions of bloody, one-ton mounds of carrion left rotting in the sun.

Farsighted legislators gave bison and cutthroats a haven in this first national park, but even here they struggle. Diseases from Europe wracked them both. More than a century ago some park bison contracted the bovine disease brucellosis, probably from neighboring domestic cattle herds. Today ranchers in the states bordering Yellowstone fear that the buffalo might give back the disease, which can cause cows to abort their calves. Since 1985 almost 7,000 bison—about double the total number of buffalo currently living in Yellowstone—have been shot or shipped to the slaughterhouse for wandering outside the invisible park border under a dubious and much-criticized policy to protect ranchers.[9] Meanwhile, who knows how many cutthroats died from whirling disease.

And still they both held on. Slower than a baby crawls, they might even be making a comeback. I visited fisheries biologist Pat Bigelow's office on the shore of Yellowstone Lake one afternoon in September 2011 after watching the lake trout netting boats dock. The old wood building is the command center for the war on lake trout. Its walls are decorated with photos of huge, dead lakers plus maps, charts, and graphs plotting the fight against this alien fish. Bigelow told me that her computer analysis showed that if netters could just yank about 200,000 lake trout out of Yellowstone Lake that summer, it might be enough to finally start driving their population down. Enough to start giving cutthroats a fighting chance.

In October park officials announced their lake trout harvest from Yellowstone Lake for the 2011 season: 220,500.

That same month Montana Fish, Wildlife, and Parks sought public feedback on a plan to relocate a few genetically pure, disease-free bison from Yellowstone to new ranges in the state, places on turf where buffalo used to roam. A couple hundred ranchers and farmers packed meetings and raised hell, thereby scuttling a part of the plan that could've created a public bison herd available to both Montana's hunters and wildlife watchers. But at those same contentious public forums some tribal members stood up and said Yellowstone's special buffalo would be welcome with them.[10] These bison had wandered out of the park in search of food during harsh winter months in 2005 and 2006, and wildlife agents corralled them in pens along the highway north of Gardiner, Montana. Veterinarians tested and retested these bison for brucellosis—more than any domestic animals on earth, state officials say—and they built a healthy herd designed for conservation and reintroduction.[11] Still, the animals remained in purgatory due to pushback from a state livestock industry that has fought hard to keep wild bison from ever returning.[12] I drove past these buffalo countless times, wondering what would become their fate.

In March 2012, sixty-one of these embattled bison were released on Montana's Fort Peck Indian Reservation almost 500 miles northeast of the park. Sioux and Assiniboine tribal members pounded drums and wailed a welcome song as the animals charged from their livestock trucks at night out onto a plains pasture where no pureblood bison had been seen since 1873.[13] This historic homecoming also marked the first time in more than 70 years that Yellowstone bison were allowed to permanently expand their range beyond the park border.[14]

On the morning I left Yellowstone for good, I met with biologist Koel in his small wooden office on the top floor of an administrative complex at Mammoth Hot Springs. I fired up my laptop computer to show him the picture of the little cutthroat I had caught in Pelican Creek. When Koel saw it, he smiled just like Voigt had.

"That trout shows no sign of whirling disease," Koel said. "And it looks like it's one to two years old, past the age range where it would be susceptible."

Another Pelican Valley survivor.

At the Pelican Creek Trailhead that day, I shook my companions' hands and thanked them. Voigt gave me a pin for my efforts. It had the word *Volunteer* written above the National Park Service seal, the one that features the snowcapped mountain and the white buffalo. I stuck it on my vest.

My pickup grumbled to life, and I rumbled down the dirt road, still wrapped in thought. A Manhattan Project of geniuses couldn't brainstorm more heinous ways to snuff out bison and cutthroats: *A parasite that eats their baby's bones! A .50-caliber rifle for every hunter in the country! Hybridization! Brucellosis! Drought! Lake trout! Edgar Howell!*

But they held on, thanks to wisdom and work. With luck, may it ever be so.

Notes

INTRODUCTION
1. Aubrey L. Haines, *The Yellowstone Story: A History of Our First National Park* (Boulder: Univ. Press of Colorado, 1996), 1:37–38.
2. Ibid., 21–22.
3. Ibid., 24.
4. Burton Harris, *John Colter: His Years in the Rockies* (Lincoln: Univ. of Nebraska Press, 1993), xii.
5. Ibid., 88.
6. Ibid., 159.
7. Merril D. Beal, *The Story of Man in Yellowstone*, Yellowstone Interpretive Series 7 (Caldwell, ID: Caxton, 1956), 40.

FIREHOLE RIVER AT BISCUIT BASIN
1. Howard Back, *The Waters of Yellowstone with Rod and Fly* (Guilford, CT: Lyons, 2000), 152.
2. Lee H. Whittlesey, *Yellowstone Place Names* (Gardiner, MT: Wonderland, 2006), 105.

OPEN SEASON
1. Patrick Trotter, *Cutthroat: Native Trout of the West*, 2nd ed. (Berkeley: Univ. of California Press, 2008), 43.
2. John D. Varley and Paul Schullery, *Yellowstone Fishes: Ecology, History, and Angling in the Park* (Mechanicsburg, PA: Stackpole Books, 1998), 8.
3. Trotter, *Cutthroat*, 300.
4. Varley and Schullery, *Yellowstone Fishes*, 26, 56.
5. Beal, *The Story of Man in Yellowstone*, 81. (Frances Fuller Victor, op. cit., 238.)
6. Orrin H. and Lorraine Bonney, *Battle Drums and Geysers: The Life and Journals of Lt. Gustavus Cheyney Doane, Soldier and Explorer of the Yellowstone and Snake River Regions* (Chicago: Sage Books, 1970), 232.
7. M. Mark Miller, *Adventures in Yellowstone: Early Travelers Tell Their Tales* (Guilford, CT: TwoDot, 2009), 137–38. (Originally from Windham Thomas Wyndham-Quin, *The Great Divide*.)
8. Ibid., 172. (Originally from Jack Bean's memoir.)

9. Henry Jacob Winser, *The Yellowstone National Park: A Manual for Tourists* (New York: G. P. Putnam's Sons, 1883), 21.
10. John Byorth, "Trout Shangri-La: Remaking the Fishing in Yellowstone National Park," *Montana: The Magazine of Western History* 52 (Summer 2002): 38–47.
11. Mary T. Townsend, "A Woman's Trout Fishing in Yellowstone Park," *Outing: An Illustrated Magazine of Sport, Travel and Recreation* 30 (May 1897): 165–77.
12. Howard Back, *The Waters of Yellowstone with Rod and Fly* (New York: Dodd, Mead, 1938), 139.

DELACY CREEK
1. Whittlesey, *Yellowstone Place Names*, 83.
2. National Park Service, U.S. Department of the Interior, "Native Fish Conservation Plan: Environmental Assessment," Yellowstone National Park (December 16, 2010): 57.

CRAWFISH CREEK
1. Whittlesey, *Yellowstone Place Names*, 76.

GIBBON RIVER
1. Whittlesey, *Yellowstone Place Names*, 117.

MADISON RIVER AT ELK MEADOWS
1. Whittlesey, *Yellowstone Place Names*, 161.

MINARET CREEK
1. National Park Service, "Native Fish Conservation Plan," 75.
2. Whittlesey, *Yellowstone Place Names*, 251–52.
3. Beal, *The Story of Man in Yellowstone*, 123.

LOWER GARDNER RIVER
1. Haines, *The Yellowstone Story*, 266.

GREBE LAKE
1. Proposed Rules, Docket Number FWS-R6-ES-2009-0065, *Federal Register* 75, no. 173 (September 8, 2010): 54, 713.
2. U.S. Fish and Wildlife Service Endangered Species, http://www.fws.gov/mountain-prairie/species/fish/grayling/grayling.htm (accessed February 10, 2012).
3. Peter Lamothe and James Magee, "Reintroducing Fluvial Arctic Grayling (*Thymallus arcticus*) to the Upper Ruby River, MT: A Progress Report," Montana Fish, Wildlife, and Parks (February 2004): 2–3.
4. Varley and Schullery, *Yellowstone Fishes*, 59–60.
5. Cal Kaya, "Arctic Grayling in Yellowstone: Status, Management, and Recent Restoration Efforts," *Yellowstone Science* 8 (Summer 2000): 14.

6. Jimmy Carter, *An Outdoor Journal: Adventures and Reflections* (New York: Bantam Books, 1988), 97–98.

7. Ray Bergman, *The Trout Fisherman's Bible*, (Lanham, MD: The Derrydale Press, 2000), 397.

SOUTH ARM OF YELLOWSTONE LAKE

1. Brian Handwerk, "Yellowstone Has Bulged As Magma Pocket Swells," *National Geographic News*, January 19, 2011. http://news.national geographic.com/news/2011/01/110119–yellowstone-park-supervolcano-eruption-magma-science/.

ALIEN INVASION

1. Varley and Schullery, *Yellowstone Fishes*, 26.

2. Sory Marocchi, Tony Remsen, and J. Val Klump, *Yellowstone Lake: Join the Expedition!* (Whitefish Bay, WI: Hammockswing, 2001), 46.

3. Byorth, "Trout Shangri-La," 38–47.

4. Paul Schullery, *Searching for Yellowstone: Ecology and Wonder in the Last Wilderness* (Helena: Montana Historical Society Press, 2004), 46.

5. Mary Ann Franke, "A Grand Experiment: 100 Years of Fisheries Management in Yellowstone, Part I," *Yellowstone Science* 4 (Fall 1996): 4.

6. Varley and Schullery, *Yellowstone Fishes*, 26.

7. Kaya, "Arctic Grayling in Yellowstone," 12.

8. National Park Service, "Native Fish Conservation Plan," 58.

9. Franke, "A Grand Experiment," 4.

10. Marocchi, Remsen, and Klump, *Yellowstone Lake*, 46.

11. Varley and Schullery, *Yellowstone Fishes*, 26.

12. Ibid., 97.

13. Todd Koel, Patricia E. Bigelow, Philip D. Doepke, et. al., "Introduced Fishes Feature: Nonnative Lake Trout Result in Yellowstone Cutthroat Trout Decline and Impacts to Bears and Anglers," *Fisheries* 30 (November 2005): 12–13.

14. Byorth, "Trout Shangri-La,"38–47.

15. George Reiger, Conversation, "The Question Arises: Is It Right to Treat a Trout Differently Than You Would Treat an Eagle or a Cougar?" *Field & Stream* 90 (May 1985): 25.

16. Robert J. Behnke, *About Trout: The Best of Robert J. Behnke from* Trout *Magazine*, (Guilford, CT: Lyons, 2007), 74.

17. National Park Service, "Native Fish Conservation Plan," 8.

18. Ibid., 8.

19. Varley and Schullery, *Yellowstone Fishes*, 102.

20. Back, *The Waters of Yellowstone with Rod and Fly*, x.

21. Charles E. Brooks, *Fishing Yellowstone Waters* (Guilford, CT: Lyons, 1984), 11.

HEART LAKE
1. Whittlesey, *Yellowstone Place Names*, 128.
2. Trotter, *Cutthroat*, 272.

TROUT LAKE
1. Whittlesey, *Yellowstone Place Names*, 253.
2. National Park Service, "Native Fish Conservation Plan," 57.
3. Haines, *The Yellowstone Story*, 304.

UPPER GARDNER RIVER AT SHEEPEATER CANYON
1. Whittlesey, *Yellowstone Place Names*, 224.

SLOUGH CREEK, UPPER MEADOWS
1. Whittlesey, *Yellowstone Place Names*, 230.
2. Lee H. Whittlesey, *Death in Yellowstone: Accidents and Foolhardiness in the First National Park* (Boulder, CO: Roberts Rinehart, 1995), 56–57.

YELLOWSTONE RIVER AT THOROFARE
1. Whittlesey, *Yellowstone Place Names*, 248.

SNAKE RIVER
1. Trotter, *Cutthroat*, 301.
2. Ibid.

GRAYLING CREEK
1. National Park Service, "Native Fish Conservation Plan," 70.

FALL RIVER
1. Whittlesey, *Yellowstone Place Names*, 103.

FAN CREEK
1. Whittlesey, *Yellowstone Place Names*, 103–4.

FUNCTIONALLY EXTINCT
1. Trotter, *Cutthroat*, 269.
2. Ibid., 270.
3. Varley and Schullery, *Yellowstone Fishes*, 21.
4. National Park Service, "Native Fish Conservation Plan," 22, 20.
5. Ibid., 23.
6. Yellowstone Fisheries & Aquatic Sciences, Annual Report 2008, 7.
7. Scientific Review Panel Evaluation of the National Park Service Lake Trout Suppression Program in Yellowstone Lake, August 25–29, 2008, Final Report (October 2009): 9.
8. Trotter, *Cutthroat*, 269.

9. George Reiger, Conversation, "What's Going On? Recent Management Decisions Regarding Fish and Waterfowl Have Many Sportsmen Puzzled and Disturbed," *Field & Stream* 100 (March 1996): 22.

10. Varley and Schullery, *Yellowstone Fishes*, 19.

11. National Park Service, "Native Fish Conservation Plan," 30.

BECHLER RIVER AT BECHLER MEADOWS

1. Whittlesey, *Yellowstone Place Names*, 47.

LAMAR RIVER AT LAMAR VALLEY

1. Michael Punke, *Last Stand: George Bird Grinnell, the Battle to Save the Buffalo and the Birth of the New West* (New York: HarperCollins, 2007), 173.

YELLOWSTONE RIVER AT LOWER GRAND CANYON

1. National Park Service Use Statistics Office, http://www.nature.nps.gov/stats/viewReport.cfm (accessed February 10, 2012).

NEZ PERCE CREEK

1. Direct quotes attributed to George Cowan in this chapter are taken from his 1920 dictation to his daughter Ethel Cowan entitled, "Indian Experiences in the Yellowstone National Park in the Year 1877 as Related by George F. Cowan."

2. Emma Cowan, "Reminiscences of Pioneer Life," *Contributions to the Historical Society of Montana* 4 (1903): 163.

3. Haines, *The Yellowstone Story*, 219.

4. Civil War Trust, "Oliver O. Howard," http://www.civilwar.org/education/history/biographies/oliver-howard.html.

5. Dee Brown, *Bury My Heart at Wounded Knee: An Indian History of the American West* (New York: Sterling, 1970), 325.

6. Whittlesey, *Yellowstone Place Names*, 116–117.

7. Sally-Jo Bowman, "From Where the Sun Now Stands: Nez Perce National Historical Park Shows How a War Nobody Wanted Changed a People's Long History Forever," *National Parks* 73 (January/February 1999): 32.

8. Haines, *The Yellowstone Story*, 220.

9. Ibid., 221.

10. Ibid., 359.

11. Ibid., 222.

12. Ibid.

13. Cowan, "Reminiscences of Pioneer Life," 171.

14. Ronald V. Rockwell, *The U.S. Army in Frontier Montana* (2009), 422.

15. Duncan McDonald, "The Nez Perce War of 1877—the Inside History From Indian Sources" *New North-West*, Deer Lodge, MT, January 1878.

16. Cowan, "Reminiscences of Pioneer Life," 173.

17. Bruce Hampton, *Children of Grace: The Nez Perce War of 1877* (Lincoln, NE: Bison Books, 2002), 229.

18. Cowan, "Reminiscences of Pioneer Life," 173.
19. A. W. Bowen, *Progressive Men of the State of Montana* (Chicago: A. W. Bowen, ca. 1902), 1:808–9.
20. William Connolly's diary, courtesy of the Northwest Museum of Arts and Culture in Spokane, WA, exact publication date and page number unknown.
21. Haines, *The Yellowstone Story*, 230.
22. Cowan, "Reminiscences of Pioneer Life," 173.
23. http://www.fs.fed.us/r1/clearwater/nezpercenht/people/yellowstone2.shtml
24. Cowan, "Reminiscences of Pioneer Life," 175.
25. Haines, *The Yellowstone Story*, 226.
26. Cowan, "Reminiscences of Pioneer Life," 183.
27. Haines, *The Yellowstone Story*, 236.
28. Brown, *Bury My Heart at Wounded Knee*, 326–30.
29. Whittlesey, *Death in Yellowstone*, 133–135.
30. Philetus W. Norris, Annual Report of the Superintendent of the Yellowstone National Park to the Secretary of the Interior for the Year 1880 (1880): 3.
31. Cowan, "Reminiscences of Pioneer Life,"159.
32. National Park Service, "Lake Area Fish Hatchery," 16.
33. Varley and Schullery, *Yellowstone Fishes*, 26.

GALLATIN RIVER
1. Whittlesey, *Yellowstone Place Names*, 111–12.

LAVA CREEK
1. Whittlesey, *Yellowstone Place Names*, 150.

SODA BUTTE CREEK
1. National Park Service, "Native Fish Conservation Plan," 75.

COUGAR CREEK
1. Wildscape, www.wildscape.com.
2. Matthew R. Sloat, Bradley B. Shepard, and Pat Clancy, "Survey of Tributaries to the Madison River from Hebgen Dam to Ennis, Montana, with an Emphasis on Distribution and Status of Westslope Cutthroat Trout," Report to Montana Department of Fish, Wildlife, and Parks, Fisheries Division (2000): 165.
3. James Magee and Austin McCullough, "Arctic Grayling Recovery Program: Montana Arctic Grayling Monitoring Report 2008," Montana Fish, Wildlife, and Parks (2008): 21–22.
4. Lamothe and Magee, "Reintroducing Fluvial Arctic Grayling (*Thymallus arcticus*) to the Upper Ruby River, MT," 28.

HELLROARING CREEK
1. Whittlesey, *Yellowstone Place Names*, 129.
2. Haines, *The Yellowstone Story*, 22–24.

BLACK CANYON OF THE YELLOWSTONE
1. Whittlesey, *Yellowstone Place Names*, 52.

CHASING RARE CUTTHROATS ON HIGH LAKE, SEDGE CREEK, AND GOOSE LAKE
1. Derek L. Rupert and Michael E. Ruhl, "Yellowstone National Park Westslope Cutthroat Trout Restoration Program: 2008 Field Strategy Session," Yellowstone Center for Resources (September 30, 2008): 1.
2. Varley and Schullery, *Yellowstone Fishes*, 26.
3. Greater Yellowstone Science Learning Center, "Westslope Cutthroat Trout," *Yellowstone Overview*, 4, http://www.greateryellowstonescience.org.
4. National Park Service, U.S. Department of the Interior, "Restoration of Westslope Cutthroat Trout in the East Fork Specimen Creek Watershed: Environmental Assessment," Yellowstone National Park (May 5, 2006): 5.
5. Greater Yellowstone Science Learning Center, "Westslope Cutthroat Trout," 4.
6. Craig Mathews and Clayton Molinero, *The Yellowstone Fly-Fishing Guide: An Authoritative Guide to the Waters of Yellowstone National Park* (Guilford, CT: Lyons, 1997), 42.
7. National Park Service, U.S. Department of the Interior, "Finding of No Significant Impact (FONSI): Restoration of Westslope Cutthroat Trout in the East Fork of Specimen Creek Watershed," Yellowstone National Park, (2006): 1. http://www.nps.gov/yell/parkmgmt/upload/westslope_fonsi.pdf.
8. Varley and Schullery, *Yellowstone Fishes*, 28.
9. Greater Yellowstone Science Learning Center, "Whirling Disease," *Greater Yellowstone Resource Brief* (September 21, 2007), http://www.greateryellowstonescience.org.

QUAGMIRE
1. Ken Retallic, *Flyfisher's Guide to Yellowstone National Park: Including Grand Teton National Park and Jackson Hole* (Belgrade, MT: Wilderness Adventures, 2005), 152–54.
2. Hiram Martin Chittenden, *The Yellowstone National Park: Historical and Descriptive* (Library of the University of California, 1895), 229.
3. Varley and Schullery, *Yellowstone Fishes*, 4, 12.
4. Kirk Johnson, "In Yellowstone, Killing One Kind of Trout to Save Another," *New York Times*, August 23, 2011.
5. Fisheries and Aquaculture Department, Devin Bartley, May 2005, http://www.fao.org/fishery/topic/14796/en.

SHOSHONE LAKE
1. Retallic, *Flyfisher's Guide to Yellowstone National Park*, 160 (Bruce Staples).

MADISON RIVER AT BARNS HOLE

1. Craig Mathews and Gary LaFontaine, *Fly Fishing the Madison* (Guilford, CT: Lyons, 2001), 17.

HOTTER AND DRIER

1. Stephen Saunders, Dan Findlay, Tom Easley, et al., "Greater Yellowstone in Peril: The Threats of Climate Disruption," The Rocky Mountain Climate Organization / Greater Yellowstone Coalition (September 2011): ii.
2. Ibid., iv.
3. *The Economist*, "The Hottest Years on Record," December 3, 2010.
4. Saunders, Findlay, Easley, et al., "Greater Yellowstone in Peril," iii.
5. Seth J. Wenger, Daniel J. Isaak, Charles H. Luce, et al., "Flow Regime, Temperature and Biotic Interactions Drive Differential Declines of Trout Species Under Climate Change," Proceedings of the National Academy of Sciences of the United States of America (2011): 6.
6. William R. L. Anderegg, James W. Prall, and Jacob Harold, et al., "Expert Credibility in Climate Change," Proceedings of the National Academy of Sciences of the United States of America, (June 21, 2010): 1

EPILOGUE: PELICAN CREEK

1. Greater Yellowstone Science Learning Center, "Whirling Disease."
2. Brian Maffly and Tom Dickson, "Learning to Live With Whirling Disease," *Montana Outdoors* 38 (March–April 2007): 20.
3. Greater Yellowstone Science Learning Center, "Whirling Disease."
4. Punke, *Last Stand*, 200–217.
5. Margaret Mary Meagher, "The Bison of Yellowstone National Park," National Park Service, U.S. Department of the Interior, chap. 3, table 2, http://www.cr.nps.gov/history/online_books/bison/chap3.htm.
6. Punke, *Last Stand*, 218–26.
7. Margaret Mary Meagher, Mark L. Taper, Christopher L. Jerde, "Recent Changes in Population Distribution: The Pelican Bison and the Domino Effect," Proceedings of the 6th Biennial Scientific Conference on the Greater Yellowstone Ecosystem (2002): 136.
8. The Trout Conservancy, "Montana's Wild Trout," http://www.montanatrout.org/native.html.
9. Buffalo Field Campaign, http://www.buffalofieldcampaign.org.
10. Richard Peterson, "Bison Relocation Finds Support at Glasgow Hearing," *Great Falls Tribune*, October 18, 2011.
11. Montana Fish, Wildlife, and Parks, "Draft Environmental Assessment on Potential Interim Locations for Brucellosis-Free Bison" (September 19, 2011), http://fwp.mt.gov/news/publicNotices/environmentalAssessments/speciesRemovalAndRelocation/pn_0055.html.
12. Matthew Brown, "Stockgrowers Advocate Slaughter, Other Means to Control Bison," *Billings Gazette*, December 16, 2011.
13. Richard Peterson, "Yellowstone Bison Return to Tribal Land," *Great Falls Tribune*, March 21, 2012.

14. The last bison transplant from Yellowstone happened in 1941 when 18 animals were moved to Utah's Henry Mountains. Today those bison number around 250 and allow Utah to claim the only free-roaming, pureblood, huntable herd in the lower 48. Odds of drawing a permit to hunt one of these animals is around 200 to 1. http://wildlife.utah.gov/hunting/biggame/pdf/bison_15.pdf.

Acknowledgments

I owe a tremendous debt of gratitude to everyone I interviewed for this book for tips, recollections, descriptions, directions, and above all, stories. A few people helped me especially by acting as idea soundboards, connecting me with sources, helping with research, hiking and/or dining with me, giving me rides, and even putting me up for an odd night. These good folks include Cristina Allgretti, Pat Bigelow, Ben Bloch and Caroline Peters, Marcie Bough, Erik Christensen, Deanna Congileo, Vince Devlin, Amy Layne Falcione, Rich and Sue Hamstra, Charle M. Hansen and the Eastern Washington Genealogical Society, Breanna Hopf, Jeff Hull, Patrick Ford, Harry and Patti Gadbow (for a great "Buttenanny!"), Heidi at the Nevada Historical Society, Shelton Johnson, George Kittrell, Todd Koel, Michael Leach, Craig Mathews, Rick McCourt, M. Mark Miller, Al Nash, Ocean Champions, Michael Phillips, Myers Reece, Jeff Reed, Molly and Rich Semenik, William and JoAnn Voigt, Paul Schullery, Laura Snyder, Dr. Chris Stetler, Natalie Storey, Carol Van Valkenburg, Ednor Therriault, Kyle Weaver, Lee H. Whittlesey, and Mark D. Williams.

Funny story: I tried very hard to interview a few famous people for this book. I made a list of more than two dozen movie stars, musicians, politicians, athletes, news anchors, and moguls who fly-fish the West, own big spreads near Yellowstone, or both. For a whole year, I pleaded with their agents, which is the type of thing I might do for fun only if I first ran out of toothpicks to jab into my eyeballs. I got so desperate I even spent money I didn't have buying tickets to public appearances that a couple of these guys had in New York and then waited around until after the events to try and talk to them. Still nothing. Finally, I tracked down a guy named Dave Strege, who wrote a book called *Celebrity Fish Talk: Tales of Fishing from an All-Star Cast*. I asked him how he got his famous folks to talk fish.

"I worked as a golf writer," he told me. "And I talked to these people before they teed up at celebrity events."

Curse this nexus of fame, fishing and golf!

One person did get right back to me: Vice President Dick Cheney. I thought the fearsome Republican might be the last person on earth to voluntarily reveal his secret Yellowstone honey hole, but Cheney granted me a fantastic interview, for which I'm very thankful. Seeking balance, I tried to find a high-ranking Democrat to interview about fishing Yellowstone. President Jimmy Carter was the obvious choice because he actually fished in Yellowstone Park while he was in office in the late 1970s and has returned many times since. I had hoped to interview Presdient Carter in the early spring, but his office informed me then that he was busy in North Korea meeting with late-dictator Kim Jong-il. Just before deadline, Carter was kind enough to give me a few words for my chapter on Grebe Lake, which I very much appreciated.

So to Carter and Cheney I wish a pretty grayling and a fat cutthroat respectively. To the rest I wish snagged nymph rigs.

Thank you to Jay Nichols and Stackpole Books. I had four pairs of dear friends marry in Montana over the summer: Chad Dundas and Courtney Ellis, Regan DeVictoria and Zazh Cline, Sean Bendickson and Kaci Bendickson, and Lido Vizzutti and Jessica Lowry-Vizzutti, whose wedding I had the pleasure of officiating. Mazel tov! I owe beers to my Montana buddies Brianne Burrowes, Corey G. Lewis, Brendan McGlynn, Melissa Mundt, Chris Porter, "Crazy" Harry Richards, and Mike Ruckstad. Thanks to the metro desk at the *New York Times* for granting me leave to report this decidedly nonurban story. Thanks also to the knucklehead reporters I compete with on the streets of New York for keeping me sharp. I am indebted to a treasured circle of friends in New York City for their support and inspiration. They include Eric Ambel and MaryLee Kortes, the folks at dearly departed Banjo Jim's and the Lakeside Lounge, Alex Battles, Mark J. Bonamo, Keith Christopher, John Holl (for getting me into the book racket), J. D. Hughes, the Goods, Charlene McPherson and Mo Goldner, Doug Montero, Matt Popola and the crew at Paddy's Service Station in Newark, NJ, Lance Rautzhan, Boo Reiners and Elena Skye, Chip Robinson, Drina and Dave Seay, Michael and Corey St. George, and Mike Storey. I owe my family thanks: Phil Schweber, Kay Vinci, Bill Innes, Gig Schweber, Erin Schweber, Sam Innes, Andrew Schweber, Norman and Mavis Schweber, and Norah Brennan. I owe all thanks to my sweetheart, Kristen Couchot, for being cool with me charging out into grizzly country for a summer to write a book about trout.

It would be impossible, I believe, to report a story like this without feeling moved to action to help Yellowstone's embattled cutthroats. Five percent of my profit from this book will be donated to the East Yellowstone Chapter of Trout Unlimited for their continuing research into new methods to control lake trout and bolster cutthroats.

Special thanks to my longtime friend Randy Ingersoll, a piano-playing Yellowstone treasure who knows more than almost anyone about secret places in the park. Thanks to my trusty pickup "Scamper," which I sold back on Craigslist. Extra special thanks to Dr. Guy R. Muto who told me enough fish stories to fill an encyclopedia.

Index

Page numbers in italics indicate illustrations.